2004

Explaining
ASEAN

Explaining
ASEAN

REGIONALISM IN
SOUTHEAST ASIA

Shaun Narine

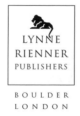

LYNNE
RIENNER
PUBLISHERS

BOULDER
LONDON

Published in the United States of America in 2002 by
Lynne Rienner Publishers, Inc.
1800 30th Street, Boulder, Colorado 80301
www.rienner.com

and in the United Kingdom by
Lynne Rienner Publishers, Inc.
3 Henrietta Street, Covent Garden, London WC2E 8LU

Library of Congress Cataloging-in-Publication Data
Narine, Shaun, 1966–
Explaining ASEAN : regionalism in Southeast Asia / Shaun Narine.
   Includes bibliographical references and index.
   ISBN 1-58826-129-8
   1. ASEAN. 2. Regionalism—Asia, Southeastern. 3. Asia, Southeastern—
Politics and government—1945– 4. Asia, Southeastern—Economic conditions.
I. Title: ASEAN. II. Title.
DS520.A873 N37   2002
341.24'73—dc21   2002020150

British Cataloguing in Publication Data
A Cataloguing in Publication record for this book
is available from the British Library.

Printed and bound in the United States of America

The paper used in this publication meets the requirements
of the American National Standard for Permanence of
Paper for Printed Library Materials Z39.48-1984.

5 4 3 2 1

Contents

Tables and Figures

Acknowledgments

In the course of writing this book, I have received support and encouragement from too many people to mention. However, a few individuals and institutions stand out as particularly deserving of my gratitude.

Amitav Acharya and David Welch provided unstinting assistance and welcome guidance when I first began to examine ASEAN as an international institution, many years ago. Their contribution to this book is indirect, but invaluable. An Izaak Walton Killam Postdoctoral Fellowship at the University of British Columbia (UBC) provided me with the time and resources necessary to revise the manuscript. I am grateful to UBC and the Killam Trust for their support. My fellowship was taken through the Institute of International Relations (IIR) at the Liu Centre. Brian Job, the director of the IIR, and the other scholars, staff, and students at the institute created a stimulating and collegial intellectual environment and a wonderful place at which to work. While at UBC, I lived at Green College. The college was an ideal environment in which to explore new ideas, meet interesting people from a variety of disciplines, and enjoy the overwhelming beauty of Vancouver. During my frequent visits to Toronto to do research, Louis Pauly and the Centre for International Studies provided me with office space and facilitated my access to the University of Toronto's considerable bibliographical resources.

Finally, I must acknowledge my heartfelt love and thanks to my parents, Amina and Haresh Narine. Through many years of education and a great deal of moving around, they have been endlessly supportive, loving, and generous.

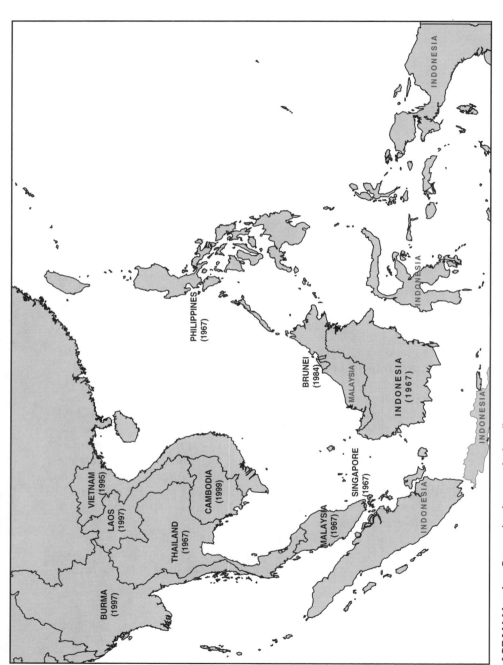

ASEAN Member States (and year admitted)

I

ASEAN:
A Regional Community?

The Association of Southeast Asian Nations (ASEAN) is difficult to understand and assess. The popular press often describes ASEAN as an economic organization. However, even a cursory examination of ASEAN's history and institutional development reveals that meaningful economic interaction has only recently become a significant part of the organization's activities. ASEAN is clearly not a security alliance. Why, then, did the organization persist throughout the Cold War period? What motivates ASEAN's expansion and reform in the post–Cold War era? And, perhaps most importantly, what are the prospects for ASEAN's continued reform and viability in the twenty-first century? The intent of this book is to answer these questions through a critical analysis of the history and institutional development of ASEAN.

Two Perspectives on ASEAN

Scholars of ASEAN hold two dominant interpretations of the organization. The first position holds that ASEAN forms the basis of a regional community of Southeast Asian states.[1] According to this argument, ASEAN embodies fundamental norms, values, and practices that have, over time, socialized the ASEAN states into adopting a shared regional identity. The second interpretation is that ASEAN is an instrument of its member states.[2] The organization is designed to pursue the narrow self-interests of its member states. From this perspective, any sense of community within Southeast Asia is illusory, at best.

This book argues that the truth of ASEAN lies between these polar positions and that, in practice, the second position is slightly closer to reality. While ASEAN is the basis of a regional identity, that identity is only one of many that define the member states. At the end of the day, the ASEAN identity is relatively weak in comparison to other identities. The norms and ideals that ASEAN embodies are important to its members; however, these norms emphasize the independence and sovereignty of states. As such, the most fundamental beliefs underpinning ASEAN actually mitigate against the creation of a strong regional community.

The first interpretive position analyzes ASEAN from a sociological perspective and argues that ASEAN's operations have created a "regional community." This community consists of states that share common norms and values. These are more than superficial norms that simply lay out the rules by which states can pursue their interests (regulatory norms); these include norms that specify the criteria by which a state knows itself. These are "constitutive" norms—they constitute states by defining the roles and identities that determine how a state understands its own interests. The processes of political and economic interaction that ASEAN has facilitated over thirty-five years have caused its members to adopt its norms as part of their own self-identities. In addition, ASEAN's norms and practices reflect a common cultural approach to regional conflict and community building. The ASEAN states share a common bond of belonging, a sense of "we feeling," that can be the basis of a security community—that is, a community of states that have abjured violent conflict between themselves. From this perspective, ASEAN represents a deeper commitment to a larger identity. Amitav Acharya emphasizes that creating "one Southeast Asia" was an aspiration of ASEAN's founders. Drawing on Benedict Anderson's concept, he argues that Southeast Asia is an example of an "imagined community"—except, in this instance, what is being imagined is not a national identity but a regional identity.[3]

Though Acharya is the most eloquent and sophisticated exponent of this position, the idea that ASEAN has "socialized" its member states into a sense of regional identity, and that this identity has significantly affected how those states deal with one another, has been a recurring and accepted theme among ASEAN analysts for a very long time. This is particularly true of experts from within Southeast Asia. Frequently, they credit ASEAN with creating political and social connections between its members, connections that have made violent conflict between them seem unthinkable. (Whether or not military conflict between ASEAN states is truly unthinkable, and for what reasons, are issues addressed later in the book.) In comparison to Southeast Asia before ASEAN, when many of its members were at odds with each other and there was a real possibility of military conflict, there is no doubt that regional relations have improved considerably.

Other scholars are far more skeptical of what ASEAN has achieved and what it can accomplish. This skepticism has always been present in analyses of ASEAN, but it has become far more pronounced in the wake of the Asian economic crisis and ASEAN's inability to respond effectively to those events. (This subject is discussed in Chapters 6 and 7.) From this more pessimistic perspective, ASEAN is, and always has been, a weak institution. Its methods of interaction do not reflect any cultural commitment to an "Asian" form of multilateralism but, instead, indicate a lack of common interests on the part of its members. ASEAN's members are committed to their own narrow national self-interests; the organization is useful to its members at various times, but does not enjoy any special regard as a symbol of regional solidarity.

One Identity Among Many

Both of the accepted perspectives touch on important elements of ASEAN's character, but neither fully or properly interprets ASEAN's fundamental nature. ASEAN is the foundation of a meaningful regional identity in Southeast Asia. This identity is not shared equally by all of the members; the level of commitment to the ASEAN identity varies from state to state, a differentiation that reflects both the circumstances of individual states and the level of socialization to ASEAN that a state has undergone. Nonetheless, the ASEAN identity is real and is shared by many, though not all, members of ASEAN. This identity is the product of interaction and communication between the ASEAN states. The fact that none of the pre-1995 ASEAN members has engaged in prolonged military conflict with any state since the creation of ASEAN is not entirely attributable to the organization, but ASEAN's existence has assisted the growth of peaceful relations and political stability within the region.

Demonstrating that a shared regional identity may exist between certain ASEAN states, however, is not enough to answer questions about ASEAN's importance to, and influence upon, its members. While an ASEAN identity does exist, it must be evaluated in relation to the other identities that shape and define the ASEAN nations. Sometimes these different identities are highly complementary, but often they are in competition. Many of these competing identities are at odds with the demands of regional identity, which is often far less important to individual ASEAN states than the national, ethnic, and other identities that shape their domestic political environment and, accordingly, affect the international politics of the region. The identities that most affect the operation of ASEAN are still being formed. Most of the ASEAN states remain deeply engaged in the process of state building; they are trying to create stable national identities out of many disparate domestic factions. Their most important concern is to maintain and promote their rights and security as sovereign states.

ASEAN's fundamental norms are directed toward protecting and enhancing the sovereignty of its member states. Sovereignty is the foundation on which ASEAN is built, is the generative institution from which all of ASEAN's other norms and practices emanate, and is continually reinforced by those norms and practices. Sovereignty enjoys the highest position in ASEAN's hierarchy of norms. In practice, this means that the ASEAN regional identity does not prevent the ASEAN states from putting narrow national interests above regional interests; in a sense, it even encourages them to do so. Although ASEAN's members have adopted the organization's norms, a strong sense of regional community is not the inevitable result. In addition, ASEAN's members often do not share economic and political philosophies, systems, or levels of development. Similarly, ASEAN states often define their security interests differently than their neighbors do. The common interests and objectives that are crucial to the formation of a strong regional institution are often missing in ASEAN.

The argument that ASEAN's norms encourage self-interested behavior may appear to unequivocally support the more skeptical interpretations of ASEAN's utility. However, the situation is not that straightforward. The commitment of the ASEAN states to the organization is rooted in a belief that ASEAN can affect regional events by influencing the normative environment. One of ASEAN's crucial functions is to promote its understanding of the norms and practices of international society to the rest of the world. ASEAN embodies principles and practices that its members strongly support. Again, however, those norms reinforce the idea that states have the right to act as they see fit within their own borders. ASEAN expects its own members to follow these principles, and if other states obey these same principles, then ASEAN can be assured of its own independence and ability to exercise their sovereign rights.

Efforts to reform ASEAN to allow greater intervention in its members' affairs are probably doomed to failure. ASEAN is not ready to be fundamentally restructured. Most of its members are not able or willing to open themselves up to external criticism and oversight. While this may imply that ASEAN is an organization in decline, the aftermath of the Asian economic crisis has created new possibilities for institutional development. The crisis spurred ASEAN not only to create new structures designed to prevent future economic upheavals but also to assist in the management of economic disruption when it occurs. More significantly, ASEAN has a major role to play in mediating and managing ASEAN Plus Three, an emerging regional institution that consists of the ASEAN-Ten plus China, Japan, and South Korea. Some supporters have presented the ASEAN Plus Three as a nascent regional financial instrument. Whatever it becomes, ASEAN will be needed to bridge the political, strategic, and historical divisions between China, Japan, and South Korea. This role will be important, but its necessity indicates that ASEAN Plus Three will have many difficulties to overcome before it can be a truly effective regional body.

As an economic institution, ASEAN is beginning to grow more effectual. It is making halting progress toward creating an ASEAN Free Trade Area (AFTA), which has led to the development of stronger formal structures within ASEAN. However, the trade of most ASEAN states remains oriented toward the global market, and this is unlikely to change soon. Therefore, ASEAN in its current incarnation can only be of limited economic significance to its members.

Most analyses of ASEAN emphasize change, both in the organization's basic structures and in the community it has attempted to create. While there is no denying that enormous change has occurred within ASEAN, it is useful to examine the consistency that has also typified ASEAN's development over the course of its history. The organization has promoted political stability in Southeast Asia, which has assisted in facilitating the region's economic development. Throughout its history, however, ASEAN's members have followed fairly consistent approaches to the organization; they have rarely or never allowed it to intrude on their self-interests, and ASEAN's basic norms have reinforced this approach. Despite efforts to reform the organization in the late 1990s, ASEAN's fundamental principles remain committed to the promotion of its members' sovereignty.

Outline of the Book

Chapter 2 presents a historical overview of ASEAN, examining the era of conflict in Southeast Asia before the creation of ASEAN in 1967 and then recounting the early years of ASEAN, from 1967 to 1978. During this period, ASEAN's basic foundations were put in place, and the resolution of the Vietnam War in 1975 pushed the organization toward its next level of development. Chapter 3 details ASEAN's efforts to reverse Vietnam's invasion of Cambodia in 1978. Most observers regard this undertaking as ASEAN's most important formative experience. During this time, ASEAN rose to international prominence. Chapter 3 explores ASEAN's accomplishments, but it also emphasizes the weaknesses in the ASEAN structure revealed by the Vietnam-Cambodia experience. ASEAN's efforts to manage this crisis were limited by its member states' divergent interests and perceptions, as well as the machinations of China and the United States.

Chapter 4 breaks with the chronological approach of the book to consider the many different facets of the security environment of Southeast Asia in the post–Cold War period. It begins by examining intra-ASEAN tensions and then discusses the roles of the United States and China in Southeast Asia. What emerges is a picture of the considerable uncertainty surrounding regional security issues. Chapter 5 looks at ASEAN's response to this uncertainty and to other forces emerging in the region in the post–Cold War era.

The chapter explains and evaluates ASEAN's efforts to expand the scope of its activities, as well as its membership, and concludes that the organization has overstepped its own capabilities and made an error in expanding its membership to all of Southeast Asia.

Chapters 6 and 7 focus on the Asian economic crisis and its impact upon ASEAN. Chapter 6 looks at the events of the crisis, then engages the debate over the causes and consequences of the economic upheaval. The crisis revealed serious deficiencies within the ASEAN states, but it was also the product of fundamental instability within the international financial system and a lack of regulation at the national and international levels. Chapter 7 considers the consequences of the economic crisis for ASEAN. When ASEAN was unable to manage the crisis, its member states rapidly abandoned any sense of regionalism and confronted the economic downturn on their own. ASEAN's impotence in the face of this major event seriously compromised its international standing. The disunity exhibited by its members shook the international community's perception of ASEAN as a coherent regional organization. ASEAN's efforts to deal with the aftermath of the crisis have also been markedly unsuccessful. Nonetheless, ASEAN is becoming the basis for a new regional institution as a result of the economic downturn. However, there remain uncomfortable questions about the continuing viability of ASEAN.

Chapter 8 concludes the book by emphasizing some of the key themes developed throughout the rest of the discussion. ASEAN was developed to enhance the sovereignty of its members. In a complex, post–Cold War era, ASEAN's relevance is directly related to its capacity to coordinate meaningful actions and policies between its members. The ASEAN states are not ready for this level of interaction, however. Creating a stronger ASEAN is counterproductive for states faced with their own institutional weaknesses, and it may be beyond their abilities to sustain a more powerful organization.

ASEAN is becoming a more vital and meaningful economic institution, and economics may be the foundation of its future activities. However, its roles as a major political and security player in Southeast Asia are now at stake. In these areas, ASEAN is risking the possibility of institutional irrelevance in the twenty-first century.

Conclusion

The intention of this book is to provide the reader with a comprehensive understanding of what ASEAN has been and then to draw on this understanding to present a clear and coherent analysis of what it is likely to become. It is important to recognize ASEAN's achievements as a collection of relatively weak states in the developing world. ASEAN's potential is enormous, both in economic and political terms. However, there are even more enormous obstacles to overcome before the organization can realize that potential.

Notes

1. Examples include Acharya, 2001; Busse, 1999; Chin, 1997; and Martin, 1987. Acharya's position on this question is not as simple as this statement may imply. He sees ASEAN as an institution in decline in the modern era.

2. See, for example, Ruland, 2000; Henderson, 1999; and Leifer, 1989. Like Acharya, Leifer's interpretation of ASEAN is more sophisticated than this simple assessment implies.

3. Acharya, 2001: 26–30.

2

Institutional Development

ASEAN's limitations as an economic and security regime prior to Vietnam's invasion of Cambodia reflected its difficulties in reaching consensus on important issues. ASEAN did make incremental progress toward different security goals, as demonstrated by the Bali Conference. Bali was a fairly impressive achievement, given the level of conflict that had existed between the ASEAN states less than a decade before. However, ASEAN was unsuccessful as an economic regime during the Cold War.

The Origins of ASEAN

The origins of ASEAN cannot be understood without first examining the history of Southeast Asia.[1] Southeast Asia in the precolonial period was rife with internal divisions and the interference of external powers. Geography made regular communication difficult between the states of the region. Nonetheless, there were interactions between the divergent parts of the region and even, arguably, the beginnings of a weak sense of community.[2] The regional societies were heavily influenced by the cultures of India and China, but no power could control Southeast Asia before the Japanese occupations of World War II. European colonialism solidified divisions within the region by orienting the colonized states toward their colonizers. In the post–World War II era, the people of Southeast Asia needed to overcome considerable barriers to a sense of regional identity.

The term "Southeast Asia" designated the theater of war commanded by Lord Louis Mountbatten during World War II.[3] Japan's expulsion of the Western colonial powers from the region led the people of Southeast Asia to believe that their independence was at hand. These expectations were disappointed by the brutal conduct of the Japanese occupiers, but once the war ended they would ensure that the process of decolonization continued.

After the war, the European powers, notably the Dutch and the French, attempted to reassert their dominance over their former Asian holdings. Indonesia had begun its struggle for independence in the prewar era, and it continued its fight against the returning Dutch, eventually gaining its independence in 1949. Vietnam began its own battle against Western domination. With the exception of Thailand, the other states of Southeast Asia remained dominated by foreign powers, but the Southeast Asian states gradually acquired actual, as well as formal, independence.[4] Despite its growing independence, Southeast Asia became a volatile dividing line in the international struggle between the United States and the Soviet Union, as well as a battleground in the conflict between China and the Soviet Union.[5]

The experience of colonialism deeply affected how the states of Southeast Asia perceived the regional environment. To differing degrees, the leaders of the region saw the international system as predatory, with powerful states waiting to exploit the internal weaknesses of weaker states. The suspicions and concerns of the Southeast Asian states also extended to one another. This perception of external threat played a fundamental role in the shaping of regionalism in Southeast Asia.

A number of attempts at creating regional organizations were made before the creation of ASEAN. These earlier attempts failed largely because they were initiated by outside powers and meant to serve the interests of external actors. Created in 1954, the Southeast Asian Treaty Organization (SEATO) was an American attempt to expand its network of anticommunist security arrangements. Only two members, the Philippines and Thailand, were actually located in Southeast Asia.[6] By the time SEATO was dissolved in 1977, it had developed a highly complex structure, but it was irrelevant to the security concerns or development of regionalism in Southeast Asia. Another regional entity that quickly failed was the Asian Pacific Council (ASPAC), the brainchild of South Korean president Park Chung-hee. Created in 1966, it expired seven years later.[7]

The Association of Southeast Asia (ASA) and Malaya-Phillipines-Indonesia (MAPHILINDO) were established in 1961 and 1963, respectively. Their membership consisted entirely of Southeast Asian states, and both were the result of regional initiatives. The members of the ASA were Malaya, the Philippines, and Thailand. The ASA was eventually neutralized by its apparent political connections to SEATO (two of the ASA's three members belonged to SEATO) and by a territorial dispute between the Philippines and Malaya.[8] Nevertheless, the ASA was important as the foundation on which ASEAN was constructed, and merits further exploration.

Malayan prime minister Tunku Abdul Rahman first advanced the idea of an indigenous regional organization comprised of Southeast Asian states in 1958. The Tunku initially advocated the creation of an anticommunist security organization. He soon realized that such an organization would divide the noncommunist states of Southeast Asia, some of which were nonaligned. He then supported the creation of a regional organization that would not be directed against any other party but would further economic and cultural cooperation. However, his habit of talking about such an organization while, in the same breath, venting his anticommunist inclinations fostered the widely held view that he was still supporting the formation of an anticommunist regional bloc.

Even as the Tunku retreated from the idea of an anticommunist bloc, Filipino leaders began trying to build a nonmilitary, anticommunist alliance among the noncommunist states of Southern Asia. Thailand's involvement in initiatives for regional organization meant that the three most pro-Western, anticommunist states in the region were at the forefront in promoting regionalism. This fact limited the appeal of the ASA, especially to Indonesia, the largest state in the region. Indonesia suspected that the Malayan proposals were an attempt by the SEATO states to link themselves to the non-SEATO states. Thus, the ASA proposal divided the noncommunist states of Southeast Asia, exactly as the Tunku had feared. In one camp were the states that actively opposed communism in general, China in particular, and saw regional economic cooperation as the way to combat these influences. In the other camp were those states, mostly of mainland Indochina, that refused to participate in any organization that even hinted at an anti-China disposition.

The ASA was established in Bangkok on July 31, 1961, at a meeting between the foreign ministers of Malaya, the Philippines, and Thailand. The Philippines and Malaya had originally envisioned an organization modeled on the European Economic Community, with strong institutional structures and obligations. Thailand, however, favored an organization with a much looser structure and without binding obligations upon its members. The other two states acquiesced to Thailand's vision, both because they required Thai participation in the ASA and because they hoped that the less formal character of the ASA would entice other Southeast Asian states into joining. It did not, but the minimal institutional structure of the ASA and its lack of state obligation carried over into ASEAN and have come to form the basis of the "ASEAN Way," an approach to regionalism that, to many observers, is at the core of ASEAN's viability.

Despite initial frenetic activity, the ASA soon ran into an insurmountable obstacle, the Philippines' claim on British North Borneo, or Sabah, which the British intended to include in the proposed Federation of Malaysia.[9] This dispute disrupted the ASA's operations in late 1962 and throughout 1963. Malaya, Singapore, Sabah, and Sarawak were amalgamated on September 16, 1963, into the state of Malaysia. The ASA was essentially paralyzed for the next three years.

MAPHILINDO was proclaimed in August 1963 but was dealt a decisive blow a month later with the creation of the Federation of Malaysia. Neither Indonesia nor the Philippines recognized Malaysia; the Philippines because of the Sabah dispute, Indonesia because it viewed Britain's creation of Malaysia as a case of an imperial power imposing its will on Southeast Asia. In response, Indonesia embarked on a policy of Konfrontasi (Confrontation) with Malaysia—and Singapore, after it was expelled from Malaysia—that lasted until 1966.[10] Nonetheless, MAPHILINDO was the first regional organization that Indonesia agreed to join.

Konfrontasi was a policy of regional disruption, initiated by the government of Indonesian nationalist leader Sukarno mostly for domestic political reasons. Konfrontasi sometimes became violent, as Indonesia attempted to undermine the stability of Malaysia by supporting guerrilla movements within the new state.[11] Konfrontasi ended when Sukarno lost power to the Indonesian military in 1966, after a failed attempt by the Communist Party of Indonesia to stage a coup d'état. The military, which was traditionally at odds with the Communists, used the opportunity to seize power and liquidate hundreds of thousands of Communists and their supporters. Sukarno was officially deposed by General Suharto in 1967.[12]

Konfrontasi underlined the disruptive potential of Indonesia as the largest and most militarily powerful state in the region.[13] Suspicion of Indonesia was a powerful factor in shaping Southeast Asian security perceptions in the post-Konfrontasi era and remains a significant factor today.[14] Konfrontasi, however, also revealed to the involved states their mutual dependency and vulnerability. Indonesian economic sanctions against Malaysia were almost as painful to Indonesia as to its intended target.[15] Suharto's government became concerned with reducing intraregional tensions and tried to reassure its neighbors that the new Indonesia would not be the destabilizing influence it had been in the past. Indonesia went from being a state largely indifferent to efforts at regional organization to a major proponent of regionalism.

The territorial and political disputes between the nations of Southeast Asia emphasized the need for a regional organization that could deal with these tensions. Outsiders saw the ASA as politically aligned to the West, an overt affiliation that Indonesia, as a leader in the nonaligned movement, wished to avoid. Indonesia also did not wish to join an organization that it had no role in creating. A new organization was required. That organization was ASEAN.

The Formation of ASEAN: 1967–1975

The participating governments officially established the Association of Southeast Asian Nations in Bangkok on August 8, 1967. Its founding members were Indonesia, Thailand, Malaysia, Singapore, and the Philippines. ASEAN's founding purpose was to ensure the survival of its members by promoting regional stability and limiting competition between them. When ASEAN was established, the greatest threats to the national security of its individual states were indigenous insurgencies that potentially invited external intervention in the region. ASEAN answered this threat in three mutually reinforcing ways. First, the ASEAN states sought to reduce the appeal of internal Communist insurgencies by promoting domestic socio-economic development, expressing this objective in the notions of "national" and "regional resilience." The idea of "national resilience" came from Indonesia and expressed the belief that a state that is internally strong does not need to fear external provocations.[16] Second, ASEAN sought to reduce the regional military influence of external actors. The Bangkok Declaration labeled foreign military bases in the region "temporary" and promoted "security from external interference" as an objective. Third, ASEAN sought to reduce intra-ASEAN competition and to improve relationships between members. The member states shared a strong consensus on the intra-ASEAN dimension of these security objectives. The provision designating foreign military bases as "temporary," however, ran into difficulties.

The original invitation to join what would become ASEAN was the Southeast Asian Association for Regional Cooperation (SEAARC) proposal. Drafted by Thailand, after consultations with Indonesia, it was issued to the other potential members in December 1966. The SEAARC proposal brought Indonesia into a regional organization without making it seem that Indonesia had asked to join. Though sponsored by Thailand, the plan expressed the Indonesian view on regional security and contained references to security matters that were not acceptable to the other Southeast Asian states. The SEAARC proposal described the member states as:

> Believing the countries of Southeast Asia share a primary responsibility for ensuring the stability and maintaining the security of the area. . . .
> Being in agreement that foreign bases are temporary in nature and should not be allowed to be used directly or indirectly to subvert the national independence of Asian countries, and that arrangements of collective defense should not be used to serve the particular interest of any of the big powers.[17]

The Philippines, Malaysia, Singapore, and Thailand all maintained security relationships with foreign powers and saw the SEAARC as a criticism of such policies. The Philippines rejected the SEAARC formulation. When the parties met in Bangkok to draft the ASEAN Declaration, the Filipinos argued that they would rather the document not refer to security matters at all than take the position advocated in the SEAARC proposal. They were strongly supported by Singapore and less strongly by Malaysia and Thailand. However, the Filipino proposal was not an acceptable solution to Indonesia. Difficult bargaining followed; in the end, the compromise reached omitted any reference to collective defense arrangements serving the interests of big powers. The two security provisions in the ASEAN Declaration's preamble read,

> CONSIDERING that the countries of South-East Asia share a primary responsibility for strengthening the economic and social stability of the region and ensuring their peaceful and progressive national development, and that they are determined to ensure their stability and security from external interference in any form or manifestation in order to preserve their national identities in accordance with the ideals and aspirations of their peoples;
>
> AFFIRMING that all foreign bases are temporary and remain only with the expressed concurrence of the countries concerned and are not intended to be used directly or indirectly to subvert the national independence and freedom of States in the area or prejudice the orderly processes of their national development; . . . [18]

The controversy over the wording of the security provisions in the ASEAN Declaration demonstrates both the importance of this issue to the member states and their considerable differences in security outlooks. Indonesia, despite undergoing a dramatic reorientation in foreign policy under Suharto, saw foreign powers targeting the region and maintained that its national security was best served by following a policy of self-reliance and nonalignment. It believed that the Southeast Asian states should follow its lead.

The other ASEAN states were not unsympathetic to the Indonesian position. They saw foreign powers as unreliable allies and recognized the appeal of controlling their own region.[19] However, they regarded this as a goal for the future. The Filipinos felt that their security was best served by maintaining their strong bilateral defense ties with the United States, which kept major military bases there. Likewise, Singapore remained dependent on protection from Britain and was home to the largest British base in the region. In 1967, the Singaporeans still believed that they could rely on direct British protection for another ten to fifteen years. Moreover, Singapore remained highly conscious of its status as an ethnic Chinese state surrounded by potentially hostile Malays; it was uneasy about proposals that would essentially leave its security in the hands of its neighbors. Malaysia and Thailand's opposition to the Indonesian position was more muted. Arnfinn Jorgenson-Dahl suggests that this restraint was tactical; as long as the Philippines and Singapore argued with Indonesia, there was no need for the other two states to become deeply embroiled in the disagreement.

The other ASEAN states eventually agreed to support the modified ASEAN Declaration because of the need to draw Indonesia into a regional bloc. According to Michael Leifer, the ASEAN states agreed to the statement on the temporary nature of foreign bases because there was no possibility of this statement becoming reality. It was a harmless statement of principle that placated Indonesia. They had no intention of actively pursuing policies that would compromise their own security. Moreover, the other ASEAN states, notably Singapore, wanted to engage external actors in the region in order to prevent Indonesian domination.[20]

All the members of ASEAN had different reasons for wanting an effective regional organization. Indonesia desired to repair its relations in the region, but it also saw ASEAN as an opportunity both to exercise regional leadership and to reduce the ability of external powers to influence events in Southeast Asia. Malaysia, Singapore, and the Philippines supported ASEAN as a way to constrain Indonesia, while providing Jakarta with a channel for its aspirations to regional preeminence. However, these states had other interests in the organization. The pullout of the British military had important security implications for Malaysia and Singapore. Besides their mutual concern over Indonesia, Malaysia and Singapore were deeply suspicious of each other. To Singapore, belonging to ASEAN symbolized that it was accepted and tolerated by its neighbors as an equal state. For Malaysia and the Philippines, ASEAN was an opportunity to enhance their national prestige. Manila also hoped that ASEAN would strengthen Filipinos' Asian identity and trading links, thereby counterbalancing the Philippines' relationship with the United States. Thailand hoped that ASEAN would become the basis for the "collective political defense" of the region, forming an organization that could supplement and perhaps eventually replace its own security relationship with the United States.[21]

Ostensibly, ASEAN was not a security-oriented structure. The Bangkok Declaration broadly states the main purposes of ASEAN as being: "to accelerate economic growth, social progress, and cultural development in the region" and "to promote regional peace and stability."[22] Despite the latter objective, ASEAN politicians made it clear from the outset that the organization would not deal directly with security matters or political controversies. However, security matters were of primary significance, for ASEAN was, in fact, a grouping of anticommunist states in a volatile region. Their common political outlook was a major factor in bringing them together, but ASEAN refused to present itself as a security bloc because it wished to avoid the polarizing effects of such a position on the other states of the region. Forming a military alliance clearly implied antagonism toward some identifiable threat. In addition, there was not enough consensus between the ASEAN states on security matters, distrust among the ASEAN states remained a problem, and the ASEAN states lacked the military power needed to form a credible bloc.[23] Nonetheless, the perception of a common external threat played an important role in ASEAN's creation and grew more important as the organization developed.

ASEAN's Organizational Structure

ASEAN was created with a fairly loose institutional structure. The Annual Ministerial Meeting (AMM) of the ASEAN foreign ministers was the organization's main decision-making body. The AMM was supported by the ASEAN Standing Committee (ASC), which handled the daily affairs of the organization. The ASC rotated annually between members and was chaired by the foreign minister of the host nation and comprised of the ambassadors of the respective ASEAN states within the host nation. ASEAN National Secretariats were created as part of the Foreign Ministries of the ASEAN states. During its formative period, the ASEAN structure produced hundreds of recommendations, but few were actually implemented, and no one group had a true overview of the organization's activities. After the Bali Summit in 1976, ASEAN was reorganized. The restructured ASEAN had the following traits:

1. ASEAN held infrequent Heads of Government meetings. Prior to 1997, the last summit was held in Singapore in 1992, which was only the fourth meeting in twenty-four years.
2. The AMM remained the de facto governing body of ASEAN. After 1976, Economic Ministers Meetings took place. These eventually became the most important decision-making forum for issues of economic cooperation. Finally, annual ASEAN-Post-Ministerial Conferences (ASEAN-PMC) with the ASEAN dialogue partners were institutionalized.[24]
3. The ASEAN Standing Committee and its associated responsibilities and relationships with the ASEAN National Secretariats remained intact.
4. A group of senior foreign ministry officials met regularly as part of the Senior Officials Meeting (SOM). The SOM had no formal standing in ASEAN's structure but was very important. It held regular intra-ASEAN political consultations and serviced the AMM. Later, the AEM established the Senior Economic Officials Meeting (SEOM) to serve a similar function on economic matters.
5. A weak central ASEAN Secretariat with limited functions and a coordinating role was established after 1976. The secretariat was underfunded and understaffed, and the secretary-general of the ASEAN Secretariat was accorded a very low status.
6. Finally, a number of economic and functional committees were established to replace the existing committees. Each committee was supported by technical secretariats and numerous lesser groups. There were five economic committees, answerable to the ASEAN Economic Ministers, and three noneconomic functional committees.[25]

**Figure 2.1 ASEAN's Organizational Structure Before the Bali Summit
(February 1976)**

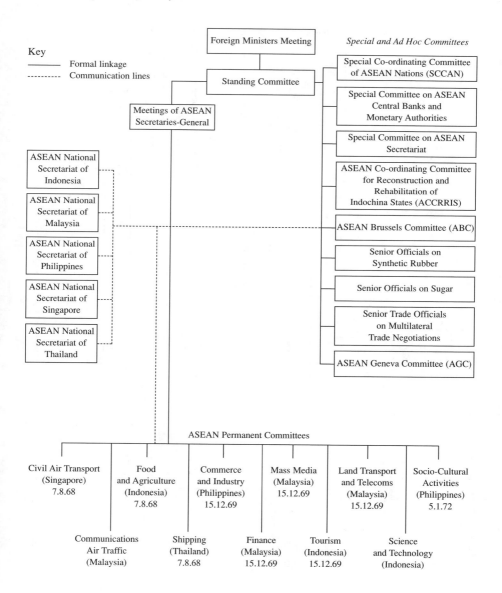

Source: ASEAN Secretariat, *ASEAN Economic Cooperation* (Singapore: ISEAS, 1997): 22.

Figure 2.2 ASEAN's Organizational Structure, 1983

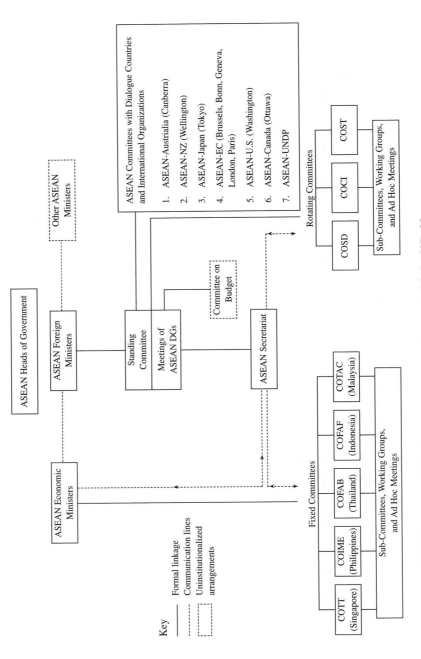

Source: ASEAN Secretariat, *ASEAN Economic Cooperation* (Singapore: ISEAS, 1997): 25.

These official and unofficial structures formed the basic components of ASEAN until it was reorganized again in 1992.[26] The restructuring begun after the Bali Conference allowed ASEAN to encompass more regional economic activity, but it remained an instrument of its member states. The ASEAN Secretariat was unable to gain a significant role in policymaking or any other function that might push the organization toward greater integration.

The ZOPFAN Proposal

ASEAN ran into problems almost immediately after its formation. The Corregidor Affair erupted in March 1968. It involved allegations that the Philippines was using the island of Corregidor as a base to train Muslim insurgents for infiltration into Sabah.[27] Diplomatic attempts to resolve the territorial dispute between Malaysia and the Philippines proved fruitless. In September 1968, the Philippine Congress passed a resolution emphasizing Philippine claims to Sabah. ASEAN meetings were canceled until May 1969, and Malaysia and the Philippines suspended diplomatic contact. In December 1969, Malaysia and the Philippines resumed normal relations; the Malaysian prime minister declared that this action showed "the great value" Malaysia placed upon ASEAN.[28] However, Malaysia's decision also reflected the dramatic changes taking place in the larger regional environment and the corresponding need for the ASEAN states to remain united.

Between 1967 and 1971, a number of international developments radically altered the regional security environment, profoundly affecting the development of ASEAN. In 1968, Britain announced that it was accelerating its withdrawal from Southeast Asia, forcing Singapore and Malaysia to rethink their security strategies. In 1969, U.S. president Richard Nixon issued the Nixon, or Guam, Doctrine, limiting U.S. involvement in Southeast Asia. To the regional states, this new policy indicated U.S. unwillingness to honor its security commitments. Also in 1969, the Soviet Union expressed a regional interest by proposing an Asian collective security system. Factors such as the reemergence of China following the Cultural Revolution, the intensifying Sino-Soviet conflict, the increasing importance of Japanese economic power, and the spread of the Vietnam War to Laos and Cambodia illustrated that Southeast Asia was undergoing rapid changes that ASEAN was completely unable to affect.[29]

Malaysia responded to the regional upheaval by proposing the "neutralization" of Southeast Asia. Malaysian politicians had debated this idea for two years, before making it an official state policy in 1970. Neutralization involved obtaining guarantees from the great powers that they would not pursue their disputes within Southeast Asia. Malaysia had recently shifted its foreign policy position to one of nonalignment, and wished to pursue that goal. Also, the détente between the United States and the Soviet Union and the easing of tensions between the United States and China convinced Malaysia that the time was right for its proposal.

Domestic political factors played an additional important role in Malaysia's advocacy of neutralization. In May 1969, Malaysia had contended with racial riots between ethnic Malays and Chinese. Neutralization accommodated emerging Chinese interests in Southeast Asia, and by reaching out to communist China, the Malaysian government hoped to promote domestic reconciliation with its own Chinese minority and to undermine the ethnic-Chinese-dominated Malayan Communist Party (MCP) at the same time. Malaysia believed that neutralization would help to create a peaceful environment that would enable it to focus on its own economic development and avoid having to take on an onerous defense burden.[30]

The Malaysian neutralization proposal was first formally articulated in September, 1970 at the Nonaligned Conference in Lusaka, Zambia. It had two distinct components:

> One was the collective neutralization of Southeast Asia by means of guarantees by the United States, the Soviet Union and China. These powers were required to accept and respect Southeast Asia as an area of neutrality, exclude the region from competition among themselves, and devise supervisory means to guarantee its neutrality. The second element required countries in the region to fully commit themselves to the principles of non-interference and non-aggression in the conduct of their inter-state relations, follow a policy of non-involvement in the rivalries among the big powers, and seek the exclusion of these rivalries from Southeast Asia.[31]

The reaction to the Malaysian proposal from the great powers was mostly negative. The United States had no desire to disengage from Southeast Asia, and the Soviet Union was seeking to play a more active role in the region. Only China agreed with the proposal, largely because its geographical proximity to Southeast Asia meant that it would not be unduly affected by neutralization.

The other ASEAN states were also opposed to the Malaysian proposal. Indonesia could not accept the neutralization of Southeast Asia through the guarantees of external powers. Indonesia wanted to exclude the great powers from Southeast Asia, not legitimize their intervention in regional affairs. The Indonesian military opposed neutralization because it implied an accommodation with China, which it saw as the main external threat to the region. Indonesia also expressed skepticism that the great powers could cooperate as guarantors of regional neutrality.[32]

The remainder of the ASEAN states opposed neutralization because they relied on foreign powers to guarantee their security. Still, ASEAN agreed to consider Malaysia's idea, especially in light of two important events in the autumn of 1971: the announcement that President Nixon would visit Beijing, which came as a complete surprise to the noncommunist regional states, and China's taking a seat at the United Nations in October, which forced the ASEAN states to decide whether or not to normalize their relations with the communist giant.

A special meeting of the foreign ministers of the ASEAN countries was held outside the ASEAN framework on November 26–27, 1971, in Kuala Lumpur. The compromise on neutralization that came out of the meeting "was an expression of creative ambiguity which did not conspicuously appear to reject Malaysia's initiative."[33] In fact, it endorsed the Indonesian vision of regional order, producing the Declaration on a Zone of Peace, Freedom and Neutrality (ZOPFAN) in Southeast Asia. The operative paragraphs of the ZOPFAN Declaration are

1. that Indonesia, Malaysia, the Philippines, Singapore and Thailand are determined to exert initially necessary efforts to secure the recognition of, and respect for, South East Asia as a Zone of Peace, Freedom and Neutrality, free from any form or manner of interference by outside Powers;
2. that South East Asian countries should make concerted efforts to broaden the areas of cooperation which would contribute to their strength, solidarity and closer relationship.[34]

The preamble mentions neutralization as "a desirable objective" and suggests that the ASEAN states should "explore ways and means of bringing about its realization." However, neutralization is only one of many options that could fulfill the declaration's objectives. Though the word "neutralization" is used in the preamble, the operative concept is really that of a political "neutrality." There is no mention of the great powers having any effective role to play in the region, though the preamble strongly implies that they should respect the sovereignty and independence of the ASEAN states.

The ZOPFAN Declaration is, therefore, a political compromise cobbled together to accommodate ASEAN states with strongly divergent strategic perspectives. According to Leifer, "To the extent that a consensus was worked out in Kuala Lumpur, it was based on a refusal to lend corporate endorsement to a Malaysian-inspired regional accommodation to China."[35] The ZOPFAN Declaration was a broad statement of intent, which imposed no legal obligations on its signatories. The Zone of Peace, Freedom and Neutrality was meant, at best, to be a long-term goal that would not undermine the existing policies and security arrangements of the ASEAN states.[36]

Following the Kuala Lumpur meeting, the ASEAN states created a Senior Officials Committee (SOC) to draw up a ZOPFAN blueprint and develop a common understanding of the interpretation of ZOPFAN. They understood the blueprint to have no practical effect nor to impose any obligations on them so long as ZOPFAN was unrealized. Muthiah Alagappa summarizes the blue-print as follows:

> ZOPFAN may be deemed to exist when the regional states are free to pur-sue national development and regional co-operation without interference from outside powers. Peace is defined as a condition in which the region is free of ideological, political, economic, armed and other forms of con-flicts. Freedom is defined as the right of states to resolve their domestic problems in whatever manner they deem appropriate and to assume the primary responsibility for security and stability in the region. Neutrality requires the regional states to maintain impartiality in their relations with the major powers and refrain from involvement, directly or indirectly, in ideological, political, economic, armed or other forms of conflict.[37]

The blueprint is a stronger reiteration of basic principles first laid out in the ASEAN Declaration, demands from the ASEAN states for the freedom to exercise unconditional sovereignty and to regulate the affairs of their own region. However, the conditions under which ZOPFAN could be achieved were ideal, and represented a lack of commitment to ZOPFAN on the part of most of the ASEAN states.

ZOPFAN stood as the "primary declaratory security policy" of ASEAN.[38] Nonetheless, it was a highly ambiguous concept. The member states had "serious reservations" about it.[39] For Thailand and the Philippines, their existing relationship with the United States was a better security guarantee than being part of a neutralized area. Singapore preferred to trust its secu-rity to a balance of great power forces in the region. Each state had a dif-ferent interpretation of what ZOPFAN meant and implied. ASEAN made very little movement toward implementing the policy. Tim Huxley argues that ZOPFAN was a statement of principles that were never meant to be taken seriously and represented what the ASEAN states understood to be "a vague long-term aspiration."[40]

ZOPFAN stands out as ASEAN's most prominent and important diplo-matic accomplishment before 1975, and it is therefore not surprising that analysts assessing ASEAN's performance at that time felt that the organi-zation had accomplished very little.[41] In retrospect, however, ASEAN may have been far more successful during this formative period than is first apparent. Michael Antolik argues that during this period of apparent inac-tivity, the ASEAN states were actually recovering from the trauma of Kon-frontasi.[42] According to Frank Frost,

> While its formal co-operative projects were limited, and its members were divided on the major question of regional security, ASEAN had enabled a pattern of regular contacts to develop among regional leaders which was reducing the likelihood of inter-state conflict and which later provided a base for a more ambitious programme of consultation and co-operation.[43]

The Bali Conference, 1976

The reduction of U.S. power in Southeast Asia and the related collapse of anticommunist regimes in South Vietnam and Cambodia in 1975 provided a powerful impetus to ASEAN's political development. The leaders of the ASEAN states viewed the rise of communist Vietnam with deep suspicion. They feared that the Vietnamese government would provide arms to indigenous communist movements in other parts of Southeast Asia, particularly Thailand, the Philippines, and Malaysia.

In the wake of this regional upheaval, ASEAN started to come together as an international organization. The organization shifted its emphasis to the promotion of economic development as the surest way of combating the internal appeal of communism in the ASEAN nations. The Indonesian government even wanted to redefine the organization as a military alliance, but the other states rejected this proposal.

The Bali Conference convened in February of 1976. It was the first meeting of the ASEAN heads of state, and it produced two important agreements, the Declaration of ASEAN Concord and the Treaty of Amity and Co-operation in Southeast Asia (TAC). These agreements represent the two dimensions to ASEAN's thinking on security. The Declaration of ASEAN Concord primarily addressed the economic side of security. It briefly mentioned areas of social and cultural cooperation but spent its greatest effort to define areas of economic cooperation, specifying four: cooperation on basic commodities, such as food and energy; cooperation in the creation of large-scale ASEAN industrial projects; cooperation in intraregional trade liberalization; and joint approaches to world economic problems. The declaration also encouraged military cooperation between its members, albeit on a non-ASEAN basis. ASEAN economic ministers had their first meeting in 1975, and, after the Bali Conference, they began to meet annually to facilitate the goals of the declaration.

The TAC dealt with the second component of security in the region. Its goals were to "promote perpetual peace, everlasting unity and co-operation among the people which would contribute to their strength, solidarity and closer relationship."[44] The TAC explicitly allowed for the accession of non-ASEAN Southeast Asian states. It obliged its signatories to settle disputes peacefully through consultation and promoted cooperation in different areas, with the objective of furthering "economic development, peace and stability in Southeast Asia."[45] The TAC was ASEAN's code of conduct for regional relations and embodied the most important norms and values governing the international behavior of the ASEAN states. It also served as a nonaggression pact between the states.

Immediately following the Bali Conference, the ASEAN states moved to implement the declaration's economic provisions. They attempted to increase economic liberalization within the region and to further economic relations with ASEAN's major trading partners. For a variety of reasons, however, ASEAN was not successful in creating significant economic cooperation between its members.

ASEAN as an Economic Organization

From the Bangkok Declaration to the Bali Conference and beyond, intra-ASEAN economic cooperation has been an important part of ASEAN's declared vision of what it wanted to become. However, ASEAN has enjoyed only limited success as an economic institution. During the Cold War era, the ASEAN economies experienced phenomenal development.[46] This impressive economic showing greatly enhanced ASEAN's political standing in the international community. The ASEAN states' economic accomplishments, however, were the result of individual achievements combined with fortuitous events in the larger international economy. Their economic success had no direct connection to ASEAN, the organization.[47]

Richard Stubbs argues that understanding the economic success of the ASEAN states requires consideration of the geopolitical factors and regional security context of Southeast Asia since the end of World War II.[48] Singapore and Malaya in particular, benefited enormously from the economic effects of the Korean War. The economic boom created by that conflict allowed them to develop extensive social and economic infrastructures and effective civil administrations, factors that established the basis for the two colonies' continuing economic success in later times. The Korean War affected the other future ASEAN states only minimally.[49]

The Vietnam War benefited the development of Thailand and Singapore. Thailand began to receive U.S. economic support as early as the mid-1950s, when the United States saw it as a bulwark against communism. Thailand used this support to develop an extensive transportation and communications infrastructure and an efficient, modern civil service. The actual U.S.-Vietnam War (1964–1974) dramatically increased the U.S. economic and military commitment to Thailand. Thailand also prospered as a source of goods for South Vietnam.

Singapore increased its exports to Vietnam during the war. Much of this trade was in petroleum products, which established Singapore as the petroleum-processing center of the region. Singapore increased its exports to other Asian countries, but its export-oriented development strategy toward the war-fuelled U.S. economy had the most profound effect for its economy. Singaporean exports to the United States jumped from $52 million in 1966 to $858 million in 1974. The government used this revenue to continue to develop Singapore's economic and social infrastructures.[50]

Japan began to invest in Southeast Asia starting in the early 1970s. At that time, the Japanese government stopped restricting overseas investment and the export of capital. Japan needed cheaper labor and land and weaker environmental standards to compete more effectively with rising Asian Newly Industrialized Countries (NICs). It needed better access to raw materials and to the economies of the ASEAN states closed by import-substitution policies. Pollution in Japan and the upward revaluation of the yen by 15 percent in December 1971 also contributed to its policy shift.

Japanese investment began to flow at just the right time for ASEAN. The economic stimulus of the Vietnam War was wearing off. Singapore and Malaysia were implementing export-oriented industrialization strategies; Thailand was planning to follow their lead. Even the Philippines and Indonesia were considering opening up their economies.

Most Japanese investment was in Indonesia, in resource-extraction projects. Singapore, which received the greatest per capita impact, Malaysia, and, to a lesser extent, Thailand, attracted Japanese investors in manufacturing industries. This upscale investment was largely attributable to the extensive infrastructures built in these countries in previous eras. Japanese capital utilized the raw materials and services of the ASEAN states, and invested in the textile, chemical, and electrical industries, in order to produce goods for export to the United States. This arrangement was the foundation of the economic success of the prosperous ASEAN states.

In the mid-1970s, Japan also began providing offical development assistance (ODA) to the ASEAN states, particularly Thailand, the "frontline" state in ASEAN's confrontation with Vietnam over Cambodia. Japan's focus on aid was partly a response to increasing anti-Japanese sentiment in the region, partly an acknowledgment of Southeast Asia's increasing strategic and economic importance to Japan, and partly a response to U.S. requests to help the anticommunist regional forces through economic assistance.[51] Thailand and Malaysia were well equipped to absorb this aid effectively, due to their developed infrastructures. The Philippines and Indonesia, for the opposite reasons, did not benefit from Japanese aid to as great a degree. During the 1980s Japan became the dominant economic actor in Southeast Asia largely as a result of its ODA. In 1980, Japanese aid to ASEAN states was U.S. $703 million; by 1989, it was $2.13 billion. In the last half of the 1980s, Japan provided the ASEAN states with 65 percent of their total bilateral aid.[52]

The Plaza Accord of 1985 had a profound effect on Japanese foreign direct investment (FDI) in the ASEAN states. The Plaza Accord was an agreement between the world's major economic powers to depreciate the value of the U.S. dollar and appreciate the Japanese yen. The increased value of the yen, combined with the need to relocate industry in order to counter possible Western protectionist measures against Japanese goods, meant that Japanese business invested in the Asian NICs. By 1986, however, Japanese foreign investment moved on to the ASEAN states, where the local currencies did not appreciate against the U.S. dollar. By 1989, ASEAN members were the major destination for Japanese foreign investment in the region.[53]

Increased Japanese investment significantly altered the nature of the trade between the ASEAN region and Japan. Japanese investors brought in enormous amounts of capital goods to establish industries. Japanese FDI led to an substantial increase in the sale of ASEAN-manufactured goods to Japan. In 1986, ASEAN nations exported $2.1 billion worth of manufactured goods to Japan. By 1989, this jumped to $6.65 billion, 27 percent of all ASEAN exports.[54]

Stubbs draws a number of important lessons from this analysis of ASEAN's economic evolution. A massive influx of capital allowed Singapore, Malaysia, and Thailand to create economic prosperity for themselves. These countries used the capital to create strong infrastructures. The will to develop this absorptive capacity arose from the countries' security positions. All three states were threatened by internal insurgencies and, in the case of Thailand, external threat. Indonesia also attracted a great deal of investment, but it lacked the infrastructure to mobilize that investment properly. The Philippines was in a similar situation. The existence of ASEAN, the organization, did not affect these economic factors. The ASEAN states' economic success was attributable to a confluence of external and internal forces, but ASEAN played no direct role in creating or managing those forces.

When ASEAN was created in 1967, most of the member states, with the exception of Singapore, pursued import-substitution policies and used tariffs and regulatory deterrents to protect their economies from external penetration. During the late 1960s, however, the Philippines, Thailand, and Malaysia shifted their economic focus to export-oriented products, while retaining import-substitution policies in selected areas. Indonesia continued its focus on import-substitution until the early 1980s. The change in policy occurred for a number of reasons. First, import substitution had a disappointing track record. It failed to generate sustained industrial or employment growth, and import replacement did not spill over into the export market, as its practitioners had hoped. Second, the other ASEAN states saw that Singapore and the emerging Asian NICs were prospering through export-oriented industrialization and, until the mid-1970s, access to an increasingly liberal world trading system. Third, international financial institutions and economists began to place a greater emphasis on exports. Despite these changes in focus, however, regulatory and other barriers still existed between the ASEAN states. Export-oriented and import-substitution policies operate in most ASEAN states in a parallel fashion even today, though these states do place greater emphasis on export industries.[55]

ASEAN tried to facilitate intergovernmental economic cooperation between its member states and developed a fairly elaborate institutional structure to do so. Eight ASEAN committees dealt directly with economic issues. Five were responsible to the ASEAN economic ministers, while three fell under the auspices of the ASEAN standing committee, which was responsible to the ASEAN foreign ministers.[56] The ASEAN Secretariat coordinated the eight committees, each of which had subcommittees and working groups operating under it. ASEAN also developed affiliations with nongovernmental economic organizations. Numerous regional private business and professional organizations were connected to ASEAN and allowed to use the "ASEAN" logo. Nonetheless, ASEAN's efforts to foster intraregional economic cooperation were stymied both by a lack of complementarity and by outright competition between most of its members.

The ASEAN states, with the exception of Singapore, traditionally produced natural resources for the first world, while importing capital goods, manufactures, and technology.[57] Japan, the United States, and the European Economic Community (EEC) were their primary economic partners. In 1985, the United States and Japan accounted for 45 percent of ASEAN's exports and 35 percent of its imports; the EEC accounted for 11 and 14 percent, respectively.[58] By contrast, intra-ASEAN trade accounted for between 15 percent and 20 percent of exports for most of the 1970s and 1980s. Most of this intra-ASEAN trade was between Singapore, which acted as an international entrepôt, and the other ASEAN states. When Singapore was removed from the trading picture, intra-ASEAN trade stood at around 5 percent.[59] In addition, the products manufactured in the ASEAN states competed for the same Western markets, dissuading intra-ASEAN economic cooperation.

In 1969, the UN Economic Commission for Asia and the Far East (ECAFE) commissioned a study team to examine the ASEAN economies. Its activities were sanctioned by ASEAN. Its final report, delivered in June 1972, served as a blueprint for subsequent ASEAN economic initiatives. The ECAFE team argued that the development potential of the ASEAN states was limited by their small internal markets. Overcoming this problem required implementing import-substitution policies on a regional, rather than national, basis. ECAFE proposed a kind of economic union to help ASEAN industries take advantage of the economies of scale available at the regional level and have freer access to the region's resources.[60]

Using the UN report as a guide, ASEAN undertook a number of initiatives to introduce intra-ASEAN trade liberalization. In 1977, after years of discussion, it introduced preferential trading arrangements (PTA), which were meant to extend trade preferences between the member states. However, the kind of products that the ASEAN states agreed to include in the PTA were often obscure, and not important enough to truly affect intra-ASEAN trade.

Some of the products, including snowplow equipment and nuclear power plants, were neither produced nor traded in the region.[61] Tariffs were reduced for products produced in ASEAN states but remained formidable enough to stifle significant trade. Numerous nontariff barriers remained in place, such as highly complex regulations designed to frustrate foreign access to the ASEAN economies. As a final measure, Article 12 of the PTA allowed states to block foreign access if domestic industries faced the prospect of "serious injury" due to foreign competition. By 1984, products included in the PTA made up only 0.04 percent of Indonesia's trade with the rest of the ASEAN states. Of the thousands of items for which Indonesia had granted tariff preferences, only nine were actually imported. The situation was similar in the other states, except the free-trade regimes of Singapore and Brunei. By 1990, despite listing almost 16,000 products, the PTA covered less than 1 percent of intra-ASEAN trade.[62]

The UN report also suggested that ASEAN create ASEAN Industrial Projects (AIPs), large industrial projects that would be jointly owned by the ASEAN states. The products of these projects would enjoy preferential access to the ASEAN economies under the PTA. The state that was home to the project would contribute 60 percent of the equity; the other four ASEAN states would provide the remaining 40 percent. Five projects were scheduled for implementation, one to each member.[63] However, only two of these projects—urea production facilities assigned to Malaysia and Indonesia—were successfully implemented, and both of these had previously been suggested as national initiatives.[64] The projects in Singapore and Thailand were abandoned for different reasons and the Philippine project was scaled down.

The AIPs failed for a number of reasons. They were government-sponsored initiatives in a region where the private sector and market were expected to lead economic growth. A report commissioned by the ASEAN Secretariat determined that the projects lacked proper feasibility studies prior to their announcement, adequate technical and financial support, commitment from some member states to implement their designated project, and interest from the private sector.[65]

Another initiative was the ASEAN Industrial Complementation scheme (AIC), first presented in 1976 and officially approved in 1981. This program was meant to develop industrial projects whose individual components would be constructed in the different ASEAN states. The private sector was recruited to develop the plan. In 1976, the ASEAN Automotive Federation (AAF) proposed two projects involving the production and distribution of automotive parts within the ASEAN countries. ASEAN's economic ministers approved one project in 1983; the other was canceled because they could not agree on how the project should be distributed among participants and the parts built by different producers were incompatible. By the end of 1985, the total value of the products traded by the only AIC was just over $1 million.[66] Again, intra-ASEAN economic cooperation failed to produce significant results. As Srikanta Chatterjee points out, "The fact that most ASEAN countries . . . managed to set up their own domestic automotive industries in collaboration with well-known multinational firms from outside ASEAN . . . points towards a certain lack of trust amongst members in matters involving mutual co-operation."[67]

A reconstituted version of the AIC was implemented in 1988, largely at the urging of Japanese automakers. This new initiative, called Brand-to-Brand Complementation (BBC), was a greater success than the original scheme. The BBC expanded to sectors other than automotive components in 1991. It provides components exchanged between participating ASEAN states with a 50 percent margin of preference over competitors. Eight auto companies have had proposals approved for three participating states, Malaysia, the Philippines, and Thailand; Indonesia decided to join the program in 1994. This version of the AIC may prove more successful and durable than its predecessor.[68]

ASEAN Industrial Joint Ventures (AIJVs) attempted to build on the fact that the ASEAN states seemed more willing to cooperate with outside actors on economic matters. This scheme permitted non-ASEAN involvement in industrial projects as long as at least two ASEAN states participated by contributing equity. The items produced by the projects were granted preferential access in the participating countries. The Basic Agreement on ASEAN Industrial Joint Ventures (BAAIJV) was approved in 1983; by 1986, nine projects had been proposed. The private sector has generally shown little interest in these ventures, however, largely because of the difficulty of getting projects approved. By the end of 1994, state bureaucracies had accepted only twenty-three proposals.

ASEAN states tried to cooperate in the provision of financial services. They also tried to coordinate policies and programs in the areas of food, agriculture, forestry, minerals and energy, transport and communication, and tourism. These endeavors created specialized bodies and many meetings, but their results were not impressive. The ASEAN states did enjoy a limited degree of success in acting as an economic bloc. To a large degree, this coherence was forced upon ASEAN by external actors who preferred to deal with the ASEAN states in this manner. As early as 1968, officials of the EEC encouraged the ASEAN states to function as an economic bloc. Interorganizational contact began in earnest in November 1971, when ASEAN and the EEC held informal talks in Brussels. Since that time, the EEC (now the European Union) and ASEAN have enjoyed strong organizational linkages.

A rare example of the ASEAN states functioning as a successful economic bloc is the case of synthetic rubber. In 1973, ASEAN became concerned that an increase in Japanese-produced synthetic rubber would adversely affect the economies of member states, especially Malaysia. The ASEAN states initiated contact with Japan on this issue, and the parties agreed to establish the ASEAN-Japan Synthetic Rubber Forum to deal with the question. Eventually, the forum adopted a memorandum of understanding that obligated Japan to support an ASEAN tire-testing laboratory in Malaysia and to provide assistance to the Rubber Research Centre in Thailand. The Rubber Forum was converted to the ASEAN-Japan Forum in March 1977. Subsequent Japanese economic support for ASEAN economic projects was stalled by intra-ASEAN squabbling. Nonetheless, this experience encouraged Japan to approach the ASEAN states as a group, something it was initially reluctant to do.[69]

In 1978, Australia announced a new international civil aviation policy, which dramatically lowered airfares between Australia and Europe, increased penalties for stopovers, and limited participation in the new policy to Australia's national airline and the airlines of the European nations directly involved. This policy excluded ASEAN airlines from a profitable route and adversely affected the income the ASEAN countries derived from tourist stopovers between Australia and Europe. The ASEAN countries saw Australia's efforts as a blatant attempt to knock the airlines of developing world states out of international civil aviation. At the time, Singapore was the ASEAN state with the most at stake. The ASEAN economic ministers adopted a common policy opposed to Australia. By 1979, the Australian government agreed to allow ASEAN airlines a share of the air traffic between Australia and Europe.

As an economic institution, ASEAN was clearly a failure during the Cold War period. The member states simply did not have the desire to cooperate, and their views on how to pursue their economic interests diverged. Even after they began to move away from import-substitution policies, they still had little reason to forge strong intra-ASEAN economic bonds, largely because their economies were oriented outward. The economic benefits to be gained by pursuing intra-ASEAN trade were negligible in comparison to trade with the rest of Asia, North America, and Europe. What economic success ASEAN did enjoy during this period was either attributable to the involvement of players outside the region, or it took place in areas where intra-ASEAN competition was not a factor. Where the narrow economic interests of individual ASEAN states were in competition, the states were unable to make the economic side of ASEAN work. As we shall see, however, the economic incentives for intra-ASEAN economic cooperation may have changed in the post–Cold War era.

ASEAN may have been economically important in a more indirect way. The existence of the organization and its ability to mitigate disputes between its members contributed to the sense of political stability in the region and made it much more attractive to foreign investment. It is unlikely that foreign business would have flocked to invest in a war zone or an area of high tensions. The extent to which the existence of ASEAN has led to this investment climate compared to the extent to which the investment climate has maintained ASEAN remains, for now, an open question.

The ASEAN Way

A fundamentally important component of ASEAN is its pattern of diplomacy. ASEAN's supporters credit the success of the organization to the "ASEAN way" of diplomacy. The ASEAN way is based upon the Malay cultural practices of *musjawarah* and *mufukat,* which Sukarno and the Indonesians introduced to Southeast Asian diplomacy. *Musjawarah* and *mufukat* are rooted in the traditional village societies of the Malay world. They represent an approach to decisionmaking that emphasizes consensus and consultation. *Musjawarah* means "that a leader should not act arbitrarily or impose his will, but rather make gentle suggestions of the path a community should follow, being careful always to consult all other participants fully and to take their views and feelings into consideration before delivering his synthesis conclusions."[70] *Mufukat* means consensus and is the goal toward which *musjawarah* is directed. *Musjuwarah* relies on the willingness of the members to be aware of the larger interests at stake in a situation. The negotiations that take place in the spirit of *musjawarah* are "not as between opponents but as between friends and brothers."[71]

Starting with this cultural disposition, ASEAN has developed the ASEAN way. The ASEAN way is about the management and containment of problems. It is a "consultative process" that is primarily motivated by the desire to create a stable intramural environment.[72] The techniques used by ASEAN to achieve this goal center around symbolism and indirect approaches to conflictual situations. ASEAN uses code words to express a variety of meanings in its diplomatic dealings. "ASEAN" itself is a code word, representing "prosperity and stability," as well as a sense of regional consciousness and socialization, depending on the context in which it is used.[73] The organization also practices a cautious diplomacy. Within ASEAN, conflicts are dealt with by postponing difficult issues, compartmentalizing an issue so that it does not interfere with other areas of cooperation, and quiet diplomacy. As a result, ASEAN is not capable of *resolving* many issues of contention between its members, but it can move those issues aside so that they do not prevent progress in other areas. ASEAN also promotes regional socialization and has facilitated contacts between the governmental and social elites of its member states. It has helped construct a sense of regional identity, as well as ties of personal obligation and familiarity among national leaders.[74]

Antolik identifies three key principles of ASEAN that all member states must adhere to in order to ensure the success of the organization. These are restraint, respect, and responsibility. *Restraint* refers to a commitment to noninterference in other states' internal affairs; *respect* between states is indicated by frequent consultation; and *responsibility* involves the consideration of each member's interests and concerns.[75] In practice, ASEAN's unified policies reflect a consensus that is usually the lowest common denominator among member states. If the ASEAN states cannot agree on a common policy, they agree to go their separate ways, while still couching their differences in a "language of solidarity" that is sufficiently ambiguous to cover over differences. ASEAN can go to great lengths to accommodate different positions within itself. However, Antolik argues that ASEAN does not exist apart from its member states and only learns insofar as they learn.[76] ASEAN is a convergence of the interests of its members.

Jorgenson-Dahl points out that there are many difficulties associated with transferring the processes of *musjawarah* and *mufukat* to the international system. First, the nature and complexity of the interests at stake at the international level are of a magnitude far beyond that of the village environment where these concepts originated. A disposition toward consensus building is helpful, but it cannot replace a convergence of interests between the negotiating states. Second, the authority vested in a village chieftain has no parallel at the international level. At the village level, the authority and prestige of the leader has an important effect on the outcome of any consensus building. By contrast, the principle of sovereign equality is a fundamental part of international relations. In the context of ASEAN, no one state can legitimately claim to be the leader. Indonesia has asserted this role, and the other ASEAN states have deferred to it. But its position reflects political realities, not institutional structures. Finally, the processes of consultation and consensus building that ASEAN emphasizes are hardly unique to Southeast Asia or Asia more generally. There are many examples of Western-created institutions that effectively function on the basis of consensus building and unanimity.[77]

This is not to argue that the "ASEAN way" and the cultural factors supposedly underlying it are irrelevant. As Jorgenson-Dahl notes, "A residue of goodwill based on feelings of brotherhood and kinship may serve the same purpose as oil on rough sea. They take the edges off the waves and make for smoother sailing."[78] Again, however, there is nothing unique about cultural commonalities forming the basis of more cooperative relations between states. Similar factors probably help to smooth relations between countries such as Canada, Britain, and the United States. What is unique about the ASEAN way is the emphasis that ASEAN's supporters place upon it as the preferred method of diplomatic conduct in Southeast Asia. In the post–Cold War period, some Asian commentators promote the

ASEAN way as the Asian way of conducting international relations. According to them, Asians as a group are culturally disposed toward handling conflict in nonconfrontational ways. They reject rigid, legalistic institutions, preferring informal mechanisms for governing their relations. These cultural preferences are most fully embodied in the ASEAN way and should be extended to encompass the relations of all Asian states.[79]

There are numerous difficulties with this argument. Presenting the ASEAN way as a manifestation of cultural preferences obfuscates the true nature of the process. The refusal of the ASEAN states to create strong, binding institutional structures is not simply an example of an Asian antipathy toward such structures. Rather, it reflects the fact that the ASEAN states do not wish to sacrifice sovereignty or independence of action to a supranational body. They do not share the level of consensus or recognition of common interests necessary to sustain strong institutional obligations.[80]

The ASEAN way is a realistically modest approach to dealing with intra-ASEAN relations. It recognizes what it is possible to achieve between states. By appealing to the lowest common denominator, it does not push the institution beyond what it can sustain. It does not allow disagreement in some areas to prevent cooperation in others. In these respects, it is a brilliant and productive approach to international relations; it is one of ASEAN's genuine strengths. However, the ASEAN way is also symptomatic of ASEAN's institutional weakness. A delicate approach to regional relations is necessary because ASEAN lacks the higher levels of community and integration that would allow it to support binding, strongly institutionalized structures. The ASEAN way may even sustain this limited sense of community by encouraging ASEAN's lowest-common-denominator approach, rather than forcing the member states to compromise to a higher level of cooperation. As we shall see, weaknesses in ASEAN's sense of community have become particularly acute in the post–Cold War era.

Conclusion

The picture of ASEAN that emerges from this historical overview is complex. ASEAN improved relations between its member states. It developed techniques of interaction that fostered cooperative relations. At the same time, it was driven by the spectre of external political threat. ASEAN's members created it in response to the fear of externally sponsored communist insurgency. Even ASEAN's desire to alleviate tensions between its members was motivated, in part, by the fear that if anticommunist Southeast Asia was divided within itself, the region would be much more vulnerable to communist subversion. ZOPFAN, the Treaty of Amity and Cooperation, and the Declaration of ASEAN Concord all responded to changes in

ASEAN's perception of external threats. As an economic institution, ASEAN was mostly unsuccessful. Economic arguments for the integration of the region did exist and were convincing, and ASEAN even made a few tentative steps toward economic integration during the Cold War period. However, the ASEAN states were unwilling to put their national interests aside for the sake of a larger regional interest. During this period, ASEAN made its greatest impact as the political expression of its members' understanding of how the regional states should conduct their relations with each other and the outside world.

Notes

1. The following discussion of the political history of Southeast Asia and ASEAN is based mostly upon the following sources: Jorgenson-Dahl, 1982; Palmer, 1991: 59–74; Irvine, 1982: 8–36, 37–69; Frost, 1990: 1–31; and Huxley, 1990: 83–111. A useful basic history of Southeast Asia is SarDesai, 1994.

2. Acharya, 2000: 17–42.

3. Other outsiders treated Southeast Asia as a distinct region well before the Allied forces arrived. The Chinese and Japanese referred to the region, respectively, as "Nanyang" and "Nanyo," both expressions meaning "the southern seas." See Jorgenson-Dahl, 1982: xii. Mountbatten's South-East Asia Command (SEAC) did not include many of the states now regarded as part of Southeast Asia. ASEAN asserts that there are ten states in Southeast Asia: Brunei, Burma, Cambodia, Indonesia, Laos, Malaysia, the Philippines, Singapore, Thailand, and Vietnam. See Emmerson, 1984: 1–21.

4. During the post–World War II period, the Philippines remained firmly allied to the United States and was home to major U.S. military installations. Though no longer formally a U.S. colony, it was still not independent of U.S. interests. Malaya (including Singapore) remained a colony of Britain until 1963.

5. Tilman, 1987: 16–19.

6. The other Asian member of SEATO was Pakistan. Besides these three and the United States, the members of SEATO were Australia, Britain, France, and New Zealand. The membership roster clearly reflected the Western orientation and interests of SEATO.

7. The members of ASPAC were Australia, Japan, Malaysia, Taiwan, New Zealand, the Philippines, South Korea, South Vietnam, and Thailand. Laos, and Cambodia opted for observer status, along with Indonesia.

8. China, the Soviet Union, and the Communist states of Indochina all denounced the ASA as an offshoot of SEATO.

9. See Leifer, 1968, and Garner Noble, 1977.

10. Ethnic Malay political leaders had accepted Singapore into Malaysia only very reluctantly. The addition of the 1.2 million Chinese of Singapore to Malaysia upset the "racial balance" of the state and made Malays less than the majority ethnic group in Malaysia. The Malaysian constitution provided special economic and political rights to Malays, as well as privileged access to education. Throughout the early part of 1965, Lee Kuan Yew, Singapore's prime minister and leader of the People's Action Party (PAP), campaigned against these policies and tried to popularize a nonethnic vision of Malaysian society. The PAP's attempts to create a multiracial

party largely failed. Its efforts appealed mostly to non-Malays and further polarized communal differences. Malay leaders felt that without special privileges their people would remain at the bottom of the social and economic ladder. Malaysian prime minister Tunku Abdal Rahman was unable to create a policy that could unite both moderate and ultraconservative Malays and contain the PAP. In the end, he ejected Singapore from the Malaysian federation rather than risk further ethnic strife. He announced Singapore's ejection from Malaysia on August 9, 1965. See Mackie, 1974: 292–297; SarDesai, 1994: 254–255.

11. Alagappa explains Konfrontasi by noting that Indonesia wished to establish an international reputation as a representative of the "emerging forces" of the developing world, as opposed to "reactionary and repressive old established forces." Malaysia was an example of "neocolonialism." Indonesian political forces portrayed Malaysia as a threat to the territorial integrity of Indonesia. Therefore, Sukarno, the Communist Party of Indonesia (PKI), and the Armed Forces of Indonesia (ABRI) all supported Konfrontasi to help establish their nationalist credentials. See Alagappa, 1991a: 18.

12. Van der Kroef, 1971: 1–45. The exact number of people killed by the military and anticommunist nationalist gangs is unclear, but it may have been more than 1 million. Ibid.: 14.

13. Konfrontasi between Indonesia and Malaysia came to an end in May 1966, after a meeting in Bangkok between the foreign ministers of the respective states. Indonesia recognized Singapore in June of 1966, but the Jakarta Agreement ending Konfrontasi and normalizing relations between Indonesia and Malaysia was not signed until August 16, 1966. See Mackie, 1974: 318–322; Garner Noble, 1977: 160–161.

14. The idea that ASEAN itself is primarily a tool designed to control Indonesia within the subregional context remains a powerful reason for the organization's continued viability today. Indonesians I interviewed generally viewed their country's commitment to ASEAN as a form of self-restraint. The Indonesians also viewed their country as too large to meet its international aspirations within ASEAN.

15. Antolik, 1990: 19.

16. Leifer, 1989: 4.

17. Quoted in Jorgenson-Dahl, 1982: 36.

18. ASEAN Declaration, Preamble, Bangkok, Thailand, August 8, 1967.

19. In an interview, a Thai academic noted that Thailand had learned to distrust SEATO during the 1960s. At that time, Thailand felt threatened by Communist insurgents in Laos. Thailand threatened to leave SEATO unless the United States agreed to defend Thailand in the event that SEATO could or would not act. The United States eventually agreed to this condition.

20. Leifer, 1989: 5–6.

21. Huxley, 1990: 84.

22. Quoted in Palmer, 1991: 65.

23. When ASEAN was first taking shape, there are indications that Indonesia suggested the organization might eventually form the basis of a regional military bloc. The ASEAN states soon arrived at the consensus that they should not emphasize military cooperation as one of the organization's functions. See Irvine, 1982: 17–18. Moreover, at the time, Indonesia was also concerned about maintaining its nonaligned status and image. See Leifer, 1989: 5.

24. The ASEAN-PMC later formed the basis of the ASEAN Regional Forum (ARF). The ARF is discussed in more detail in Chapter 6.

25. This assessment of ASEAN's institutional redesign is based upon Chin, 1995: 431–432.

26. Irvine, 1982: 55–61.

27. The Corregidor Affair involved the killing, apparently by their officers, of twelve to sixty recruits being trained at a secret army camp on the island of Corregidor, in Manila Bay. The recruits were Muslim, and some had been told that their assignment might be the infiltration of Sabah. See Jorgenson-Dahl, 1982: 197–198; Garner Noble, 1977: 165–171.

28. Irvine, 1982: 20.

29. Hanggi, 1991: 12.

30. This account of ZOPFAN and the circumstances surrounding its creation is based primarily on Leifer, 1989: 52–60; Alagappa, 1991b: 272–275; Hanggi, 1991: 12–20; Irvine, 1982: 23–29; Huxley, 1993: 16–18.

31. Alagappa, 1991b: 272.

32. According to Alagappa, Indonesia was "cool but not opposed" to Malaysia's proposal. It saw the concept of neutralization as generally in keeping with its own policies of nonalignment. Indonesia interpreted the Malaysian proposal as an attempt to regulate the activities of external powers and advance the declaration's designation of all foreign military bases in the region as "temporary." Nonetheless, Indonesia's overall opposition to the proposal was far stronger than any mitigating considerations. Alagappa, 1991b: 272–273.

33. Leifer, 1989: 58.

34. Zone of Peace, Freedom and Neutrality Declaration, Kuala Lumpur, Malaysia, November 27, 1971.

35. Leifer, 1989: 59.

36. Another agreement came out of the Kuala Lumpur meeting. This is the "agreement on consultations for a common approach to political issues affecting Southeast Asia." This agreement institutionalized the habit of consulting with ASEAN that has since become one of the most important elements of ASEAN's unity and effectiveness. Ibid.: 58–59; Hanggi, 1991: 17; Huxley, 1993: 16.

37. Alagappa, 1991b: 274.

38. Rolls, 1991: 325.

39. Frost, 1990: 6.

40. Huxley, 1993: 16.

41. Frost, 1990: 7.

42. Antolik, 1990: 159.

43. Frost, 1990: 7.

44. Ibid.: 9.

45. Ibid.

46. In 1987, Singapore had a per capita income of U.S. $7,325. This was much higher than Taiwan ($4,573) or South Korea ($2,826). In the same year, Malaysia and Thailand were classified as near NICs, while the Philippines and Indonesia remained relatively poor countries. Brunei, which joined ASEAN in 1984, had the highest per capita income in ASEAN, though solely as a result of its oil wealth. See Stubbs, 1989: 518.

47. See Castro, 1982: 70–91; Tyabji, 1990: 32–57; and Chatterjee, 1990: 58–82.

48. Stubbs, 1989: 517–540.

49. For details of the effects of the Korean War on the economies of Singapore and Malaya, see Stubbs, 1989: 520–526.

50. The Philippines also benefited from the U.S.-Vietnam War but was unable to turn the U.S. war expenditure into long-term infrastructural gains, as in Thailand. Stubbs, 1989: 530.

51. Stubbs, 1991: 657–658.

52. Ibid.: 658.

53. Ibid.: 659–660. Stubbs cites the following figures: Japanese FDI in Thailand went from $46 million in 1985 to $1.28 billion in 1989; in Singapore, from $494 million in 1987 to $1.9 billion in 1989; and in Malaysia, from $163 million in 1987 to $975 million in 1990.

54. Ibid.: 660–661. Stubbs points out that the ASEAN states proceeded to push Japan into the role of a regional leader on economic issues. While ASEAN was prepared to follow the Japanese lead in some areas, it required that Japan remain constrained by the U.S. regional presence.

55. Arif and Hill, 1985: 19; Castro, 1982: 72.

56. One of the factors contributing to ASEAN's early inability to make progress in the economic field was that ASEAN's economic initiatives were directed by the foreign ministers of the ASEAN states. Economic ministers rarely took part in ASEAN discussions. Castro, 1990: 74–75.

57. During the 1970s and 1980s, ASEAN supplied over 80 percent of the world's natural rubber and abaca fibre, 70 percent of its tin, 60 percent of its palm oil, and 50 percent of its copra. Castro, 1982: 71.

58. Chatterjee, 1990: 64.

59. Ibid.

60. This account of the UN report is based primarily on Castro, 1982: 75–77; Suriyamongkol, 1988: 56–62; Jorgenson-Dahl, 1982: 142–145; and Ravenhill, 1995: 851–853.

61. The Philippines listed snowplow equipment and Indonesia included nuclear power plants. Ravenhill says that these sorts of actions turned the PTA into a "farce." Ravenhill, 1995: 853.

62. Ibid.

63. The allocated projects were the following: Indonesia, urea project; Malaysia, urea project; Philippines, copper fabrication project; Singapore, Hepatitis B vaccine project; and Thailand, rock salt–soda ash project. Chatterjee, 1990: 68.

64. Ravenhill, 1995: 852.

65. Ibid. The lack of commitment of the ASEAN states to the AIPs is demonstrated by the fact that ASEAN states would neither guarantee markets to the products produced by AIPs nor promise to refrain from developing the same industries on a national level, which would then compete with the regional AIPs. Suriyamongkol, 1988: 210–215, 226.

66. Chatterjee, 1990: 69–70.

67. Ibid.: 70.

68. Ravenhill, 1995: 852.

69. The end of the Vietnam War and the successful conclusion of the Bali Conference also encouraged Japan to deal with ASEAN as a group rather than with individual states on a bilateral basis, which had been its preference. See Sudo, 1991: 20–21.

70. Quoted by Jorgenson-Dahl, 1982: 166.

71. Indonesian foreign minister Subandrio, quoted by Jorgenson-Dahl, 1982: 166.

72. Antolik, 1990: 9–10.

73. Ibid.: 94–96.

74. In a confidential interview, an academic told me that informal contacts between diplomats in ASEAN were instrumental in defusing tensions between the Philippines and Indonesia created by the holding of a human rights conference on East Timor in the Philippines. These contacts prompted the Philippines' government to obstruct the conference. This is a rather dubious example of intra-ASEAN cooperation.

75. Antolik, 1990: 8–10, 156–157; Rolls, 1991: 316. As an example of intra-ASEAN "responsibility," Antolik cites Singapore's relations with its neighbors regarding the treatment of ASEAN nationals in Singapore. In the past, Singapore has executed both Indonesian and Thai nationals, despite the protests of their respective governments. Antolik argues that such insensitivity on the part of the Singaporean government would not occur again. However, this did occur again: the execution of a Filipina national in Singapore in March of 1995 created a genuine crisis within ASEAN at the time. See "Anger of a Nation," 1995.

76. Antolik, 1990: 10.

77. Jorgenson-Dahl, 1982: 165–167. Jorgenson-Dahl cites the failed League of Nations as an example of the requirement of unanimity at work in a broader-based international institution. He also mentions the Council of Europe and the Council of NATO as requiring unanimity in some cases.

78. Ibid.: 167.

79. While there may be some validity to this cultural argument, it may have more to do with form than content (as indicated by the history of war and conflict in Asia).

80. Malaysia and the Philippines first wished to construct the ASA as a strong institution with binding obligations. Thailand vetoed this idea and pushed for a less binding structure. The decision to implement a loose structure reflected political realities, not cultural considerations. Jorgenson-Dahl, 1982: 20.

3

Vietnam's Invasion of Cambodia

Many observers consider ASEAN's management of the Vietnamese invasion of Cambodia (known at the time as Kampuchea) to be the high-water mark in the organization's diplomatic history. The Vietnamese occupation lasted from 1978 to 1990. During this period, ASEAN emerged as a significant international and regional actor. Much of the argument that ASEAN can play a major role in the security and economic arrangements of the Asia-Pacific is based upon a highly favorable interpretation of ASEAN's handling of the invasion. According to this interpretation, ASEAN's management of this issue demonstrated its ability to be a coherent and effective regional organization.

Even though ASEAN did exhibit a high degree of diplomatic cohesion during this formative period, it was also dogged by consistent disagreements between its member states. Key ASEAN states had differing perceptions of the regional threat and different strategies on how to approach it. The Vietnam experience is more instructive and pertinent as an indication of the limitations of intra-ASEAN cooperation than it is as a measure of ASEAN's solidarity.

The Interwar Period

The establishment of communist regimes in Vietnam, Cambodia, and Laos in 1975 forced ASEAN to decide how to approach Indochina. The 1976 Bali Conference and the associated ASEAN Declaration of Concord and the TAC were part of an overall strategy to consolidate regional security, while extending an olive branch to Vietnam (now the Socialist Republic of Vietnam, or SRV) and its allies.[1] In mid-1975, ASEAN proposed the establishment of cooperative relations with communist Indochina, an offer it left open until 1978, but it was not yet willing to open its membership to the communist states. Vietnam was suspicious of ASEAN, however, and refused to establish relations with the organization. Instead, it pursued bilateral relations with the different ASEAN states. Vietnam had not forgotten about the involvement of some ASEAN members, Thailand and the Philippines, in the U.S. war effort against North Vietnam (the Democratic Republic of Vietnam, or DRV). It believed ASEAN to be an indirect tool of U.S. imperialism. Nonetheless, individual ASEAN states and the SRV were able to establish diplomatic and commercial ties.[2]

Vietnam's approach to regional issues reflected both its sense of its importance in the region, given its victory over the United States, and its perception of ASEAN as U.S. instrument. In 1976, Vietnam expressed what was interpreted in the ASEAN capitals as a desire to support revolutionary movements throughout the region. Vietnam also called for the development of "genuine neutrality" in Southeast Asia. The use of the term "genuine neutrality" offended the ASEAN states, which heard in the phrase the implication that Malaysia and the Philippines could not be considered neutral until they removed the foreign bases on their soil. At a meeting of the Non-Aligned Movement (NAM) in August 1976, Vietnam and its communist allies explicitly rejected ZOPFAN as a model for regional security in Southeast Asia. In late 1977 and early 1978, Vietnam suggested the formation of a new Southeast Asian organization, based on the principles of "peace, independence, and neutrality." In May 1978, Vietnam presented its own regional vision at the United Nations. It called for the declaration of Southeast Asia as a Zone of Peace, Independence and Genuine Neutrality (ZOPIGN), an obvious counterpart to ASEAN's ZOPFAN.

In the face of Vietnamese hostility toward its regional vision, ASEAN closed ranks and reiterated its commitment to ZOPFAN. Given the opposition of the Indochinese states and its own internal ambivalence toward ZOPFAN, ASEAN was incapable of making tangible progress on its initiatives. However, the sense of threat within ASEAN was not as pressing as it had been immediately after the communist victory in Vietnam. Since 1975, it had become clear that the Khmer Rouge (KR), which ruled Kampuchea, was fiercely independent and would not be part of a Vietnamese-dominated communist bloc in Indochina. ASEAN welcomed this inter-communist balance of power on the mainland, as it made it easier for the organization to accommodate conflicting security perspectives between its members. Thailand was happy with a situation that prevented Vietnam from dominating Indochina and maintained Kampuchea as a buffer between Thailand and Vietnam. Indonesia was satisfied with the growing Sino-Vietnamese tensions, which impeded Chinese influence in Southeast Asia.

By August 1977, the intra-communist conflict began to escalate. The KR provoked a series of military conflicts on the Vietnam-Kampuchea border. By the end of 1977, Vietnam and Kampuchea had suspended diplomatic relations. Each started preparing for war and seeking outside assistance. Kampuchea turned to China; Vietnam strengthened its ties to the Soviet Union. Both sides began to court ASEAN. Despite its inability to articulate a concerted approach to regional security and a decided lack of progress toward economic cooperation, ASEAN found itself the focus of considerable diplomatic attention.

This attention was part of a trend that started in 1977. Outside powers had begun to view the organization as a bulwark against communist Indochina. Japanese prime minister Fukuda attended ASEAN's tenth anniversary meeting in 1977. The meeting also initiated ASEAN's dialogue with actors from outside the region. This international attention increased ASEAN's prestige, and the competition between the communist powers for ASEAN's support enhanced ASEAN's diplomatic credentials. The more foreign actors treated ASEAN as a diplomatic community, the more it responded as though it were a coherent body.

In July 1978, Vietnamese foreign minister Phan Hien toured Southeast Asia. He declared that Vietnam now regarded ASEAN as a regional economic organization, rather than a U.S. puppet. He announced Vietnam's support for ZOPFAN, while calling for discussions on ZOPIGN. In September and October, Vietnamese premier Pham Van Dong visited the ASEAN capitals. In each nation, he offered to sign a bilateral treaty of friendship and nonaggression; he also pledged that Vietnam would not provide any support to regional insurgencies. ASEAN coordinated its response to the Vietnamese initiatives and collectively agreed to decline the offers of nonaggression treaties.[3]

Kampuchea launched its own diplomatic initiative with the assistance of China. Deng Xiaoping himself visited Thailand in December 1978, to support the Kampucheans.[4] By this time, the intelligence agencies of the ASEAN states knew that both Vietnam and Kampuchea had been equipped for war by their external supporters and that the conflict in Indochina was becoming more intense. On November 3, 1978, Vietnam signed a twenty-five-year Treaty of Friendship and Co-operation with the Soviet Union. On December 25, Vietnam began its invasion and occupation of Kampuchea.

Vietnam's Role

The Vietnamese decision to invade Cambodia was the outcome of a long history of antagonistic Communist Party relationships within Indochina.[5] Even before the end of the Vietnam War, KR factions were engaged in military conflict with the Vietnamese Communists. Differences in doctrine, history, culture, and the demands of strategic imperatives combined to create hostility between the two groups. After 1975, different Vietnamese

actions and initiatives, especially the Vietnamese call for a "special relationship" between the countries of Indochina, confirmed KR fears that Vietnam aspired to be the Indochinese hegemon. Relations worsened, and the
KR launched a number of commando raids on Vietnam, which ultimately
provoked the Vietnamese invasion.[6]

History had taught Vietnam to think of Indochina as a "single strategic
unit."[7] France and the United States had frequently used Laos and Cambodia as staging grounds for attacks. The Vietnamese determined that their
own peace, security, and independence were contingent on having friendly
governments in their neighbor states. Vietnam's attempts to ensure this outcome antagonized Kampuchea, which perceived Vietnam's ambitions as a
threat and moved closer to China to balance Vietnam. Vietnam already
regarded China's designs in Southeast Asia with considerable suspicion, and
it moved closer to the Soviet Union even as it grew increasingly estranged
from China. China attempted to mediate the conflict, fearing that the Soviet
Union would exploit the rift. However, after 1975, open conflict between the
KR and Vietnam led the parties to break diplomatic relations. This development forced China to choose between the two. By February 1978, China
denounced "hegemony" in Indochina (a reference to Vietnamese ambitions)
and increased its provision of weapons to the KR, which from Vietnam's
perspective confirmed that Kampuchea was an instrument of Chinese domination in the region. Vietnam moved closer to the Soviets, joining the
Council for Mutual Economic Assistance (COMECON) in June 1978. China
responded by suspending all remaining aid to Vietnam. Finally, the USSR-
Vietnam Treaty of Friendship and Cooperation of November 1978 gave
Vietnam a superpower protector against China and its Kampuchean ally. The
treaty opened the door to the Vietnamese invasion of Kampuchea, and the
conflict moved to the forefront of continuing Soviet-Chinese competition.[8]

Vietnam's long-term strategy in Kampuchea was to create a state that
was self-reliant but allied to Hanoi. The Vietnamese saw two possible
"traps" that they wanted to avoid. The first was creating a Kampuchean
regime dependent on Vietnam for its survival. The second was withdrawing
from Kampuchea too early, thereby allowing the return of the KR and, by
extension, China. To avoid the risk of Kampuchean dependence, Vietnam
announced a policy of gradual troop withdrawals, beginning in February
1982. These withdrawals were designed to force the new Kampuchean government forces to fend for themselves. To deal with the the possibility of a
KR return, Vietnam launched a series of devastating attacks on Kampuchean resistance encampments in Thailand during the 1984–1985 dry
season. The objective of these attacks was to cripple the resistance, allowing Vietnam to withdraw completely from the area by 1990 while giving
the People's Republic of Kampuchea (PRK) the opportunity to consolidate
its own military gains. Vietnam also advanced plans for economic integration between it and Kampuchea, in order to ensure the PRK's survival.

Vietnam counted on its gradual troop withdrawals to placate international opposition and to draw attention away from questions about the legitimacy of the Kampuchean government. If the sight of Vietnamese troops withdrawing was not enough to distract the world from the conflict altogether, it might be enough to refocus world attention on how to prevent the return to power of the Khmer Rouge (KR). Either way, Vietnam believed that it could block the return of the KR. It could still achieve the larger goals of its intervention.[9]

Vietnam tried to play to contradicting threat perceptions and the concerns of some ASEAN states, notably Indonesia and Malaysia, about the intrusion of external powers into Southeast Asia. This strategy met with limited success, in part because of Vietnam's clumsiness in attempting to sow discord within ASEAN. In the short term, Vietnam's attempts to foment disunity actually drew ASEAN together more strongly.[10] In the long term, however, the significant differences in perceptions about security interests between ASEAN states created tensions within the organization over its handling of Vietnam.

The Roles and Interests of the Great Powers

The Cambodian conflict attracted a great deal of attention from the great powers because it began at a time of considerable tension between the Soviet Union and China. The U.S. retreat from Vietnam left a power vacuum in Southeast Asia that the Soviets and Chinese tried to fill. Already confronted by a Soviet presence on its northern border, China was concerned about keeping its southern flank free of Soviet influence. Vietnam could not, therefore, form a relationship with the Soviet Union without aggravating China. By February 1979, when China invaded Vietnam in response to its invasion of Kampuchea, there were numerous areas of contention between the two countries, including territorial disputes. The most important single factor accounting for Chinese hostility, however, was Vietnam's growing relationship with China's primary rival, the Soviet Union.

China's strategic response to these developments was to "bleed" Vietnam and, by extension, the Soviet Union. After its punitive invasion in February–March 1979, China continued to apply military pressure on Vietnam in an effort to exhaust Vietnam's economic and military ability to maintain its occupation.[11] China supported the KR in a guerrilla war designed to mire Vietnam in an unwinnable conflict until it was drained and the Soviet Union had lost its desire to underwrite the occupation. China demanded the complete and unconditional withdrawal of Vietnamese troops from Kampuchea as part of a delaying tactic designed to keep Vietnam engaged in the struggle. To implement its strategy, China needed to improve relations with the ASEAN states, especially the frontline state of Thailand. Chinese weapons could then cross Thailand and reach the KR. The conflict also provided China with opportunities to better its relations with ASEAN, to engage the ASEAN states in a united front against Vietnam, and to act as a guarantor of peace and stability in Southeast Asia.

The Soviet Union's behavior was defined by its rivalry with China and its desire to exploit the decline of U.S. power. Vietnam needed Soviet support. In exchange for that support, the Soviet Union gained considerable prestige in its competition with China for intercommunist primacy. It also acquired a strategic foothold in a region from which it had been excluded. In March 1979, Vietnam allowed the Soviet Union the use of base facilities at Cam Ranh Bay; in 1980, the Soviets were granted access to an airfield at Danang. These developments permitted the extension of Soviet military power into the Indian Ocean and Persian Gulf, and formed the cornerstone of a Soviet-Vietnamese alliance against their mutual enemies, China and the United States.

U.S. interests in the conflict were less direct than those of China and the Soviet Union. The United States perceived the Vietnamese invasion as a threat to Thailand, as a challenge to its strategic reliability in the region, and as an opportunity to cement a partnership with China against the Soviet Union. It responded to the invasion by tightening its economic embargo on Vietnam, expanding its military presence in the region, and increasing arms sales to the ASEAN states. Initially, the United States was highly supportive of China's intransigent stand against Vietnam, but congressional pressure later forced the U.S. government to distance itself from the KR and to become more sensitive to the spread of Chinese influence in Southeast Asia. Nonetheless, U.S. support was essential in strengthening ASEAN's resistance to the Vietnamese invasion.

Issues and conflicts particular to other actors in this situation also played important roles in perpetuating the war in Kampuchea, but the interests of the great powers kept the conflict going. All three great powers benefited from the situation. Vietnam's aggression provided China with an opportunity to exercise power and influence in the region. The war also gave China and the United States an opportunity to damage the Soviet Union. The Soviets, by contrast, gained an unprecedented foothold in the region that they could maintain as long as Vietnam remained dependent on their support.[12]

ASEAN's Response

The Vietnamese invasion had an immediate and dramatic effect on ASEAN. ASEAN's previous institutional development had largely been in response to the perceived security threat from Vietnam. Now, it appeared that Vietnam was living up to its neighbors' greatest fears. Moreover, the invasion occurred only a few months after Vietnamese premier Pham Van Dong's visit to the ASEAN states and his assurances that Vietnam would respect the principles of territorial sovereignty and noninterference. In the eyes of the ASEAN leaders, the attack on the state of Kampuchea was a breach of faith.[13]

Vietnam's invasion and occupation of Cambodia violated two of ASEAN's fundamental security norms: (1) states shall not interfere in the domestic affairs of other states; (2) states shall not use force to resolve political disputes.[14] While the ASEAN states could agree on the general principles at stake and the need to reverse the Vietnamese invasion, their divergent strategic perspectives created friction within ASEAN over how to achieve that goal.

Thailand was the ASEAN state most directly threatened by the Vietnamese invasion, which radically altered the regional balance of power by destroying Kampuchea as a buffer state between Thailand and Vietnam. Thailand was not afraid of a Vietnamese military invasion, but it was historically opposed to Vietnamese dominance in Indochina, which threatened its own aspirations. More directly, it was concerned that Vietnam would undermine its national security by supporting insurgency and secession, especially in northeastern Thailand.

Thailand's primary response to the invasion was to call on the great powers. ASEAN was a part of Thailand's diplomatic response to Vietnam, but it was only a secondary factor in the Thais' overall strategy. The organization could not provide the raw power necessary to roll back the Vietnamese invasion; such power was only available from much larger players. In January 1979, Thailand struck a secret bargain with China whereby it facilitated Chinese material support to the deposed KR. In exchange, China abandoned its support for the Communist Party of Thailand. In February, Thai prime minister Kriangsak Chomanan visited Washington to secure a reiteration of U.S. security guarantees to Thailand. It was on the basis of the support of these great powers that Thailand decided to oppose Vietnam's actions.[15]

Singapore's strategic perspective was ostensibly influenced by the Soviet Union's support for the Vietnamese invasion. However, Singaporean calculations were also more subtle. Singapore believed that a stable balance of power in the region required the involvement of the United States. By presenting the Vietnamese action as an example of Soviet expansionism, it attempted to draw U.S. attention. Singapore still adhered to the domino theory of communist expansion, and Vietnam's huge supply of captured U.S. weapons gave rise to fears that Vietnam would use those arms to support regional insurgency. Singapore regarded itself as highly vulnerable; it could not afford to lose the buffer states between it and Vietnam.[16]

Indonesia took a much different perspective on the invasion from the outset. Some observers have suggested that, initially, Thailand needed to convince Indonesia to oppose Vietnamese actions.[17] Despite being deeply hostile to communism and having maritime territorial disputes with Vietnam, Indonesia was still well disposed to the SRV. There are several major reasons for Indonesia's initial reluctance to condemn Vietnam. First, Indonesia was sympathetic to Vietnam's security concerns. As a nation that had to wage a prolonged anticolonial war before it gained independence, Indonesia believed it understood Vietnamese fears. Second, to Indonesia, it was unclear that Vietnam was a threat to regional security, and even if it was, it only constituted a short-term threat. Indonesia viewed China as the real long-term security threat and hoped that Vietnam could help check the expansion of Chinese influence into Southeast Asia.[18] In addition, Indonesia resented the ASEAN agenda being set by Thailand.

Despite its reservations about the general direction of ASEAN corporate policy toward Vietnam, however, Indonesia had a number of reasons for supporting ASEAN. First, Indonesia needed to demonstrate that it could be a regional player. With the shadow of Konfrontasi still hanging over, it could not afford to undermine ASEAN. Second, Indonesia continued to view ASEAN as an instrument through which it could exercise regional influence. Finally, the Indonesians recognized that Thailand was quite willing to abandon ASEAN if the organization did not support its position against Vietnam. Losing Thailand would disrupt ASEAN and push the Thais into an even closer relationship with China. For these reasons, Indonesia was willing to submerge its own immediate interests for the sake of ASEAN solidarity and to try to work within ASEAN to resolve the Kampuchean situation.

Like Indonesia, Malaysia considered China to be the paramount long-term threat to the region, and saw Vietnam as a possible counterweight to Chinese influence. Local insurgencies in Malaysia continued to gain their greatest support from ethnic Chinese, and the PRC had refused to renounce its support of the Communist Party of Malaya. Moreover, Malaysia perceived the outflow of ethnic-Chinese boat people from Vietnam that was occurring at the time of the Cambodian conflict as a threat to its ethnic balance.

The Philippines, due to its geographic isolation, did not feel particularly threatened by either Vietnam or China. It had serious communist and Muslim insurgencies with which to contend; it was not overly concerned with hypothetical threats from external actors. However, the Philippines had a well-established legalistic outlook in international relations; it could not excuse Vietnam's actions. Moreover, ASEAN was fundamental to the Philippines' strategy of building its regional identity. Therefore, the Philippines would not dissent from the ASEAN consensus.

Despite the lack of an organizational strategic consensus, ASEAN could not ignore the blatant violation of principle Vietnam's invasion represented. Nonetheless, ASEAN's initial statements on the invasion were quite diplomatic, reflecting Indonesia's perspective and the desire to keep channels of communication open with Vietnam. The organization met in Bangkok on January 12–13, 1979, and issued a statement calling for the "immediate and total withdrawal of the foreign forces from Kampuchean territory."[19] In February–March 1979, ASEAN responded to China's punitive assault on Vietnam by calling for the withdrawal of all foreign forces from both Vietnam and Cambodia.

From 1979 to 1980, ASEAN applied political and economic pressure to Vietnam and its client government of Kampuchea. It focused its diplomatic efforts on international forums such as the United Nations and the Non-Aligned Movement. Its political goal was to deny the new People's Republic of Kampuchea (PRK) international recognition and access to international aid. ASEAN also sought to deny Vietnam access to economic aid from the West and Japan. In order to maintain the pressure on Vietnam, ASEAN kept the conflict in the international public eye, working to define the terms of the international debate. ASEAN established the orthodoxy that the Vietnamese invasion caused the Cambodian conflict, which could only be resolved therefore if Vietnam withdrew.

ASEAN was quite successful in garnering support for its diplomatic and economic agenda in international forums. Its activities also promoted cooperation within the organization. Operating as a bloc on the international stage taught the ASEAN states how to refine internal consultation and policy coordination. Nonetheless, ASEAN remained divided on how to achieve its stated goals. While the ASEAN states could agree on political and economic pressures against Vietnam, they disagreed on the form of military pressure.

In September 1979, Vietnam and its allies tried, unsuccessfully, to replace Democratic Kampuchea (DK) with the PRK as the country's representative at the UN. ASEAN rallied opposition to this move and succeeded in coordinating a 91–21 vote in favor of a resolution calling for a cease-fire, the withdrawal of foreign forces, and the convening of an international conference on the conflict. ASEAN's diplomatic success reflected not only its own efforts but also the organization's inclusion in a larger informal international coalition opposed to Vietnam and the Soviet Union. ASEAN received vigorous diplomatic support from China for its initiatives. Chinese willingness to provide military support for the KR was also essential in maintaining ASEAN's initial opposition to Vietnam's actions. Without access to Chinese military backing, it is doubtful that Thailand would have opposed the invasion of Cambodia on the basis of ASEAN's diplomatic support alone. The rapprochement between the United States and China, based on a common opposition to the Soviet Union, was also at work. The United States responded to the invasion by implementing economic sanctions against Vietnam. Despite concerns with driving Vietnam more firmly into the arms of the Soviet Union, Japan and the European Community followed suit.

ASEAN's ability to adopt a common policy toward Vietnam concealed internal disagreements over whose security interests were being served. Indonesia and Malaysia persisted in their view that ASEAN's corporate policy furthered Chinese interests by punishing Vietnam and would compound regional problems in the long term. They also feared that Vietnam was being driven more tightly into the Soviet orbit. The Soviet access to military facilities in Vietnam was symptomatic of this development. ASEAN's policies not only drew the organization into the Sino-Soviet conflict but also were bound to lead to an intensification of that conflict in Southeast Asia. The final outcome would either be a weakened Vietnam subject to Chinese influence, or a weakened Vietnam increasingly dependent on the Soviet Union, which would reinforce the Thailand-China relationship. The idea of ZOPFAN would never become a reality, and Southeast Asia would continue as the focus of great-power rivalry.[20]

In March 1980, these growing concerns led to a meeting between President Suharto of Indonesia and Prime Minister Hussein Onn of Malaysia in the Malaysian town of Kuantan.[21] Indonesia and Malaysia believed that Vietnam could be convinced to withdraw from Cambodia if its "legitimate" security needs were taken into account. The resulting Kuantan Declaration stated that Southeast Asia could only be a zone of peace if Vietnam were freed of Chinese and Soviet influence, something that could only be achieved by recognizing Vietnam's legitimate interest in the political character of Kampuchea. In effect, the declaration was the application of ZOPFAN to the Cambodian conflict.

The Kuantan Declaration implicitly accepted Vietnam's hegemonic status in Indochina. As such, it was completely unacceptable to Bangkok. Hanoi rejected the declaration, too; it was not about to abandon its close relationship to the Soviet Union. The Kuantan Declaration, which had disturbed the surface political cohesion of ASEAN, became a political embarrassment that was rapidly buried. Nonetheless, the political and strategic logic underlying the declaration persisted and continued to create tensions within ASEAN, albeit in a more muted form.[22]

Subsequent developments temporarily mitigated intra-ASEAN divisions. In June 1980, the Thai government, with the approval of the United Nations, initiated a policy of "voluntary repatriation" of Kampuchean refugees from camps within Thailand. Along the way, a KR-controlled camp was repatriated, strengthening KR forces within Kampuchea. The Kampuchean government denounced this action as a hostile plot; Vietnam embarked on a limited military campaign to stop the repatriations, which involved incursions into Thailand and engagement of Thai forces. Vietnam's actions were not just meant to end the repatriation process but also to redefine the terms of the international debate on Kampuchea. Vietnam sought to demonstrate that the only source of conflict in the region was on the Thailand-Kampuchea border and that conflict would cease once Thailand recognized the new Kampuchean government. Whatever its reasons, Vietnam's actions caused ASEAN to close ranks behind Thailand once again.

The International Conference on Kampuchea

A major liability for ASEAN's position on Kampuchea was its need to support the Khmer Rouge as the legitimate government of Kampuchea. Due to the KR's history of atrocity, it was not well regarded either inside or outside Kampuchea. The prospect of the KR's return to power terrified most Kampucheans and hardened Vietnam's resistance to political compromise to end the conflict. ASEAN's implicit support for the KR was weakening international support for its position.[23] However, the KR was the only viable military opposition to Vietnam in Kampuchea.

ASEAN tried creating a noncommunist alternative to the Khmer Rouge, but, at the time, there were no credible candidates for such a role. Prince Norodom Sihanouk of Cambodia had not yet committed himself to lead a resistance movement. The Khmer People's National Liberation Front (KPNLF), led by Son Sann, had just been formed, but it lacked a viable military. The KR could not be ignored. ASEAN's plan was to create a coalition that could incorporate the KR and dilute its identity. However, noncommunist forces had to be convinced to work with the KR, which was hardly inclined to join a coalition meant to usurp its leadership position. China was also unprepared to push the KR in this direction.

Nonetheless, ASEAN persisted in its efforts to find a political solution to the Cambodian conflict. In June 1981, ASEAN adopted a compromise between the Indonesian and Thai positions. It attempted to accommodate Vietnam's security concerns by presenting a formula for the resolution of the conflict that called for the disarming of all Kampuchean factions by a UN force dispatched to supervise Vietnam's withdrawal of forces. ASEAN apparently hoped to moderate Vietnam's intransigence by offering the possibility that Kampuchea might be reclaimed by a noncommunist alternative to the KR, some group that would enjoy popular support and not threaten Vietnam's security. Practically speaking, this solution would have required disarming the KR and constructing a political coalition between disparate factions, tasks easier said than done. Still, ASEAN indicated a willingness to be flexible in its diplomacy and open to Vietnamese interests.

ASEAN successfully lobbied for an International Conference on Kampuchea (ICK), which was held in New York in July 1981 under the auspices of the UN. In an attempt to accommodate Vietnam's security concerns, the

ICK was deliberately linked to ZOPFAN, which Vietnam had accepted as a basis of discussing regional security. ASEAN tried to ensure as wide participation as possible by including Vietnam and three different Khmer factions as participants in the ICK.[24] Vietnam boycotted the proceedings, however, because the UN continued to recognize the DK as the legitimate Kampuchean government. The Soviet Union and Laos also declined to attend. Moreover, ASEAN's effort to appear evenhanded by soliciting the participation of nongovernmental representation from the Phnom Penh regime was blocked by China. Still, ninety-two countries attended the ICK. On the surface, this was a remarkable success for ASEAN diplomacy and greatly enhanced ASEAN's international profile and prestige. The outcome of the conference, however, illustrated the concrete limits of ASEAN's influence over Southeast Asian security.

Following its proposal of the previous month, ASEAN tried to make the conference a constructive dialogue with Vietnam. It suggested disarming all Khmer factions before holding internationally supervised elections in Kampuchea. This plan, however, was opposed by China, with U.S. support. As discussed above, China and the United States had their own reasons for perpetuating the Cambodian conflict. China was determined to follow its policy of attrition against the society and government of Vietnam and, by extension, the Soviet Union. It had no interest in accommodating Vietnamese concerns. The United States tacitly supported China's policy as part of its own strategy against the Soviet Union.

The final ICK strategy proposed the following points:

1. An agreement on cease-fire by all parties to the conflict in Kampuchea and withdrawal of all foreign forces from Kampuchea in the shortest time possible under the supervision and verification of a United Nations peace-keeping force observer group;
2. appropriate arrangements to ensure that armed Kampuchean factions will not be able to prevent or disrupt the holding of free elections, or intimidate or coerce the population in the electoral process; such arrangements should also ensure that they will respect of the [*sic*] free elections;
3. appropriate measures for the maintenance of law and order in Kampuchea and the holding of free elections, following the withdrawal of all foreign forces from the country and before the establishment of a new government resulting from those elections;
4. the holding of free elections under United Nations supervision which will allow the Kampuchean people to exercise their right of self-determination and elect a government of their own choice; all Kampucheans will have the right to participate in the elections.[25]

The ICK became the legal and moral basis for a settlement of the Cambodian conflict. It was too inflexible, however, to be the true basis of a political resolution. Its failure to require the disarmament of Kampuchean factions rendered it essentially useless at the time it was proposed. On the other hand, it served China's purposes of prolonging the conflict and facilitating its strategy of "bleeding Vietnam white." ASEAN states interested in negotiating an end to the conflict, however, had to find ways around the ICK.

ASEAN's experience in New York clearly outlined the limits of its abilities to affect regional security. Michael Leifer characterizes the outcome of the ICK as a "diplomatic defeat" for ASEAN.[26] Without the cooperation of the great powers, it could not steer events in the direction that it found most desirable. Despite its efforts at accommodation, it was stymied by more powerful actors.

The Coalition Government of Democratic Kampuchea

Following the ICK, China did accept the need to broaden the base of political resistance to Vietnam. While it would not support measures to reduce the power of the Khmer Rouge, it realized the risk of losing international support for the anti-Vietnamese forces if the KR's presence was not moderated. Under Singapore's leadership, ASEAN followed up the ICK by increasing its efforts to unite various Khmer opposition forces into a coalition government. In July 1982, the KPNLF and the Armée Nationale Sihanoukiste (ANS), the military arm of a new political movement supporting Prince Sihanouk, agreed to combine with the Khmer Rouge to form the Coalition Government of Democratic Kampuchea (CGDK).[27] ASEAN hoped that the noncommunist elements of the CGDK would draw away enough support among the Kampuchean refugees and peasantry to cause the KR's demise. It also hoped that the noncommunist factions would attract international support that might allow them to gain a military advantage over the KR. This hope proved to be something of a fantasy. The KR and its Chinese sponsor were hardly prepared to stand by and watch the KR lose its military edge.

ASEAN directed its international efforts toward gathering support and credibility for the CGDK. Its diplomacy was very successful, as evidenced by the ever-increasing majorities in support of ASEAN's annual UN resolution calling for the withdrawal of foreign forces from Kampuchea.[28] Within Kampuchea, the CGDK was less successful. It showed little sign of developing enough popular support to threaten the PRK government. As a military body, the noncommunist segments of the CGDK were largely ineffective. Moreover, the CGDK was unable to form a unified command. The KR vigorously maintained its exclusive control over its own areas of operation and habitually attacked its CGDK allies to keep them off balance.

By the middle of 1984, CGDK military operations, mostly conducted by the Khmer Rouge, had created a high degree of insecurity within Kampuchea. In the latter half of 1984 and into 1985, however, the Vietnam Peoples' Army launched a series of offensive initiatives that drove CGDK forces out of their border encampments. The KPNLF and ANS were virtually eliminated as military players; the KR withdrew into the interior of Kampuchea. The KR remained a formidable guerrilla force. It continued to enjoy access to sanctuaries in Thailand and an unlimited flow of arms from China. It could not overthrow the Phnom Penh regime, but it remained an obstacle to peace.

The Resolution of the Conflict

Despite considerable discussion between the involved parties, the situation settled into a deadlock. Between 1984 and 1987, various diplomatic initiatives on the part of ASEAN and other parties failed to break the stalemate. In 1985 ASEAN, through Malaysia, proposed a series of "proximity talks" to bring the different Kampuchean factions together through a neutral intermediary. However, Thailand insisted that the proposal be changed to include Vietnam, not the PRK, as one of the contending parties, which was in keeping with ASEAN's stated position that the Cambodian conflict was fundamentally about the Vietnamese invasion and could not be considered a civil conflict. Vietnam refused to accept this modification, and the proposal lapsed.

During this period, Indonesia became increasingly frustrated with ASEAN's policies, the constraints those policies placed upon its own activities, and its own loss of influence within ASEAN. Thailand was virtually exercising a veto over ASEAN's corporate direction; Malaysia had undergone a change of leadership and was no longer a reliable supporter. Indonesia began to pursue some of its own initiatives regarding Vietnam and Kampuchea at the formal and informal levels.[29] Statements by Indonesian officials indicated the country's unique security perspective and seemed to undermine ASEAN's united front. Indonesia continued to return to the ASEAN fold whenever it appeared to break ranks, but its actions indicated its growing impatience with the organization. In an effort to accommodate Indonesia, ASEAN designated it the "interlocutor of ASEAN" with Vietnam, with the mission of exploring diplomatic contacts. These intramural tensions were exacerbated by ASEAN's inability to affect the situation in Kampuchean significantly.

In 1987, circumstances began to change, and the major actors began to reassess their positions. The Soviet Union and China even held direct talks on Kampuchea in 1988. The two nations had been tentatively exploring ways to improve relations since 1982–1983, but the Vietnam-Kampuchea situation had always been a major stumbling block. Mikhail Gorbachev's rise to power in the Soviet Union in 1985, and the subsequent overtures he made to China as part of his larger plan to improve the Soviet economy, made constructive talks on the future of Kampuchea possible.[30]

Vietnam, which in 1985 had declared its intention to remove its forces from Kampuchea by 1990, increased the pace of its withdrawal in 1988. Soviet pressure played a role in this accelerated withdrawal. With the shift in Soviet attitudes and leadership, Vietnam could not continue to rely solely on support from the USSR. Vietnam had its own reasons for wanting to get out of Kampuchea. Economically, its Southeast Asian neighbors were leaving it behind. It was committed to economic reforms, but it could only initiate them with outside help. The economic and political consequences of its actions in Kampuchea were having a concrete effect upon its own development. China had cut off aid to Vietnam in 1976; Japan and other Western countries stopped aid after the invasion of Cambodia (partly in response to pressure from ASEAN and the United States). The United States also continued to block Vietnam's access to aid from international organizations. Though economic restructuring during the 1980s had begun to ease some aspects of Vietnam's economic crisis, the country could not afford to fight a perpetual war.

Within this rapidly changing environment, ASEAN contributed to the diplomatic process by sponsoring the Jakarta Informal Meetings between the Kampuchean disputants. In July 1987, Indonesia and Vietnam, as representatives of their respective "blocs," agreed to a format for informal discussion that involved breaking the Cambodian conflict into internal and external dimensions. The internal element would allow the different Kampuchean factions to deal with one another; the external element would allow ASEAN and Vietnam to discuss the international consequences of the existing situation.[31] This compromise almost failed as a result of KR obstructionism, until Prince Sihanouk took leave from the presidency of the CGDK to hold private talks with Premier Hun Sen of the PRK in December 1987 and January 1988. Sihanouk's apparent willingness to abandon the CGDK, which would have caused the collapse of the coalition government and completely delegitimized the KR, galvanized ASEAN, China, and the United States into adopting more flexible negotiating positions.[32]

The Jakarta Informal Meetings followed in July 1988 (JIM I) and February 1989 (JIM II). At JIM I, the involved parties reached an agreement to link the withdrawal of Vietnamese troops from Kampuchea with the cessation of external aid to all Kampuchean factions. They reaffirmed this connection at JIM II but emphasized, as demanded by ASEAN, that the linkage be contingent on finding a comprehensive solution that included an internal settlement. These meetings highlighted the considerable disagreements about the fate of the KR, postwar governance and power sharing, particularly among the Kampuchean factions.

Around this same time, a change in Thai policy also had a profound effect on ASEAN's policies toward Vietnam. In August 1988, Chatichai Choonhaven assumed office as the new prime minister of Thailand. Chatichai came to power declaring his intention of turning Indochina from a "battlefield to a trading market."[33] Chatichai represented emerging business interests and intellectual elites, both of whom strongly disagreed with Thailand's established policy toward Vietnam. His New Look Diplomacy followed from the idea that the situation in Indochina was radically different in 1988 than it had been in 1978. Given the decline of the Soviet Union, Vietnam was no longer a real threat to the region. Without that immediate danger, Thailand's interests were best served by pursuing economic opportunities in Indochina, using its status as the most economically successful state in the region to advantage. Thai business desired unfettered access to the resources of Indochina, and it hoped to make Thailand the financial service center of the region. Initially, there was resistance to the New Look Diplomacy from within the Thai Foreign Ministry, which had long formulated policy on the assumption that Vietnam was an ever-present threat. Factions in the Thai military also presented some difficulties. However, by November 1989, the Foreign Ministry was willing to declare that the new "business of diplomacy is business."[34]

Thailand used the failure of the JIM talks and the apparent inability of established diplomatic means to resolve the Kampuchean issue to justify its foreign policy turnaround. The attitude of the new Thai government was that the diplomatic hard line on Vietnam had proven both ineffective and out of date. Thailand, for domestic economic and political reasons, reversed itself on the questions of Vietnam and Cambodia. It essentially adopted the Indonesian position on the conflict. This reversal, however, took place without any consultation with ASEAN and therefore collapsed the appearance of an ASEAN united front. It undermined Indonesian diplomacy, which had been trying to maintain this image of ASEAN solidarity while it was negotiating with Vietnam. The Thai initiative rewarded the Vietnamese with economic benefits without gaining from them corresponding concessions on Kampuchea. The implications of Thailand's diplomatic transformation will be explored further below.[35]

In January 1989, China and Vietnam conducted their first face-to-face talks in nine years. Vietnam agreed to the complete withdrawal of its troops from Kampuchea no later than September 1989, in exchange for the normalization of its relations with China. This Vietnamese promise was contingent on a political solution to the conflict. On May 8–10, 1989, China and Vietnam reached a "basic agreement" on the "international aspect" of the conflict in Cambodia (returned from "Kampuchea" to its former name in April 1989), though they remained far apart on the "internal aspect." This agreement cleared the way for the Soviet Union to normalize relations with China, given that China dropped its insistence that the Soviet Union abandon all support for Vietnam before normalization could occur. For Vietnam, the Sino-Soviet rapprochement held out the hope that Chinese-Vietnamese relations could be similarly delinked from events in Cambodia.

To the Vietnamese, it appeared that the Cambodian situation was heading toward a favorable settlement. The détente between the superpowers and ASEAN's desire for regional peace and stability combined with Vietnam's troop withdrawals to create a settlement that would see the elimination of the KR and "the establishment of a zone of peace and cooperation in Southeast Asia for all countries in the region."[36] This did not happen, however, as China and the United States refused to delink an internal settlement in Cambodia from normalization of their relations with Vietnam.

The divisions between the different parties to the conflict were clearly laid out during the Paris International Conference on Cambodia (PICC) in July 1989. The external actors were not yet ready to abandon their respective allies in order to force a peace. ASEAN, the United States, and China continued to insist on linking the external and internal dimensions of the Cambodian conflict to force Vietnam to settle on terms more favorable to the Cambodian resistance. Vietnam and the Soviet Union, by contrast, insisted that the conflict's external aspects be dealt with first, in the hope that suspending the provision of arms to the KR in exchange for Vietnam's troop withdrawal would allow the PRK to prevail within Cambodia. It was clear that no side yet had the political will to truly resolve the situation. The divisions between the Cambodian factions themselves remained especially pronounced.[37]

Following the failure of the PICC, the great powers developed a growing consensus over how to resolve the conflict. Starting in January 1990, the United Nations Security Council "Perm-Five" held a series of six meetings. These culminated on August 28, 1990, with the issuing of a five-part document that laid out the program by which the UN would oversee the resolution of the Cambodian conflict. The UN process committed the great powers to ending the Cambodian situation and provided China with a way to back away from the KR. The United States and the European Community had, by this time, changed their votes on the question of Cambodian representation at the UN. Both were opposed to indirectly supporting the KR. To avoid further isolation, China pledged not to facilitate the KR's return to power by the use of force.[38]

After the PICC, ASEAN was in "disarray."[39] Singapore had taken a very hard line toward Vietnam and Cambodia, as had Thai foreign minister Siddhi Savetsila, to the dismay of Prime Minister Chatichai. Chatichai continued his own initiatives, however, with the assistance of General Chaovalit Yongchiyudh, and supported Australian calls for a JIM III. According to Michael Haas, Indonesian foreign minister Ali Alatas felt upstaged by

Chatichai and personally responsible for the failure of the PICC; he was reluctant to continue the effort and expense of staking so much Indonesian diplomacy and prestige on a resolution of the Cambodian situation.[40] The Indonesian Defense Ministry suggested that Indonesia might soon have to embrace the Cambodian government, even if it meant abandoning ASEAN. Alatas was reluctant to convene another JIM, but he did call an Informal Meeting on Cambodia, which took place under PICC auspices and included all of the JIM participants.[41] After this meeting, however, Jakarta faded from the scene as an active participant in the peace process; the Perm-Five now dominated the situation.

Even as the rest of the world came together on the issue of Cambodia, the Cambodians themselves remained deeply divided. On the surface, it appeared that they were making progress toward peace. Prince Sihanouk and Hun Sen agreed to the establishment of a Supreme National Council (SNC) that would be invested with Cambodian sovereignty in the period before national elections. On September 9, 1990, the competing Cambodian factions agreed in principle to the UN framework for peace and to the establishment of the SNC. Delegates were named to the SNC. Finally, meeting in Paris on December 21–22, 1990, all of the Cambodian factions, including the KR, pledged to accept the Perm-Five "framework document" and accede to UN authority in implementing the document.[42]

In fact, Cambodian acceptance of the Perm-Five settlement and UN authority was highly qualified. The government of the State of Cambodia (SOC) refused to cede administrative control of the state to the UN and still insisted on excluding the KR leadership from political participation. Vietnam supported the SOC on these matters. While Hanoi officially accepted the Perm-Five plan, it also criticized the plan for dealing with internal Cambodian matters and, contradictorily, for not acting to eliminate the KR. Largely out of its continued concern with the KR, Vietnam decided not to pressure the SOC into accepting the UN plan, despite the obvious advantages that would accrue to Vietnam if the Cambodian conflict were resolved. As noted earlier, Vietnam viewed Indochina as a single security unit and saw the SOC as the only guarantee against a return of the KR. Vietnam could not run the risk that the KR would return to power by controlling Prince Sihanouk if he won the elections.

Despite their considerable interest in resolving the Cambodian situation, the Vietnamese continued to insist on the elimination of the KR. By the end of the 1980s and beginning of the 1990s, the decline and fall of the Soviet Empire in Eastern Europe was dramatically affecting Vietnam, which could no longer depend upon Soviet economic and political support. Soviet aid to Vietnam, which had run at between $1 billion and $2 billion a year for over a decade, dropped to $110 million in 1991.[43] Hanoi needed new trading partners. To this end, it increased its efforts to delink the Cambodian issue from its relations with other states.

At the same time, China was growing increasingly isolated within the international community. China and Vietnam were two of the few remaining hard-line socialist states, a fact that brought the two nations closer together. The reduction of the Soviet presence in Vietnam mitigated Chinese-Vietnamese tensions. China and Vietnam improved their economic linkages, especially following the withdrawal of Vietnamese troops from Cambodia. Vietnam hoped that China would agree to a formal improvement in relations without regard to Cambodia. China, however, continued to insist on a favorable resolution in Cambodia before it would normalize relations with Vietnam.

Vietnam had more luck in improving its standing with the ASEAN states. Despite the lack of a Cambodian settlement, Vietnam's economic relations with the ASEAN states, particularly Indonesia, Malaysia, and Thailand, increased considerably. In November 1990, President Suharto of Indonesia visited Hanoi. The visit culminated in the signing of an accord on economic, scientific, and technical cooperation between the two countries. The foreign ministers of Vietnam and Indonesia also made it clear that neither side intended to allow the Cambodian situation to dominate their relations. Vietnam repeated a desire to accede to ASEAN's Treaty of Amity and Cooperation and eventually to join ASEAN.

Vietnam's dealings with Malaysia were very productive. Vietnam supported Malaysian diplomatic initiatives for the Southeast Asian region. In March 1991, Malaysia became the first ASEAN state to open a consulate in Ho Chi Minh City; it also resumed grant aid that had been suspended since 1978 and promised to help Vietnam develop its oil industry.

Of the ASEAN states, Vietnam's dealings with Thailand were most ambitious and strongly reciprocated. In October 1990, Vietnamese foreign minister Thach called for a summit meeting between Premier Do Muoi of Vietnam and Prime Minister Chatichai Choonhaven of Thailand. Thailand agreed. During this period, Vietnam and Thailand began discussing numerous economic arrangements and formal treaties. Even the joint development of oil reserves in overlapping territories was on the table. For Thailand, its interest in improved relations with Vietnam was fuelled by its need to export processed and semiprocessed goods in exchange for abundant Vietnamese raw materials. Thailand also hoped to serve as a channel for financial resources to Vietnam and as a source of reconstruction aid to Indochina. The Thai military overthrew Chatichai in February 1991, but even this coup did not change the Thai government's general tone toward Vietnam. Other than postponing the summit meeting, the generals maintained most of the previous government's Vietnam initiatives. In March 1991, coup leader General Suchinda Khongsomphong announced his intention to visit Hanoi.

Vietnam's approach to ASEAN reflected a long-term strategy to wean itself from dependence on any single power and to get around the effects of the U.S. economic embargo. Its goal was to develop economic and political connections with the ASEAN states, despite the Cambodian issue. It hoped gradually to build a bridge from ASEAN into the Asia-Pacific and share in the prosperity of the region as a whole. Vietnam also intended to join ASEAN eventually and participate in whatever influence ASEAN might exercise in international forums. Being part of ASEAN would allow Vietnam to contribute to efforts to offset China's influence in the region. In 1994, the United States normalized relations with Vietnam, and the country began to attract considerable foreign investment. In July 1995, Vietnam joined ASEAN.

A number of factors contributed to the resolution of the international or "external" aspects of the Cambodian situation. During the 1980s, economic matters began to take precedence over the preoccupation with regional security within Southeast Asia. The growing openness between the Soviet Union and China also played a fundamental part in reducing Southeast Asian states' perception of the Cambodian situation as a threat to regional security. No longer was the Sino-Soviet competition being played out in Southeast Asia's backyard. Forces and interests particular to the region were also at work. The removal of Vietnamese troops from Cambodia allowed the ASEAN states to see the Cambodian situation as an obstacle to regional peace and prosperity that was better ignored if it could not be resolved. Increasingly, Indonesia, Malaysia, and Thailand were making it clear that they did not intend to allow the Cambodian problem to prevent them from reaping the benefits of trade with Vietnam. This determination played into Vietnamese hands, but Vietnam itself was genuinely committed to economic reforms designed to gain it access to the burgeoning economies of ASEAN and the Asia-Pacific. By the time the Paris Peace Treaty was signed on October 22, 1991, no external actor had an interest in keeping the Cambodian conflict alive.[44] The UN plan afforded all of the parties external to the Cambodian conflict the opportunity to withdraw from the situation with their prestige and interests intact. The plan reflected the consensus in the international community that Cambodia should be removed as a stumbling block to better relations both between the superpowers and within the region. With the treaty all the involved parties could claim some kind of victory while returning the conflict to the hands of the Cambodians. It also represented the justification necessary to legitimize doing business with Vietnam. The surest measure of the resolution of the conflict between ASEAN and Vietnam was Vietnam's decision to join ASEAN .

The Effects of the Cambodian Conflict

ASEAN's institutional development was enhanced by the organization's experience with the invasion of Cambodia. Initially, the individual interests of member states and the need to defend institutional principles forced ASEAN to articulate a coherent corporate position. The need to coordinate policy greatly improved the mechanisms and habits of consultation and cooperation within ASEAN, and it fostered the further evolution of the "ASEAN way." Moreover, the organization's increased international profile encouraged intra-ASEAN unity. The ASEAN states enjoyed the taste of real international influence that their role in the Cambodian conflict attracted. They realized that they could only maintain this influence if they continued to act as a unified whole.

It is easy to overstate ASEAN's accomplishments during this period, however. It is true that ASEAN exhibited a high degree of institutional coherence. Beneath the facade of institutional unity, however, significant disagreements created internal tensions. Moreover, ASEAN's effectiveness as an institution can only be understood in light of the international context underlying ASEAN's confrontation with Vietnam.

ASEAN was the tip of a diplomatic iceberg created to oppose Vietnam's actions and, by extension, the Soviet Union's ambitions in Southeast Asia. Without the diplomatic and military support of the United States and, especially, China, ASEAN would not have been able to oppose Vietnam. The invasion would quickly have become a fait accompli, and the ASEAN states would have learned to live with it. The great powers were essential to ASEAN's ability to become engaged in the conflict.

At the same time, the great powers limited what ASEAN could accomplish. At the 1981 ICK, for example, neither China nor the United States had any interest in resolving the Cambodian conflict, and they sabotaged ASEAN's efforts to create a viable diplomatic solution. ASEAN was powerless to promote its own initiatives if its great power supporters opposed them. A resolution to the Cambodian situation only became possible as the Soviet Union underwent radical reform and mended its relations with China. Without Soviet support Vietnam was unable to sustain its occupation. By the time of the JIMs, all of the external powers involved in Cambodia were looking for ways either to resolve the conflict or to remove it as an obstacle to improving their own relations. Under these conditions, ASEAN was able to exercise a limited degree of independent influence. While ASEAN was able to make a diplomatic contribution at this time, the major events of the situation remained beyond its influence. The PICC, while a useful contribution to the resolution of the conflict, still failed. The international aspects of the Cambodian situation were finally resolved through the actions of the Perm-Five of the UN Security Council.

ASEAN's diplomacy and institutional effectiveness must be understood from within this context. Its successful attempts to rally international opposition to Vietnamese actions reflected its own efforts and determination; however, these factors only mattered to a limited degree. China, the United States, and the Soviet Union set the parameters of the Cambodian conflict. Thus, the response to the conflict is not simply an example of

ASEAN learning to exercise international influence through institutional coherence; it is a lesson about the limits of small powers. Despite these limitations, the ASEAN states gained a level of prominence and diplomatic influence that they had never enjoyed before, and far more than they would have attracted as individual states. The lesson of the Vietnam experience— the limits of small powers—must be tempered with a certain degree of optimism about ASEAN's effectiveness.

ASEAN's actions during the Cambodian conflict also symbolically undermined ZOPFAN. ZOPFAN asserted ASEAN's vision of a regional order free of the interference of outside powers and managed by the ASEAN states. To deal effectively with the threat of Vietnam and the Soviet Union, however, ASEAN took sides in a conflict between the great powers, allying itself with the United States and China. ASEAN could not manage its regional security environment on its own terms.

ASEAN's response to the Vietnamese invasion is also not a clear example of the organization learning the political and diplomatic virtues of unity, as some observers suggest. ASEAN was never as unified as it appeared. Instead, divergent strategic perspectives, particularly between Indonesia and Thailand, divided it. These tensions were repressed, which was a considerable accomplishment in itself. However, they always remained and became more prominent as the conflict dragged on.

Thailand's diplomatic about-face in 1988 is, perhaps, the most telling part of the story of ASEAN's dealings with Vietnam over Cambodia. Thailand adopted a position in relation to Vietnam that was much closer to the Indonesian position, but its doing so without consulting its ASEAN partners served to undermine rather than promote ASEAN unity. Thailand acted on the basis of its narrowly defined self-interests. The Thais' decision demonstrated a number of important weaknesses within the ASEAN structure, which have profound implications for the future.

For almost a decade, the situation in Vietnam preoccupied ASEAN's institutional activities. As the frontline state, Thailand essentially set the policies that ASEAN followed. It was deeply involved in the processes of consultation and consensus that characterize the ASEAN way. Yet, on coming to power, the new Thai government ignored ASEAN procedure, gave little thought to the effects of its actions on ASEAN's unity, and reversed its policies on the issue that dominated ASEAN's activities. This behavior indicated that the sense of community that ASEAN supposedly built among its members did not go very deep and was, therefore, much more fragile than it seemed. A change in governing elites within Thailand was all that was necessary to undermine ASEAN's coherence. The intraregional commitment to ASEAN may be dependent on far too few people within the member states. As leadership changes occur and as new elites demand to be heard within the member states, ASEAN may face a growing crisis of unity.

Among ASEAN's foreign policy elites, some express the view that ASEAN's stand on Cambodia was the organization's "finest hour" and is not likely to be repeated. Its position, they argue, was sustained by the common interest of the member states in protecting an important regional principle. Such a unifying regional issue may not arise again. Moreover, Vietnam's invasion of Cambodia was too issue-specific to be the foundation on which ASEAN could build cooperation. The invasion taught ASEAN's members how to cooperate over a particular problem, but that did not lead to a more general supportive regional framework.[45]

Conclusion

ASEAN learned a great deal from its concerted opposition to Vietnam's invasion of Cambodia. Its members discovered the diplomatic benefits of being part of a larger organization, and it grew considerably as an institution. The habits of cooperation and consultation became an ingrained part of the ASEAN process. However, ASEAN also ran solidly into its own limitations. Its ability to affect regional security was constrained by the parameters set by the great powers. ASEAN needed to call on outside support in order to be an effective and credible opposition to Vietnamese aspirations. In the end, even the extent to which ASEAN itself was a coherent organization is questionable. The ASEAN states' common interest in opposing Vietnam was strained by conflicting perceptions of long-term regional security and their own economic and political interests. Thailand's diplomatic about-face, in many ways, undermined the processes of consultation and consensus building that are ASEAN's most important achievements. ASEAN did not emerge from its Vietnam-Cambodia experience as a unified and coherent international institution. Attempts to interpret ASEAN on the basis of this assumption fail to appreciate the true nature of the divisions—and the unity—that underlie the organization.

Notes

1. North and South Vietnam did not formally reunify until 1976. At that time, the country was renamed the Socialist Republic of Vietnam. Thayer, 1990: 143.
2. Ibid.: 143–145; Leifer, 1989: 74–75, 78–79.
3. Chanda, 1990: 76–77; Jorgenson-Dahl, 1982: 125–127.
4. According to Evans and Rowley, China had tried to restrain the scope and intensity of Kampuchea's attacks on Vietnam, to little effect. By the time Deng Xiaoping visited Bangkok in 1978, he was predicting that Vietnam would invade Kampuchea and was really attempting to interest Thailand and the other ASEAN states in supporting an armed insurgency against a Vietnam-backed regime in Phnom Penh. See Evans and Rowley, 1990: 140–141.

5. Cambodia was renamed Kampuchea in 1975. The country's name was changed from the People's Republic of Kampuchea back to the State of Cambodia on April 30, 1989. This was done as part of an attempt to improve relations between the Cambodian government and the deposed Prince Sihanouk. See Haas, 1991: 141. The use of these names in this book reflect these historical events.

6. See Turley, 1993: 167–193; Evans and Rowley, 1990: 181–300. For a full account of the events leading up to the Vietnamese invasion of Cambodia and its immediate aftermath, see Chanda, 1986, and Evans and Rowley, 1990: 81–111. A detailed chronological account of the Vietnamese invasion and the roles and responses of the different international actors, including ASEAN, is found in Haas, 1991.

7. Turley, 1993: 171; Evans and Rowley, 1990: 86–87.

8. Turley, 1993: 169. For a different analysis, see Amer, 1993: 314–331. Amer emphasizes the exodus of ethnic Chinese from Vietnam during the late 1970s as a crucial factor in explaining the deterioration of China-Vietnam relations. Evans and Rowley concur with this analysis. Vietnam's decision to ally itself with the Soviet Union was the decisive strategic event that solidified China's enmity toward Vietnam, but China-Vietnam relations were already deeply strained by the continuing conflict over the cultural identities and political loyalties of the ethnic Chinese (Hoa) in Vietnam. Evans and Rowley, 1990: 48–54, 302.

9. Turley, 1993: 173. For a detailed account of the Vietnamese occupation of Cambodia, see M. Martin, 1994.

10. Thayer, 1990: 148; Leifer, 1989: 106–107; Antolik, 1990: 119–120.

11. China's "punitive invasion" achieved most of China's immediate military objectives within Vietnam, but at an unacceptably high price. According to Vietnam, more than 20,000 Chinese were killed, and the total number of Chinese casualties was over 60,000. The military action actually demonstrated the weaknesses of China's People's Liberation Army (PLA). Compared to China, Vietnam possessed superior weaponry and logistics. China's 200,000 troops were contained by half as many of Vietnam's regional troops and militias. Only in one battle did Vietnam commit one of its main force divisions. Evans and Rowley, 1990: 115–117.

12. Turley, 1993: 176. China wanted the Soviet Union out of East Asia even as the Soviets were determined to assert themselves as a great power in the region. However, as early as 1983, both sides were making efforts to improve their relations. Evans and Rowley, 1990: 233–235.

13. Frost, 1990: 15–16; Antolik, 1990: 116; Leifer, 1989: 90.

14. Alagappa, 1993: 452.

15. Communist Laos shared a common border with Thailand and a subordinate relationship to Vietnam. Thailand had no choice but to accept the loss of Laos as a buffer state, however, because no external power was opposed to the arrangement. Leifer, 1989: 96–97.

16. Ibid.: 72, 92; Haas, 1991: 97–98. Leifer says that Singapore was "wary" of China but was more concerned about Vietnam, for the reasons cited. Moreover, Singapore recognized that the United States would be less inclined toward recognizing a Chinese threat to the region, given the U.S.-China rapprochement.

17. This information was given to me in the course of a confidential interview with an academic observer in Thailand. A Thai Foreign Ministry official told me that Thailand had to convince Indonesia that a serious issue of principle was stake.

18. Huxley, 1993: 14.

19. Quoted in Leifer, 1989: 94. Mochtar Kusuumaatmadja, Indonesia's foreign minister issued ASEAN's earliest official statement about the invasion on January

9, in his capacity as chairman of the ASEAN Standing Committee. This statement deplored the escalation of conflict in Indochina but was less condemnatory of Vietnam than the statement of January 14.

20. Leifer, 1989: 102–103. Another factor that contributed to ASEAN's united front against Vietnam during this period was the problem of the "boat people." Throughout 1978–1979, Vietnam allowed the mass exodus of a significant part of its ethnic-Chinese population. Malaysia feared the influx of ethnic Chinese would disrupt its internal communal balance. Its policy of pushing boat people back out to sea and on to Indonesia strained relations with its larger neighbor. Indonesia also feared the ethnic and political impact of the Vietnamese-Chinese refugees. Singapore, which did not want to become an ethnic-Chinese haven, only accepted refugees if they were in transit to a third country. ASEAN further closed ranks against Vietnam as a result of this situation. Even here, however, differences in strategic perspective became apparent. Indonesia and Malaysia, which saw China as the major regional security threat, were sympathetic to what they saw as Vietnam's security concerns about its ethnic Chinese population. Singapore, by contrast, portrayed the boat people as part of a Vietnam-Soviet Union plot to destabilize the region. The end result, however, was that Vietnam alienated the ASEAN states most sympathetic to its position. Leifer, 1989: 98–99; Evans and Rowley, 1990: 48–54.

21. President Suharto and Prime Minister Hussein were also motivated by a concern over political instability in Thailand. A recent transfer of power within Thailand from prime minister General Kriangsak to General Prem Tinsulanond had been peaceful, but the result of factional infighting within the Thai military. Leifer, 1989: 105–106.

22. Ibid.: 106–107. Thayer suggests that Vietnam was more open to the Kuantan Declaration, which it saw as an opportunity to exploit the evident divisions within ASEAN. Vietnamese foreign minister Nguyen Co Thach visited Malaysia in May 1980 and declared the Kampuchean situation open for discussion in light of the Kuantan Declaration. Any potential progress, however, was ended by Vietnam's subsequent military actions against Thailand. Thayer, 1990: 148–149.

23. In 1979, Britain withdrew its recognition of the DK; in 1980; Australia followed suit, and India established diplomatic relations with the regime in Phnom Penh. Leifer, 1989: 110. However, both Britain and Australia promised ASEAN that they would not recognize the PRK, on the grounds that, even though it controlled Kampuchea, it was dependent on Vietnam for its survival. Evans and Rowley, 1990: 192.

24. These were the factions led by Prince Sihanouk, Son Sann, and the PRK government of Heng Samrin; the Khmer Rouge was not included.

25. Quoted in Thayer, 1990: 149–150.

26. Leifer, 1989: 117.

27. China only supported the idea of the CGDK once ASEAN agreed to an arrangement that would protect the interests of the DK in the event of the coalition's dissolution.

28. Between 1979–1988, the votes for and against the ASEAN resolution in the UN were 97–23 (1980), 100–25 (1981), 105–23 (1982), 105–23 (1983), 110–22 (1984), 114–21 (1985), 115–21 (1986), 117–21 (1987), and 122–19 (1988). (Abstentions not listed.) Thayer, 1990: 160.

29. For example, in 1980 and 1981, Indonesian Defense Minister Benny Murdani went to Vietnam to renew contacts with the Vietnamese military; in 1982, Jakarta approached the United States about normalizing relations with Vietnam as a first step toward getting Vietnamese troops out of Cambodia, only to discover that

Washington had taken the position of no normalization without Vietnamese troop withdrawal first. In 1983, Indonesia used its good offices to facilitate contacts between Thailand and Vietnam and, in 1984, was designated ASEAN's official "interlocutor" with Vietnam, Haas, 1991:169.

30. Alagappa, 1990: 266–271.

31. This period of Indonesian-sponsored diplomacy, which preceded the JIM meetings, is referred to as "cocktail diplomacy." See Van der Kroef, 1988: 300–320.

32. Turley, 1993: 178. Sihanouk and Hun Sen's talks ultimately broke down over the issues of the disarming of the Khmer Rouge and the fate of the PRK. Sihanouk then tried to resign permanently from the presidency of the CGDK but resumed the office after pressure from China. See Evans and Rowley, 1990: 280–284. Abdulgaffar Peang-Meth credits this meeting as initiating a true dialogue for peace in the region. See Abdulgaffar, 1992: 37.

33. Quoted in Um, 1991: 246. Thailand's shift in policy toward Vietnam and Kampuchea had started under the previous prime minister, General Prem Tinsulanond, who had been in power since 1980. During that time, Prem had left foreign policy to his foreign minister Siddhi Sawetsila, who adopted a hard-line position against Vietnam. In 1987 and 1988, however, Prem's contacts with the new Soviet government convinced him that the USSR was genuinely trying to resolve the Kampuchean issue. At this time, the commander-in-chief of the armed forces, General Chaovalit Yongchiyudh, viewed the Kampuchean conflict as a civil war and made diplomatic overtures to Vietnam and the Soviet Union. Chatichai came to power supporting Chaovalit's initiatives. See Evans and Rowley, 1990: 264–265.

34. Quoted in Um, 1991: 246. For a time, the Thai Foreign Ministry, under Foreign Minister Siddhi, remained strongly opposed to Chatichai's efforts. It *did* consider the effect of Thailand's diplomatic shift on ASEAN and Thailand's other allies. Moreover, Thailand's actions attracted threats from the United States and condemnation from its ASEAN partners. However, this did not stop Chatichai's initiatives. See Evans and Rowley, 1990: 288–289. The Thai Foreign Ministry under Siddhi actively sabotaged Chatichai's various diplomatic initiatives during late 1989 by quietly refusing to pursue them. See Haas, 1991: 216–217. Siddhi was kept on by Chatichai because he needed Siddhi's political support as part of a coalition government. However, Siddhi was forced to resign in 1990 for domestic political reasons. The new foreign minister, Subin Pinkayan, agreed with Chatichai that the war in Cambodia was over, as far as Thailand was concerned. See ibid.: 264; Evans and Rowley, 1990: 265.

35. For an analysis of the events and political factors surrounding Thailand's change in policy, See Van der Kroef, 1990: 227–238; Evans and Rowley, 1990: 263–266; Haas, 1991: 262–264.

36. Vietnamese foreign minister Nguyen Co Thach, quoted in Turley, 1993: 179.

37. For more on the Paris International Conference on Cambodia, see Haas, 1991: 190–208.

38. Turley, 1993: 180. The U.S. policy on Cambodia became increasingly confused after the PICC; eventually, it became politically unacceptable at home for the United States to continue supporting the Khmer Rouge. See Haas, 1991: 251–257. The European Community, pushed by Italy, agreed in February 1990 never again to vote to support the CGDK as Cambodia's representative at the UN because of its inclusion of the Khmer Rouge. However, the EC maintained its trade embargo of Vietnam and Cambodia to avoid alienating ASEAN. See ibid.: 220.

39. Ibid.: 262.

40. Haas, 1991: 266.

41. The IMC met at Jakarta on February 26–28, 1990 and was cochaired by Indonesia and France. The meeting considered an Australian plan to place Cambodian sovereignty in the UN during a transitional period; this plan had formed the basis for earlier discussions by the Perm-Five. The meeting helped to create a greater commitment to the plan on the part of the participating states, despite being denigrated by the French, who left the delegates feeling that they were insignificant in the face of great-power politics. See ibid.: 216–222.

42. Abdulgaffar, 1992: 33–46.

43. Turley, 1993: 182.

44. The Paris Peace Treaty created the United Nations Transitional Authority in Cambodia (UNTAC), which was given the responsibility of disarming the different Cambodian factions, repatriating Cambodian refugees, and supervising the holding of free and fair elections by summer 1993. The government of the State of Cambodia remained the primary administrative structure in Cambodia, while Cambodian sovereignty was placed in the Supreme National Council.

45. Interview with an academic analyst in Bangkok, Thailand, January 25, 1995; interview with academic analyst in Jakarta, Indonesia, February 22, 1995.

4

The Security Environment

The end of the Cold War dissolved the political and ideological foundations supporting and reinforcing interstate relations in Southeast Asia. Since then, ASEAN has had to redefine itself in a new era under radically different circumstances.

Security remains the most decisive factor pushing ASEAN's organizational development, but the future shape of regional relations in the Asia Pacific is difficult to foresee. The evidence concerning the future actions of the ASEAN states and the major players is inconclusive and contingent on numerous factors. Such uncertainty, however, is at the heart of much of ASEAN's institutional development in the post–Cold War era. Many of ASEAN's actions in the 1990s were predicated on the belief that the organization could affect the security, economic, and political architecture of the Asia Pacific in this uncertain time.

The Intraregional Security Environment

The Cold War shaped ASEAN. The ASEAN states learned to cooperate because of a shared concern with communist insurgency and the associated external threats from communist states in the region. This common threat meant that Thailand, a state historically concerned with Indochina, found itself in alliance with the states of maritime Southeast Asia. Later, after the Vietnam invasion of Cambodia, maritime Southeast Asia focused on the security concerns of Indochina. Ganesan has argued that in the post–Cold War era, ASEAN members are returning to more historical patterns of concern.[1] The end of the Cold War has seriously altered the perception of threat.[2] Has ASEAN passed beyond the stage where it needs external threats to keep it together, or have new threats emerged which will provide a new focus for ASEAN's activities?

Intra-ASEAN relations remain complex, even after thirty-five years of interaction. The established ASEAN states are far more comfortable with each other today than in 1967. Genuine community building has taken place in Southeast Asia. However, the ASEAN states still have many issues of dispute, and some members regard others as potential threats to their own security. It is unlikely that violent conflict will develop between the ASEAN states, but the reasons for that have more to do with political and economic expediency than a sense of regional community.

Was There an Intra-ASEAN Arms Race?

Throughout the 1990s, a large body of literature developed around the question of whether or not an arms race was occurring between the members of ASEAN. Analysts noted that the ASEAN states were spending far more on modern weaponry in the post–Cold War period than they had during the Cold War.[3] The intra-ASEAN arms buildup came to a brief halt with the Asian economic crisis of 1997, but it has continued since. Whether or not there was an intra-ASEAN arms race during this earlier period is an important indication of ASEAN's viability as a security community. Most analysts studying the ASEAN arms buildup came to the conclusion that there was not an intra-ASEAN arms race. Numerous factors combined to cause the ASEAN countries to increase their military spending. Mutual suspicion and intra-ASEAN tensions were among these but were not enough, by themselves, to account for the military buildup.

In looking at this question, Amitav Acharya measured defense expenditures in three ways: through current and constant prices, as a percentage of gross domestic product (GDP), and on a per capita basis. Measured in their national currencies, the defense budgets of the ASEAN states generally rose. However, when measured in terms of constant U.S. dollars, some states showed declines in military spending over some years. Nonetheless, taking ASEAN members as a whole, there was a definite upward trend in defense spending between 1987 and 1991.[4] This upward trend continued throughout the 1990s.[5] (See Table 4.1 on page 71.)

Measuring by GDP, the picture was also inconsistent. While the overall level of actual military spending in ASEAN rose, the rate of spending as a percentage of GDP actually declined, especially in Indonesia, Malaysia, and Thailand. This decline in military spending reflected the increased GDP base of the economically prosperous ASEAN states. Measured on a per capita basis, defense expenditures reflected the intraregional disparities of wealth and population. With the exception of Singapore, the per capita defense expenditures of the ASEAN states generally declined during the post–Cold War period, indicating that the ASEAN military buildup was not excessive. While ASEAN states increased their military procurements, they did not do so at the expense of other economic development.[6]

Anwar argued that, despite their rapid acquisition of military hardware, the ASEAN states were not in an arms race. Technically, an arms race requires that each side acquire weaponry with the objective of gaining a strategic advantage over the other. The gradual emergence of a near security community within ASEAN and the fact that the same ASEAN states supposedly in competition also conduct bilateral security exercises point to another interpretation: "What has been happening in ASEAN . . . is not so much an arms race, which can only occur between potential enemies, as an 'interactive' acquisition between friendly ASEAN states where the military planners tend to adopt the 'worst case scenario' approach."[7] Nonetheless, "interactive" acquisitions may be arms races by any other name. While armed conflict between ASEAN states may have been highly improbable, it was not impossible, a view apparently shared by ASEAN military planners, if by no one else.[8]

The ASEAN arms buildup of the 1980s and 1990s was the result of interactive, semi-interactive and noninteractive factors. The interactive factors were the unresolved territorial disputes and conflicts over maritime borders that exist between many ASEAN states.[9] To differing degrees, these disputes remain as sources of tension within ASEAN.[10] Historically based ethnic and political tensions also still play a role in some intra-ASEAN relations.[11] Singapore still plans its defense strategies on the assumption that Malaysia and Indonesia are its primary sources of threat.[12] The most delicate military relationship within ASEAN is between Malaysia and Singapore, though Malaysia has also been involved in tense maritime and territorial conflicts with the Philippines and Thailand.

Another interactive factor contributing to the arms buildup was a concern with "bargaining power" in the event of low-level conflicts within the region.[13] ASEAN states did not want to be at a strategic disadvantage with each other when discussing intra-ASEAN disputes. Other factors include imitation and prestige. Sophisticated new weapons are a source of prestige, and ASEAN states acquired weapons similar to their neighbors' simply so that they would not be left behind.

Among the semi-interactive and noninteractive factors was a continuing concern for internal security. During the late 1980s and early 1990s, while the ASEAN states were reorienting their militaries toward external threats, many of them were still battling internal insurgencies. Arms purchases, especially in the case of Indonesia, reflected this reality. Another major consideration was the desire for greater self-reliance in the face of less-reliable external security guarantees. With the reduction of U.S. forces in the region, and the corresponding fear of a lack of commitment to their security by the United States, the ASEAN states tried to modernize obsolete defense systems in order to better deal with regional uncertainty. Regional balance-of-power concerns were connected to the desire for self-reliance. The ASEAN states, to differing degrees, have been—and remain—apprehensive about the future military roles of China, India, and Japan in Southeast Asia. ASEAN states were arming for the future, with the possible intention of pooling their resources to counter any potential extraregional threat.

Technology transfers contributed to the military buildup. Defense acquisitions were increasingly tied to joint ventures and other arrangements designed to transfer technology and provide other economic benefits to the ASEAN states. Supply-side pressures also played a role. The end of the Cold War meant the loss of traditional arms markets, but weapons-supplier states still needed to sell weapons. Sophisticated first- and second-hand weaponry became available on the world market for cut-rate prices. The newly wealthy states of Southeast Asia were natural customers for such products. Weapons producers in the former Soviet bloc became significant competitors with the West in the arms market in Southeast Asia. Another major consideration was the effect of economic prosperity. The ASEAN states bought new weaponry because many of them could afford to do so. Also, in many ASEAN states, military purchases reflected attempts to placate the military and intraservice politics, and corrupt political leaders and others could also benefit economically from arms purchases.

Finally, the ASEAN states acquired greater maritime responsibilities. All the ASEAN states claimed their 200-nautical-mile Exclusive Economic Zones (EEZs) and extended their territorial waters to twelve nautical miles from shore, as permitted by the 1982 United Nations Convention on the Law of the Sea (UNCLOS). These expanded claims frequently overlap with one another. Before the recurrence of domestic political instability in the late 1990s, most ASEAN states generally believed that they had internal insurgency under control and turned their attention toward patrolling and controlling their maritime claims. This required that they have sophisticated, modern naval capabilities.

Even if ASEAN was engaged in an internal arms race, it may not have been as dangerous as it appeared. The actual threat attached to an ASEAN arms race depended on the ASEAN states' ability to maintain the weaponry that they purchased. J.N. Mak notes the critical difference between purchasing military "hardware" and actually improving the conventional military "capability" of a state:

> The ASEAN defense build-up is more than merely the acquisition of glamorous, high-profile, high-tech weaponry. A qualitative judgment of the relative effectiveness of the ASEAN armed forces is difficult to make. Purchasing a weapons system is perhaps the easiest part of any weapons-management program. It is considerably more difficult to make the right fundamental choice, and it is even harder to integrate, maintain and operate a weapons system efficiently and effectively in the face of sophisticated opposition.[14]

Maintaining and utilizing these systems effectively requires good infrastructure, and an educated population able to learn the technical skills necessary to operate complex equipment. The absence of this "maintenance culture" is common to all of the ASEAN states, except Singapore.[15] Whatever concerns the ASEAN arms buildup may have reflected, the probability of sustained military conflict in Southeast Asia was never very great, simply because of the technical limitations of the region's different armed forces.

ASEAN defense spending has continued to grow, with the exception of the period immediately following the start of the economic crisis (see Table 4.1). During the crisis, Singapore was the one ASEAN country to increase its defense spending, but it was also the only one in the position to do so. The crisis forced most of the ASEAN states to cancel expensive arms purchases. However, those ASEAN states that could afford to do so renewed these purchases once the economic downturn began to reverse. Indonesia is the ASEAN country that has had the most difficult time in rebounding from the crisis, which is reflected in its declining military spending. The crisis also exacerbated existing tensions between ASEAN states, particularly Singapore, Malaysia, and Indonesia.

ASEAN as a Security Community

The ASEAN states enjoy extensive social and political interactions, engaging in numerous bilateral military arrangements and, sometimes, joint military exercises.[16] Despite these interactions, ASEAN is not quite a Deutschian "security community." Acharya draws on Karl Deutsch's work to define a security community as having the following characteristics:

a. strict and observed norms concerning non-use of force, with long-term prospects for war avoidance;
b. no competitive arms acquisitions and war-planning within the grouping;
c. institutions and processes (formal or informal) for the pacific settlement of disputes; and
d. significant functional interdependence, integration and co-operation.[17]

Table 4.1   Defense Expenditures in Southeast Asia (U.S.$ billions)

	Brunei	Indonesia	Malaysia	Philippines	Singapore	Thailand
1994	.258	2.4	3.1	1.1	3.1	3.6
1995	.268	4.4	3.5	1.4	4.0	4.0
1996	.337	4.7	3.6	1.5	4.0	4.3
1997	.378	4.8	3.4	1.4	4.6	3.3
1998	.378	.95	1.9	1.5	4.8	2.1
1999	.402	1.5	3.2	1.6	4.7	2.6

Source: International Institute for Strategic Studies (1997–2000). *The Military Balance* (Oxford: Oxford University Press).

ASEAN possesses many of these characteristics on the surface. How deeply they affect its behavior is less clear. The ASEAN states seem committed to the renunciation of force. Still, intra-ASEAN tensions contributed to "competitive arms acquisitions," even if the tensions were not decisive factors in themselves. ASEAN has not allowed internal conflicts to block political cooperation. Nonetheless, conflicts do exist and run the risk of becoming active problems in the future.

As an instrument for the "pacific settlement" of disputes, ASEAN has an indirect effect. The ASEAN way avoids and works around conflict but does not resolve it. This method of diplomacy has proven effective within ASEAN, but it indicates the limitations of what the organization can accommodate and, perhaps, the fragility of its structures. ASEAN does have a conflict-resolution mechanism, but it has never been utilized. Finally, ASEAN is clearly not an interdependent or integrated economic organization. Economic interdependence is not presently a foundation on which to build an ASEAN security community. By these criteria, ASEAN is not a traditional security community.

The fact that ASEAN is not a security community increases the potential for internal conflict. ASEAN's cooperative endeavors and confidence-building measures were most important during the Cold War, when the ASEAN states were responding to an obvious threat. With the end of the Cold War, many analysts were concerned that various territorial disputes and traditional suspicions would reappear and create problems within the institution.[18] The fear of an intra-ASEAN arms race, however overblown, reflected this concern. So far, however, ASEAN has managed its emerging conflicts, with varying degrees of success.[19]

Among the continuing conflicts is a dispute between Thailand and Myanmar over Myanmarese policies that have led to an outflow of refugees to Thailand. Myanmar's occasional military incursions into Thailand to pursue or attack rebel forces have heightened tensions. Because of its concern with Myanmar, Thailand wants ASEAN to address the domestic policies of its members when those policies have regional effects. These reform efforts have, so far, proven unsuccessful, but they have put the issue on ASEAN's agenda. (This subject is discussed in more detail in Chapter 7.) Bangkok's impatience with Myanmar has increased with the election of democratic governments in Thailand. Recently, there have been indications that Thailand is supporting insurgency within Myanmar, a clear violation of ASEAN's primary purpose.

During the 1990s, disputes over fishing and illegal Thai immigrants to Malaysia complicated relations between Thailand and Malaysia. In 1995, a Malaysian gunboat fired on a Thai trawler caught illegally fishing, killing two Thai fishermen. Thailand also suspects that Malaysia may be offering clandestine support to Muslim separatists in the south. Malaysia has strongly denied this charge, but, in 1998, it refused to hand over to Thai authorities a separatist leader caught carrying explosives. Malaysia and Thailand also have territorial disputes. In all of these cases, being part of ASEAN probably helped to defuse tensions and bring flare-ups to peaceful conclusions. Nonetheless, ASEAN membership has not stopped violence from occurring nor has it settled any of the issues.

Indonesia and Malaysia's have contended over control of the islands of Ligitan and Sipidan. There have been lesser arguments over the demarcation of the land border between Kalimantan and the Malaysian states of Sabah and Sarawak. Indonesia suspects that Malaysia may be supporting separatists in Aceh. The most serious dispute between the two countries is over illegal immigrants. During the economic crisis of 1997, Malaysia began rounding up illegal immigrants, mostly Indonesians, for mass deportation. Despite these substantive issues, Indonesia and Malaysia enjoy generally good relations.

The most volatile and potentially explosive relationship between the established ASEAN states is between Singapore and Malaysia. The historical ethnic tensions between these two countries have never been resolved and often resurface. Persistent territorial disputes include the conflict over the Horsburg Lighthouse in the Straits of Johor, presently held by Singapore. In 1998, Malaysia withdrew from the annual Five Power Defence Arrangement (FPDA) exercises, citing economic reasons but admitting that deteriorating relations with Singapore affected its decision. Malaysia resumed participation in the FPDA in 1999. Malaysia has also accused Singapore of invading its airspace. In September 1998, without prior notification, it withdrew permission for Singaporean military aircraft to use Malaysian airspace. Other disputes over the development of land that Malaysia owns within Singapore and the location of Customs, Immigration, and Quarantine checkpoints have also soured relations between the two neighbors. In mid-1996, and again in 1998, undiplomatic comments made by Singaporean senior minister Lee Kuan Yew about Malaysia and its historical connections with Singapore worsened a relationship already strained by policy differences over the economic crisis. Singapore and Malaysia share the strongest economic relationship within ASEAN. This mutual vulnerability has not prevented conflict from developing, but it may prevent tensions from leading to protracted conflict.

In 1998, Lee worsened Singapore's relations with Indonesia by commenting that "the market" would be uncomfortable with Indonesian vice president B.J. Habibie's assumption of the presidency. Habibie retaliated by belittling Singapore and referring to its leaders as "racists." Abdurrahman Wahid, the president of Indonesia after Habibie, started out with good relations with Singapore, but he lashed out at the Singaporean leadership after the ASEAN Informal Summit in November 2000. Wahid accused Singapore of opposing Indonesia's attempts to include East Timor and Papua New Guinea in ASEAN. Wahid also suggested that the Singaporean leadership was racist toward Malays and that Indonesia and Malaysia should join forces to cut off Singapore's water supply. While a subsequent meeting between the foreign ministers of the two states smoothed over these problems, Singapore's relations with Indonesia soured and reinforced Singapore's insecurity about its place in Southeast Asia.[20]

The ASEAN states have made definite progress in their relationships, though the exchanges between Singapore and its two largest neighbors raise legitimate questions about the extent of that progress. The ASEAN states may not constitute a security community, but they have improved their level of communication and interaction. A sign of progress is that Malaysia and the Philippines have exchanged defense-related information, logistic support, and training, something that the territorial dispute over Sabah had made impossible until recently. In addition, Indonesia and Malaysia have agreed to send their dispute over Ligitan and Sipadan islands to the International Court of Justice (ICJ). The Singapore-Malaysia dispute over the Horsburg Lighthouse was also referred to the ICJ. These developments may indicate that belonging to ASEAN is pushing its members toward resolution, rather than avoidance, of their conflicts. It also suggests that a complete communications breakdown would need to occur before ASEAN states would engage in a serious military conflict. Even so, ASEAN is not yet a security community.

The United States in Southeast Asia

Before September 11, 2001, Asians were concerned that the United States would withdraw from the Asia Pacific, leaving a security vacuum and the possibility of regional political instability as various historical suspicions, grievances, and unresolved conflicts between Asian states bubbled to the surface. They were also concerned that the United States was adopting a confrontational stance toward China, a development that would place its East Asian allies in a difficult position.[21] On September 11, 2001, however, major terrorist attacks on the United States altered the U.S. engagement with the Asia-Pacific and, indeed, the rest of the world. Precisely how U.S. policy in the region has changed, however, and its long-term effects, remain unclear. The priorities in the U.S. "War on Terrorism" are not necessarily beneficial to peace and security in Southeast Asia, or to the international system as a whole.

In 1969, Richard Nixon articulated the Guam Doctrine, a policy that placed greater responsibility for the internal security of Asian states in the hands of their own governments. Throughout the 1970s, with the end of the

Vietnam War and the emergence of communist Indochina, U.S. influence in the region declined, though it remained stable throughout the 1980s, in response to Vietnam's invasion of Kampuchea.

Most ASEAN states remained dependent upon U.S. security links throughout the 1970s and 1980s to ensure their own security. The unofficial ASEAN-U.S. security relationship deepened during the 1980s, in response to Vietnam's actions. Clark Air Force Base and the Subic Bay naval facilities in the Philippines were the main means of projecting U.S. force in the region.[22] The end of the Cold War and budgetary restraints caused the United States to reassess its strategic deployment. It did not regard the maintenance of regional bases as necessary for it to assert itself in Southeast Asia. The eruption of Mount Pinatubo in the Philippines in July 1991, which destroyed Clark Air Force Base, and the Philippine Senate's rejection of a "Treaty of Friendship, Cooperation and Security" meant the end of the permanent U.S. military presence in the Philippines. Its last forces left in November 1992.

U.S. military power had helped maintain regional stability, so the prospect of a U.S. withdrawal from Southeast Asia worried all of the ASEAN states. By the end of the 1980s, the prospect of Chinese expansionism and other issues emerged as security concerns for the future. The ASEAN states took steps to encourage continued U.S. engagement in Southeast Asia. Starting in 1989, Singapore allowed more visits by U.S. warships and combat aircraft, then signed a memorandum of understanding, which allowed the stationing of U.S. military personnel in Singapore. In 1992, the Singaporean government approved the transfer of the U.S. Navy's logistic headquarters from the Philippines to Singapore. Brunei and the United States also began working toward the signing of a memorandum of understanding.[23] Military relationships with the United States were a sensitive topic in Malaysia and Indonesia. Even these states, however, acknowledged the value of the U.S. presence in Southeast Asia and took measures to encourage it. Thailand and the United States continued to enjoy a close military relationship. In the Philippines, the Mutual Defense Treaty remained in effect, and the Philippines promised the United States access to its military bases. Philippine president Fidel Ramos urged the United States to remain militarily engaged in Southeast Asia, and joint exercises between the two states continued.

ASEAN's efforts to keep the Americans involved in the region underlined its perception that the United States was not reliably engaged in the Asia Pacific. Following the Cold War, the United States had no clear sense of how to deal with the Asia Pacific. The U.S. security structure in the Asia Pacific is based upon the "San Francisco system," a series of treaties aligning the United States to various Asian states in an effort to contain communism.[24] However, some analysts have expressed significant doubts as to the viability of the San Francisco system in the post–Cold War environment.[25] The George H.W. Bush administration (1989–1992) insisted on maintaining the San Francisco system as the foundation for regional security relationships and rejected calls for new, multilateral security arrangements. However, the United States set military goals that could not be met, given the resources it was actually willing to invest in the region.[26] The lack of strategic vision and apparent inability to adapt to changing circumstances undermined Asian confidence in U.S. regional commitment.

The Bill Clinton administration (1993–2000) was more open to multilateral initiatives than the Bush regime. The administration's objectives in Asia, however, were contradictory and ill-defined.[27] President Clinton had little personal interest in Asian affairs. The United States articulated a policy of "enlargement" with Asia, which focused on expanding "the community of market democracies."[28] Asians rejected this initiative as an example of cultural imperialism and political interference. The U.S. policy of "engagement" was later introduced as an approach to working with regional allies to prevent the development of security threats. However, it was also based on the San Francisco system, at a time when there was no clear, common threat to justify the alliance system. The United States did not possess the economic or political resources to dominate the Asia Pacific. It had to develop an approach to Asia that both recognized the its relative decline in power and influence, the emergence of new powers, and the vital U.S. interests that were at stake in Asia.[29]

The U.S.-Japanese Mutual Security Treaty (MST) was strengthened in 1996. However, there remains the possibility that it may be held hostage to economic and nationalistic disputes between the two countries. The undermining of the U.S.-Japanese security relationship, which is the backbone of security in the region, would have profound effects on the larger Asia Pacific.[30] The United States planned to gradually reduce its deployment in East Asia, locating its forces in Japan and South Korea, while maintaining a force level sufficient to reassure its regional allies. It promised to station about 100,000 military personnel in Asia for "the foreseeable future."[31]

The events of September 11th may have changed U.S. calculations in respect to the Asia Pacific, though how is still unclear. The United States now has a definite threat against which to direct its military force and strategic planning. However, terrorism cannot be stopped by conventional warfare, a reality that the U.S. government seems determined to ignore. This strategic blindness may, in the long run, be destabilizing to Asia.

Dealing with the Dragon: The "China Threat"

Throughout the 1960s, the ASEAN states viewed the People's Republic of China (PRC) as a source of revolutionary unrest, and they were suspicious of its relationship with the ethnic Chinese of Southeast Asia. During the 1970s, China pursued a more orthodox, "government to government" diplomacy with its ASEAN neighbors. It established diplomatic links with Thailand, the Philippines, and Malaysia. During the 1980s, the ASEAN countries generally saw China as a stabilizing force in the region. China was allied with the United States against the Soviet Union, it was ASEAN's partner in confronting Vietnam in Cambodia, and it was preoccupied with its own economic development. ASEAN-China trade increased during this period. Indonesia, the ASEAN state most suspicious of China, restored diplomatic relations in August 1990; Singapore and Brunei followed suit in 1991.[32]

Even during this period, however, some ASEAN states viewed China with concern. Differing perceptions of China greatly complicated ASEAN's diplomatic initiatives regarding Vietnam. As early as the 1970s, ASEAN governments expressed unease about China's growing capability to assert its territorial claims in the South China Sea. In the post–Cold War period, the South China Sea has become a potential flashpoint for future conflict. However, China's desire to build strong economic and political ties with its Asian neighbors may offer ASEAN the possibility of influencing Chinese behavior.

China's Security Perceptions and Interests

Circumstances are forcing China to redefine its understanding of the international system and its role in it.[33] China sees the post–Cold War world as a period of transition toward a multipolar world system. The PRC vaguely defines the goals of its foreign policy as "development and peace."[34] China's leaders emphasize that foreign policy must serve the country's domestic goals and further its modernization programs. China has articulated a number of official foreign policy positions. First, it is pursuing a "good neighbor" policy with Asian states. Second, it has adopted an "omnidirectional" diplomatic policy meaning a concerted attempt to improve relations with all states. As part of this policy, it opposes "hegemonism" from any state. China wishes to play a more active role in promoting world peace. These positions are designed to create a peaceful, stable environment in which China can pursue its economic ends.[35]

China's understanding of a multipolar international system is one "in which the major powers can develop friendly ties with each other and in which non-zero-sum games are the norm."[36] The Chinese conception of "multipolar" includes not only major global powers but also regional powers and organizations that exercise influence within specific geographical areas. This system is preferable to one that is dominated by a single power, and China is committed to doing what it can—with the help of European and Asian allies—to encourage its development. It believes that an international society consisting of "one superpower, many strong powers" is the best check on U.S. hegemony.[37] China has also altered its attitude toward multilateral institutions. In the 1980s, it gradually adopted a more positive stance toward the United Nations, and it has played a constructive role within the Security Council. In respect to regional organizations, it has accepted economic multilateralism within the Asia Pacific, though it remains far more guarded about regional security regimes.[38]

China's attitude toward ASEAN reflects these broader concerns. It considers ASEAN to be a possible "pole" within the multipolar international system. ASEAN possesses enormous economic capacity and has demonstrated considerable diplomatic potential through such initiatives as the ASEAN Regional Forum, the ASEAN Free Trade Area, and its role in APEC.[39] Beijing regards ASEAN's economic downturn during the Asian Crisis as a temporary setback and is presently negotiating a free-trade arrangement with Southeast Asia. China also recognizes the important intermediary roles that ASEAN plays in the ARF and other regional forums. China also shares interests with the ASEAN states in resisting Western pressures on such issues as human rights. Based on their common identity and common views on democracy and human rights, it seeks cooperation with the ASEAN states to support a multipolar international system and to oppose U.S. hegemony.[40]

Despite its more complex interpretation of the international system, the dominant outlook on international politics in Beijing remains a realpolitik, or balance-of-power, approach.[41] This is particularly true among the military.[42] Chinese leaders believe that the relations between the United States, Japan, and China will shape the future Asian order. There are indications that more "liberal," less conflict-oriented interpretations of the international system are emerging within China. However, these views are clearly less popular among Chineses leaders than the traditional realist position.[43] Fundamentally, China's contemporary foreign policy and international outlook is shaped by its "century of humiliation," the period from 1842 to 1949 when China was subjected to domination and abuse from European powers, the United States, and, later, Japan. China's self-perception is deeply rooted in its sense of itself as a great civilization bullied and humiliated by powerful outsiders. These experiences are the foundation of China's understanding of the international system and are not easily set aside. These recent historical experiences fuel powerful nationalist feelings that are evoked whenever Chinese feel that their state is subject to international pressures.

China's relations with Japan are complex. China recognizes its need for Japanese foreign investment if it is to fulfill its own economic goals, but Beijing also views Japan as its major long-term rival for political influence in East Asia. In the twenty-first century, China believes that Japan will inevitably seek to assert a political and security role in Asia that is commensurate with its economic and technological power. Like most Asian nations, China also fears that Japan will reemerge as a militaristic power.[44] China follows Japan's military and security initiatives closely.[45] Chinese observers feel that Japan is incrementally rolling back the legal and political barriers preventing it from deploying military forces internationally. They see the redefined U.S.-Japan MST (1996) and Japan's Four-Year National Defense Buildup Program (1995) as key examples of this trend. At present, most Chinese military analysts see Japan as playing a junior role as part of a U.S. alliance to keep China in check. Over time, Chinese strategists see Japan breaking free of U.S. influence.[46] China's long-term fear is that the U.S. military will eventually leave Japan, and the MST will be terminated, thereby removing a significant barrier to Japan's military growth. Japan may even ask the United States to leave and terminate the treaty itself because it comes to see the U.S. presence as an impediment to its own international role. An independent Japanese military capability will have a destabilizing effect on the region and will likely lead to a pronounced regional arms race. If Japan decides to acquire nuclear weapons, as a response to North Korea or some elements in the Commonwealth of Independent States (CIS), overall regional stability will be seriously affected. This interpretation of Japanese interests may appear alarmist, but it is the dominant view within Chinese political circles, and it is shared to varying degrees by those in many other Asian states. It is difficult to overestimate the extent to which Chinese military planners and many political leaders distrust Japan. This dislike and distrust is powerfully felt within the general Chinese population as well.[47]

China regards the United States as its greatest security concern in the contemporary era. With the decline of the Cold War and in the aftermath of the Tiananmen Square uprising, China-U.S. relations were deeply strained. As with Japan, China acknowledges that it needs U.S. economic and technological support to attain its goal of full modernization. However, China believes that the United States is trying to impose its version of human rights, democracy, and capitalism on China, as well as the rest of the world. China sees the United States as an expansionist, hegemonic power pursuing global domination. It is attempting to solidify its global hegemony through domination of the world's economic and financial systems and the export of its economic and political ideologies. It is willing to pursue its global agenda through the use of military force, as indicated by its strengthening of various military alliances and defense partnerships, and the use of "humanitarian intervention" to further U.S. political goals. This interpretation of U.S. actions and motivations is widespread within Chinese society and has become particularly strong in the aftermath of NATO's war against the former Yugoslavia in 1999.[48] China fears that the United States is trying to foment a process of "peaceful evolution" within China, aimed at undermining the political and ideological institutions of the Chinese state.

While forcing such "peaceful evolution" may be beyond U.S. capability, Beijing is concerned that the United States continues to view China as a "threat" and a potential military adversary. China feels that the United States is trying to use the superior resources of its Asian allies, especially Japan, to block any other power from gaining a dominant regional position. Thus, while China sees the immediate withdrawal of U.S. power from Asia as a destabilizing influence, a growing number of analysts argue that U.S. forces should withdraw gradually, leaving Asians to settle Asian problems.[49]

China articulates a foreign policy that appears to be reasonable and accommodating. Other Asian states, however, are concerned about ambiguities in Chinese policy and are unwilling to take Chinese assurances of peaceful intent at face value. Among scholars of the Asia Pacific, a considerable debate over Chinese intentions has developed in recent years. Denny Roy identifies three arguments in favor of viewing China as a threat to the stability of the Asia Pacific and five counterarguments.[50] The arguments in favor of the "China threat" are,

1. *China's military buildup:* Since the end of the Cold War, China has rapidly increased its military expenditures and purchased weaponry that enhances its ability to project force into the region.
2. *Chinese Communist Party values:* Critics of China complain that it practices values that are opposed to the general trends of the international system.[51]
3. *Great powers behave like great powers:* If China achieves its economic and military potential, it will be a great power comparable to the United States at the start of the twentieth century. As an economic and political giant, China will establish hegemonic control over its environment.[52]

The arguments against viewing China as a threat are the following:

1. *Constraints against assertive behavior:* China needs a stable, peaceful and friendly international environment to ensure its goal of economic development. China has many domestic problems, such as economic displacement and a decaying environment. It must cope with these internal problems; it will not have the time for making trouble outside its borders.[53]
2. *A benign track record:* Historically, China has rarely invaded neighboring states.[54] Chinese regimes have usually been satisfied with accepting tribute from the surrounding states and spreading the benefits of their "superior" culture without physically impinging upon their neighbors.[55]
3. *China's military spending is not excessive:* Prior to 1990, the Chinese military was given a relatively low priority. Its weaponry is

largely outdated and needs to be replaced. China's military buildup is a routine and necessary upgrading of an essential service.[56]

4. *Anti-China prejudice:* Proponents of the Chinese threat are either afraid of the "other" or are promoting a hidden agenda. The United States is often accused of wanting to prevent China's emergence as an economic and political rival.

5. *Security benefits outweigh dangers:* A strong China is less threatening than a weak China. A weak China would be insecure and unstable; a strong China would be confident and better able to govern effectively.

Jing-Dong Yuan points out that the military buildup in China was under way well before the decline of the Soviet Union.[57] Thus, it is best interpreted as a necessary modernization of China's People's Liberation Army (PLA), made possible by economic growth and a "buyers' market" in armaments. In addition, Yuan argues, the current Chinese military buildup may be unsustainable. China has limited resources, and the expense, time, and training involved in building a truly modern military are enormous. Nonetheless, China may be investing in those resources. U.S. intelligence agencies believe that China's actual defense budget is at least two to three times what the Chinese admit. Moreover, there are many significant aspects of China's defense spending that are not included in the actual budget. The International Monetary Fund's reevaluation of China's economy on the basis of purchasing power parity (PPP) effectively tripled the dollar value of China's GDP. Thus, if China's 1992 reported defense budget was $12 billion, and this figure is really only about half of the actual defense budget, then China's actual defense expenditures in 1992 were between $36 billion and $72 billion.[58] Using slightly different figures, Richard Bernstein and Ross Munro argue that, taking into account PPP and the other factors cited above, a "conservative estimate of China's actual military expenditures would be at least ten times the officially announced level," putting it around $87 billion per year.[59] Arguments about current Chinese capabilities miss the essential point: regional states are far more nervous about what China does thirty to fifty years from now than in the immediate future.

Historically, China has not been an expansionist power. However, history may not be a good guide to Chinese interests in the modern era. The realities of modern military conflict and international trade require China to protect and defend its national interests over a much larger physical space than in the past. Previously, China was not overly concerned with its maritime frontier. Today, however, protecting its coastal regions and keeping open sealanes of trade and communication are essential to China's national security and could cause China to impinge on its neighbors' territories. This analysis does not require that China be an aggressive state, just that the scope and nature of its interests increase as China grows in power.[60]

The notion that traditional Chinese Confucian and martial values will prevent China from "bullying" its weaker neighbors is interesting, but unconvincing. The idea that Chinese values will restrain the state is strongly reminiscent of American ideals about the special moral character of U.S. foreign policy. This has not prevented the United States from bullying and abusing its Latin American neighbors. Historian John Garver notes that "The self-perception of China as a pacific, non-threatening country that wishes nothing more than to be allowed to live in peace with its neighbours is extremely common in China, among both the elite and ordinary people."[61] At the same time, China regards only two of the fifteen military actions it has undertaken during its modern tenure as a state to have occurred on foreign soil.[62] Sheng Lijun argues that "status-enhancement" has always been a major motivating force behind China's foreign policy.[63] China has consistently played international politics with the objective of creating a level of influence in keeping with its own vision of its global importance.

An alternative interpretation of China's long-term evolution is a liberal argument that focuses on China's internal democratization and external dependence on the goodwill of the world community. First, economic liberalization will lead to greater "democratization," causing China to become a more pacific power. However, the connection between capitalism and democracy is tenuous and complicated. It is just as likely that China will evolve into a "soft authoritarian" state, where the state holds the reins of power while allowing economic freedom.[64] Moreover, the "popular will" does not necessarily lead to peaceful policies. This is especially true when the influence of growing Chinese nationalism is factored into the equation. There is no reason to think that a democratic Chinese government would be less adamant on questions like Taiwan and the Spratly Islands than the present Communist government is. The present Chinese government carefully controls the expression of mass sentiments, fearful that such expressions could be directed against its rule. A democratically elected government that enjoyed popular legitimacy would not have to be as concerned about reining in mass sentiments. As Fei-Ling Wang writes,

> a "democratic" regime in Beijing, free from the debilitating concerns for its own survival but likely driven by popular emotions, could make the rising Chinese power a much more assertive, impatient, belligerent, even aggressive force, at least during the unstable period of fast ascendance to the ranks of a world-class power. A democratizing China with apparent and perhaps justifiable strategic concerns and demands may actually be much more likely to become a systemic challenger.[65]

The second component of the liberal argument states that interdependence with the outside world will force China to moderate its behavior.

China depends on the technology, capital, and markets of the international community in order to prosper. Economic interdependence, however, can lead to conflict as well as cooperation. Attempts to use economic levers to control China may backfire, antagonizing China and causing it to take the resources it needs from its neighbors. While this scenario is highly unlikely—China needs foreign capital and technology more than resources, at least for now—it does indicate a weakness with the "enmeshment" strategy of dealing with China.

A more telling argument against the pacifying influence of interdependence on China is that the international community is afraid of "isolating" China. Nations have proven reluctant to implement sanctions against the Chinese because China is too large a market for international business to overlook. China's attractiveness to the international business community— and China's corresponding immunity to outside pressure—will increase in the future. The international community's rush to invest in China will not create a dependent, controllable state. Indeed, the entire point of China's good neighbor foreign policy is eventually to create a powerful Chinese state that can take its rightful place in the world. China has no desire or intention to remain dependent upon, or vulnerable to, the outside world. In the long term, the only way the interdependence argument is credible is if China's present state of relative weakness allows the international community to so penetrate China's economy that no future Chinese government would see an advantage to engaging in regional conflicts. The PRC leadership, however, is unlikely to allow this to happen. There are powerful forces motivating Chinese actions other than economics, most notably nationalism.

Another possibility is that the present period of interdependence may provide a window of opportunity through which the states of the Asia Pacific can "socialize" China into becoming a responsible, cooperative regional actor. This logic underpins many of the institution-building efforts in the region. However, the effects of socialization should not be over- estimated. China can be a responsible international citizen that still demands that the international community accommodate its interests and perspectives. Moreover, China is a country that has a powerful sense of itself as a civilization. China may well socialize the rest of the region toward its own set of preferences.

Any discussion about China and the Asia Pacific must account for China's considerable internal problems. China has 20 percent of the world's population but only 7 percent of its arable land. Much of this land is now being lost to construction booms around cities; China will soon become one of the world's largest importers of food. Massive environmental degrada- tion has accompanied economic change, and the situation is bound to worsen as China's energy consumption shoots up. Crime has skyrocketed across the country.[66] Whether these problems are an argument for or against the idea of China as a regional threat depends on how one looks at the issue. Environmental, economic, and social concerns may occupy Chinese attention and resources and constrain China's foreign policy. At the very least, they may ensure that China maintains a good neighbor policy toward the Asia Pacific for the foreseeable future. This argument implies that China will remain a relatively weak state, dependent upon the outside world for its continuing economic success and, by extension, political survival.

On the other hand, economic progress is largely responsible for the decentralization of power that China is now experiencing. As the Chinese economy has prospered, Beijing has lost much of its authority to the economically dynamic coastal provinces, which actively defy central government policies and edicts in favor of their own initiatives. In addition, China is fragmenting along economic and geographical lines. The prosperous southern coastal provinces are more economically connected to other East Asian nations than they are to other parts of China. The poorer northern provinces resent the increasing disparities of wealth within the country. This geographic disparity is also causing massive economic migration. The central government is caught in a delicate situation where its attempts to assert control run the risk of undercutting the economic progress on which its legitimacy and political stability rest. If China's economic growth slows, the social forces boiling under the surface may explode. The Chinese leadership is reforming the state apparatus to better deal with the problems created by rapid economic development. The PRC needs to develop its own capacity before it can effectively govern these forces. This will take considerable time and effort, if it is possible at all.[67] In the short term, these tensions may encourage aggressive nationalism to shore up domestic unity, or they may result in a backlash against economic openness.

The South China Sea Conflict

Much of the ASEAN states' present concern with China centers around Chinese behavior in the disputed Spratly Islands.[68] The Spratlys are an archipelago stretching across more than 250,000 square kilometers of the South China Sea and consisting of more than 230 landmasses, of which 20 are islands.[69] The Spratlys are claimed in their entirety by China, Taiwan, and Vietnam; the Philippines, Brunei, and Malaysia all claim selected areas of the Spratlys falling within their territorial waters. With the exception of Brunei, all of the claimants have established a military presence on the islands. Indonesia does not claim any part of the Spratlys, but the exclusive economic zone around the Natuna Islands (which Indonesia disputes with Vietnam) overlaps with Chinese claims.[70] Vietnam controls between twenty-one and twenty-four islands in the Spratly chain. China holds seven, while Taiwan occupies Itu Aba, the single largest island in the archipelago. The Philippines holds eight islands, and Malaysia controls three atolls.

The recent history of the Spratly Islands has involved significant incidents of violence. In 1974, China evicted South Vietnam from some of the Spratlys by force; in 1988, China and Vietnam fought a major naval battle over the Spratlys that resulted in seventy-two Vietnamese deaths and the sinking of three Vietnamese ships.[71] The possibility that China will use violence against Vietnam in the future must be weighed against the much more conciliatory tone of recent Chinese-Vietnamese relations and the fact that Vietnam has joined ASEAN. Given its economic objectives and its associated good neighbor foreign policy, China has been quite restrained in its dealings with ASEAN. Nonetheless, any Sino-Vietnamese conflict over the Spratlys may involve the Philippines and Malaysia, due to the overlapping nature of the different claims. The most recent Chinese provocations in the Spratly Islands involved the Philippines and shattered the myth that China would act aggressively only toward Vietnam. In February 1995, China's occupation of the Philippines-claimed Mischief Reef, located 170 kilometers from the Philippines, came to light.[72] China had built structures on the reef in 1994. The Philippines responded by destroying Chinese sovereignty markers that had been placed on other landmasses within the Philippines' EEZ.[73]

The Spratlys are important to all claimants because of their strategic and economic potential. Strategically, the islands could serve as staging areas for military operations capable of monitoring and disrupting shipping through some of the busiest ports in the world. Economically, the area contains vast fishing grounds and, perhaps, mineral deposits. The Spratlys may also have enormous oil and gas potential. China has estimated the South China Sea to hold more than $1 trillion worth of resources.[74] The need to develop these resources may force China to be more accommodating to its neighbors in the region; it would be very difficult to encourage foreign oil companies to drill for resources in the middle of a war zone. Alternatively, the need to control natural resources in order to maintain its economic momentum may push China to assert its hegemony over the South China Sea.

The reasons for the Chinese focus on the South China Sea are more complex than they may appear.[75] China claims that the entire South China Sea falls under Chinese sovereignty. It argues that its right to the area goes back to the Xia dynasty, which purportedly ruled China from around 2100 to 1766 B.C.[76] Chen Jie argues that foreigners do not fully appreciate the intensity of the emotion with which China claims the Spratly Islands. According to Chen,

> In [Chinese] eyes, the nature of the dispute is crystal clear: initially taking advantage of China's turbulent domestic politics and its preoccupation

with superpower threats, regional countries have occupied China's islands and reefs, carved up its sea areas, and looted its marine resources. While other regional countries perceive China in recent years as aggressive and provocative in the South China Sea, Beijing intrinsically sees its assertive policy as a long-overdue and legitimate action to protect its territorial integrity.[77]

What China can achieve in the short term, however, is constrained by its present need for good relations with its neighbors.

China has developed a "three nos" policy in regard to the Spratlys: no specification of its claims, no multilateral negotiations, and no "internationalization" of the issue, including the involvement of outside powers. China has made a commitment to settle peacefully its claims over the Spratly Islands, and it has even broached the idea of putting aside the issue of sovereignty and jointly developing the area with the other claimants. However, for China, "joint development" means "development of the entire South China Sea, including gas and oil production on other claimants' continental shelves—and then only after its sovereignty over the whole maritime area has been recognised. . . . China's idea of joint development seems to be foreign participation in the development of China's resources— as opposed to a pooling of rights to resources in disputed areas, the more conventional mode of joint development."[78]

China's opposition to a multilateral approach to the problem reflects, in part, its desire to maintain the size and power advantage it possesses in any bilateral negotiations with other disputants. China's refusal to specify the exact nature and basis of its claims to the South China Sea probably reflects its realization of the difficulties in justifying its claims historically and under existing international law.[79]

China has strengthened its military capabilities in the region and tried to reinforce its legal position on the Spratlys. On February 25, 1992, China passed a law on its territorial waters that claimed all of the islets in the South China Sea. The legislation converted the waters around the Paracel and Spratly islands into territorial waters and sanctioned the use of force to protect this "coastal zone."[80] In May 1992, Beijing announced that it had entered an agreement with the U.S.-based oil company Crestone Energy Corporation, to explore for oil off the Vietnamese coast. Crestone said that it was assured that its activities would be protected by the Chinese navy.

Facing mounting apprehension on the part of regional states in 1992, China offered, once again, to negotiate the Spratlys dispute and renounce the use of force. However, ASEAN was unconvinced and that year issued the Manila (or ASEAN) Declaration on the South China Sea, ASEAN's first formal declaration dealing with regional security. The declaration called for all parties to settle disputes in the region peacefully and cooperate in operations in the area. China's response to the Manila Declaration and its subsequent behavior increased uncertainty within ASEAN over China's long-term regional objectives. China agreed, in principle, to the Manila Declaration, but it did not pledge to abide by it. At an ASEAN-China consultation meeting held in July 1995, China agreed to resolve the dispute according to accepted international law. However, China also reiterated its "undisputable sovereignty" over the Spratlys and asserted that its national laws declaring this sovereignty would have to play a role in resolving the conflict.[81]

Since 1990, Indonesia has sponsored a series of annual, multilateral workshops on conflict resolution, entitled "Managing Potential Conflicts in the South China Sea."[82] Academics and government officials (in an unofficial capacity) from the ASEAN states, the Indochina region, and China attend these talks. The talks do not deal with disputes but are meant to facilitate cooperation in the South China Sea on a broad range of topics. The organizers hope that learning to cooperate on noncontentious issues in the South China Sea will build confidence among the disputants and create cooperation on more controversial issues.[83]

The workshops have contributed to confidence building and the facilitation of contacts between regional states. However, they have been more notable for what they have not achieved. Besides rejecting suggestions to formalize the workshops, the participating states have been unable to agree on basic confidence-building measures, such as halting military expansion or creating transparency. Moreover, as the states meet and learn more about their respective positions, their differences become clearer. It appears that only Vietnam and the Philippines are committed to the workshop process; the other parties (China, Taiwan, and Malaysia) seem more interested in stalling the process. Such a tactic suggests that the workshops and similar diplomatic efforts are diversions to occupy the different actors while they follow policies that consolidate their military and bargaining positions. In the long run, these workshops may become a powerful tool for defusing conflict over the Spratlys; for now, however, the evidence is inconclusive.

There are also legal reasons to believe that any negotiated settlement to the Spratly Islands conflict is very unlikely. Even agreeing to negotiate the issue of sovereignty over the Spratlys compromises the comprehensive claims on the islands asserted by China, Vietnam, and Taiwan. Claimants in the dispute often invoke UNCLOS, but UNCLOS is of very limited application to the situation; it is not designed to resolve territorial disputes but to "provide a standard against which any co-operative arrangement regarding the Spratlys should be measured."[84]

ASEAN has had difficulty in presenting a united front over the Spratlys. The 1992 ASEAN Manila Declaration on the South China Sea was hailed as an important step forward on the issue for ASEAN. However, the declaration essentially reiterated the points agreed to at the Bandung Workshop in 1991, calling on all participants to the South China Sea dispute to exercise self-restraint and not make provocative moves in the area. Moreover, the declaration was only achieved after the Philippines applied considerable pressure on its ASEAN allies, and it was still far less than what the Philippines wanted. The declaration was reworded four times, so as not to embarrass the Chinese.[85] ASEAN frequently cites the Manila Declaration as the basis for action on the South China Sea. Nonetheless, it is difficult for ASEAN to forge a common position on this issue because of the ASEAN states' own competing claims on the Spratlys, as well as the continuing divisions within the organization on how to approach China. After the Chinese action on Mischief Reef in 1995, ASEAN issued only a weak protest statement, which neither named China nor specified any violation of the Manila Declaration. A month later at a consultation meeting in Hangzhou, there was no mention of the incident either.[86]

In October–November 1998, Philippine reconnaissance aircraft discovered that China had resumed construction on Mischief Reef. China continued to build on the disputed reef, rebuffing Filipino demands that it dismantle the structures, halt construction, and allow access. In response, the Philippines resolved to upgrade its military and follow a strategy of internationalizing the dispute. The Philippines raised the matter at the second Asia-Europe (ASEM) meeting in Berlin and the Inter-Parliamentary Union meeting in Brussels. The Philippines also started making preparations to take its dispute with China to the International Tribunal on the Law of the Sea.

ASEAN's response to China in 1998–1999 was even weaker than it had been in 1995. At the time, the organization and the region were caught up in dealing with the effects of the Asian economic crisis. ASEAN's refusal to come to the support of the Philippines was lamented by foreign minister, Lauro Baja, Jr. Baja described the Philippines as being "an orphan in its campaign" to internationalize the South China Sea. According to him, "even some of our ASEAN friends are either mute, timid or cannot go beyond espousal of general principle of peaceful settlement of disputes and polite words of understanding given in the corridors or meeting rooms. Understandably, they may have their own agenda to pursue."[87] At the ASEAN-China meeting in April 1999, ASEAN could only get Beijing's agreement that it would give "serious" consideration to a new regional code of conduct, developed by the Philippines, regarding the South China Sea. It was not clear how the code would differ from the 1992 ASEAN Declaration on the South China Sea and the 1997 ASEAN-China joint statement on the South China Sea, though the Philippines suggested that the code would be a more binding instrument. China, however, has described the code as a political rather than legal document. In March 2000, China finally endorsed the code, but it is still under negotiation.[88]

The draft code has not been made public. Reportedly, it has three elements: all claimants should settle disputes peacefully and in accordance with international law; currently unoccupied shoals and islands should remain vacant; and there should not be any further construction of buildings or structures. The Philippines presented it at the Third ASEAN Informal Summit in November 1999, but it was not formally adopted by ASEAN due to a lack of consensus. This failure underlined the continuing dissension within ASEAN over the status of the Spratlys and indicated conflicting strategies to dealing with China. Vietnam wanted to include the Paracel Islands in the code of conduct, but most of the other ASEAN states were not willing to confront China (which has also claimed the Paracels) on the issue. ASEAN's muted approach to Chinese provocations does not bode well for ASEAN's effectiveness in dealing with China in the future.[89]

ASEAN's ability to lead the way toward a resolution of the Spratlys conflict is further compromised by its failure to resolve the issue among its member states. China is not the only state that has actively pursued its interests in acquiring maritime territory in the Spratly Islands chain. With the exception of Brunei, all of the claimants have deployed troops to the Spratlys and undertaken other measures to enhance their claims to sovereignty. These claims have, unavoidably, impinged on the claims of others.

The development of the ASEAN Regional Forum (ARF) may encourage a negotiated settlement to the conflict. Despite China's opposition to internationalizing the Spratlys issue, the ASEAN states managed to raise the question of the South China Sea in the 1995 meeting of the ARF. Increased tensions and backward movement at later times, however, also offset China's apparent concessions and forward movement on the Spratlys issue. China has kept detailed discussion of the Spratlys issue off the ARF's agenda. When the Thai chairman tried to raise the issue at the 2000 meeting of the ARF, the Chinese foreign minister refused to entertain any discussion of the South China Sea and stated that China would "never" debate the Spratlys issue in a broad multilateral forum.[90]

China and Southeast Asia

At present, China lacks the military competence to be a genuine threat to the Asia Pacific. It may flex its muscles in the South China Sea and the Straits of Taiwan, but it lacks the capability to dominate the region. The ASEAN states believe that China can be socially and politically integrated into the larger region in a manner that will mitigate its disruptive effects. In the best-case scenario, China, ASEAN, and other regional actors may eventually find the common ground on which to construct a regional identity. Nonetheless, China presents a significant challenge for ASEAN. As it grows more powerful, regional states will feel the impact of its economic, political, and security preferences when they formulate their own policies. At the other extreme, if China fragments, it may utilize aggressive nationalism to maintain national unity.[91]

Chang Pao-Min talks of a "perceptional gap" between China and the states of Southeast Asia.[92] The historical relationship between China and its Southeast Asian neighbors was that of a superior culture relating to inferiors in its sphere of influence. The Southeast Asians, who paid tribute to China in return for protection and assistance, accepted this relationship. China had no interest in dominating its neighbors, and was well regarded in the region as a benign power. The advent of Western colonialism broke this relationship. China was humiliated by the West and unable to protect its tributary states, who began to look at the West as the new standard of strength. Chinese immigration to Southeast Asia and subsequent economic success led to animosity between ethnic Chinese and local peoples.[93] The dynamics of the Cold War turned communist China and the Southeast Asian states against each other and further undermined China's traditional image in the eyes of the Southeast Asians. Decolonization strengthened nationalist feelings in Southeast Asian states, which were determined to never be subservient to external powers again.

By contrast, China maintained a largely traditional view of its relationship with Southeast Asia. Indeed, Chinese animosity to the region during the Cold War was a reaction against the intrusion of an external power, the United States, into the traditional Chinese sphere of influence; it was not directed against the people of the region. China continues to see itself as the preeminent state of the region, without fully recognizing how its smaller neighbors' attitudes have changed. If China tries to assert its understanding of its historical role in the region, it will exacerbate existing tensions.

Denny Roy characterizes ASEAN's corporate policy toward China as one of "appeasement," a position that holds that "China's development cannot be hindered or even significantly influenced by outside countries. China's emergence as a superpower should therefore be accepted, and the best way the region can prepare for this eventuality is avoid making China angry."[94] In this formulation, the supporters of appeasement hope that China can be integrated into the international system, but they rely upon Chinese self-restraint rather than any coercive measures to ensure this outcome. Any attempts to use coercion are doomed to fail and will backfire by alienating China. Ultimately, the economic power of interdependence is supposed to tame China.[95]

The ASEAN states have, for the most part, been highly accommodating of China. Geography makes it impossible for them to ignore the reality of China as a regional power.[96] However, it is simplistic to characterize ASEAN's policy toward China as strictly one of appeasement. ASEAN is trying to be nonconfrontational by following a dual-track process. One track involves bringing China into the region through the use of economic and institutional linkages.[97] The other involves encouraging the creation of a balance of power in the region. Keeping the United States engaged in the region is a crucial part of ASEAN's security strategy. Some ASEAN states are quietly encouraging Japan to become more involved in regional security arrangements. The ASEAN states now consider ZOPFAN, which called for the isolation of Southeast Asia from great-power politics, to be an obsolete concept. ASEAN is too connected to the world economy to pursue an isolationist security policy.[98] As the situation in the Spratly Islands indicates, ASEAN does consider China to be a potential problem. For now, however, the ASEAN states are trying to keep all their options open. They are engaged in economic relations with China, even as they strengthen their ties to other powers and promote regional solidarity to demonstrate that they will not be coerced.

Even so, different ASEAN states have different individual interests relating to China. This division has the potential to fracture ASEAN. If China behaved aggressively in the region, would Thailand and Singapore maintain intra-ASEAN unity, or would their separate economic and political interests cause them to break ranks? It is very possible that these ASEAN states would need to be convinced that it is in their interests to take a strong stand against China, something very difficult to do, especially if China continues to increase its economic and political dominance of the region. ASEAN's ambivalence on the Spratlys issue underlines the competing interests and perceptions regarding China within the organization, which cripple ASEAN's ability to reach a consensus on how to deal with China.

The weight of the evidence inclines toward a more benign view of China's intentions in Southeast Asia. It has refrained from the use of violence in the South China Sea, and it remains at the negotiating table. During the Asian economic crisis, China effectively played the part of a responsible regional power and potential leader (see Chapter 7). These events will significantly affect the perception of the "China threat" in Southeast Asia.

The Aftermath of September 11th

The September 11th terrorist attacks on the United States radically altered its international security priorities. For the United States, the post–Cold War order is now defined by the "War on Terrorism." This new war, if poorly handled, has the potential to seriously undermine international stability. However, many analysts have argued that the terrorist attacks have created common ground and new possibilities for cooperation between the United States and other major powers.[99] How these factors will interact remains to be seen.

Before September 11th, the new George W. Bush administration pursued a unilateral approach to international relations that displayed a blunt disregard for the perspectives or interests of other nations, including U.S.

allies. In the immediate aftermath of the terrorist attack, many commentators expressed considerable optimism that the United States would adopt a multilateral approach to world affairs. The administration set about creating an international coalition against terrorism, and, with the exception of a few early gaffes, worked to reassure the Islamic world that its conflict was not a war against Islam. The United States put new energy into resolving the Arab-Israeli conflict, implicitly recognizing that the unresolved issue of Palestinian oppression was fuelling sympathy for terrorism in the Islamic world. The early reaction of the major Asian powers to the terrorist attacks was also encouraging. Russia and China quickly threw their support behind the United States. Both countries had ongoing disputes with Islamic movements, which they had long characterized as "terrorist," and now emphasized their common interests with the United States.

Southeast Asian countries, for the most part, offered the United States strong support. However, Indonesia and Malaysia, in particular, were guarded and inconsistent in their approach to U.S. actions. Indonesia, under new president Megawati Sukarno-Putri, initially offered unqualified support. This endorsement was very important, coming from the world's largest Islamic country. The president soon backtracked, however, and adopted a more qualified position in light of domestic opposition from numerous Islamic groups. By contrast, the Philippines enthusiastically embraced the United States and encouraged its involvement in dealing with Islamic domestic insurgency in Mindanao. The Philippines promised the United States access to its military facilities; already, there are reports of U.S. "advisers" assisting the Philippine military in facing Muslim insurgency. Singapore also offered unqualified support, while Thailand was more circumspect.[100]

Arguing that dealing effectively with terrorism required cooperation and coordination from many different nations, the United States initially supported hopes that it would adopt a broadly multilateral approach to its war on terrorism. The Al-Qaeda terrorist network, which the United States accused of orchestrating the attacks, functions in more than thirty countries and must be addressed through international police action. Therefore, having multilateral cooperation, particularly in Islamic countries, would appear imperative. However, the Bush administration soon began reverting to its unilateral ways. The United States launched a war against Afghanistan for sheltering the terrorists it believed responsible for the attack. The early success of that war strengthened the unilateralists within the Bush administration. At the time of this writing, there is a serious debate going on in the United States about launching further military actions against Iraq and other countries it considers to be havens for terrorism. If the United States takes these actions, it will lose its support in the Islamic world and run the real risk of creating a true religious and cultural war. While this will not take the form of overt conflict, it will strengthen hostility toward the West in many parts of the world. Moreover, the idea that the United States will attack wherever it wants to ensure its own security has the potential to undermine international law if other states adopt similar principles and justifications for aggression.

How the United States and China decide to deal with each other is the most crucial question in Asia Pacific regional relations in the twenty-first century. The Chinese believe that the United States is deeply uncomfortable with the emergence of a new great power that it did not have a hand in creating and controlling, as in the cases of Japan and Germany. There is considerable merit in this interpretation of U.S. actions. It is clear that the United States sees China as a potential competitor and is reacting accordingly. Before September 11th, the Bush White House was already confused over how to deal with a competitor that is also a major trading partner. Nonetheless, the administration expressed its intention to pursue the creation of a missile defense shield for the United States, disregarding Chinese protests. China firmly believed that the proposed missile shield was directed at it, despite U.S. denials, and was meant to render China's nuclear arsenal ineffective against the United States. It was clear that a U.S. decision to create a shield could easily set off a nuclear arms race in Asia.

Initially, the September 11th attacks created the possibility that the United States would take Chinese concerns more seriously, in the interests of maintaining a broader coalition against terrorism. However, in December 2001, the United States announced that it was abrogating the Anti-Ballistic Missile (ABM) Treaty, which forbade the development of defensive technologies that could undermine the nuclear deterrent of an opposing state. Russia believes that its nuclear arsenal is still large enough to ensure its effectiveness against U.S. defenses. China's response to this decision has, so far, been measured. However, as a matter of security, China will almost certainly increase its nuclear capability. This will force India to do the same, which will force Pakistan to react. These reactions will greatly increase tension in all of Asia, including the ASEAN region.

The U.S. war against terrorism may have a direct effect on Southeast Asia. If the Islamic world comes to see this conflict as a war against Islam, it could divide ASEAN itself along religious and cultural lines. Indonesia needs economic support from the West, but its identity as an Islamic state is a paramount consideration. If Indonesia, and possibly Malaysia, end up alienated from their fellow ASEAN members because of the perception of a U.S. war against Islam, ASEAN may pay the price in disunity and dysfunctionality. At the very least, this issue has the potential to add another layer of complexity to intra-ASEAN relations, further diluting the organization's ability to speak with one voice.

The war may also undermine the value of the U.S. security presence in the Asia Pacific. It is too early to tell if the United States will increase its military engagement in Southeast Asia. However, if it does so, its presence may no longer be the stabilizing factor that it once was, at least in the Islamic states. The U.S. ability to play honest broker in the region was contingent on its role as an outside power with no strong regional interests. If it sees Southeast Asia as another battlefront against terrorism, it will no longer be an objective outside actor. Moreover, much depends on how the United States regards the rise of democratic Islamic movements. If it decides to regard Islamic political movements as inherently threatening, it runs the risk of alienating and radicalizing many people in parts of the Islamic world who turn to political Islam as a legitimate expression of social conscience and reform. Dealing with these issues requires a depth of cultural and political sensitivity that the United States has rarely exhibited. If the United States does alienate Islamic ASEAN states, they may well turn to China. While China has its own Islamic uprisings to confront, it is not interested in confronting terrorism beyond its borders.

The U.S. war on terrorism is still too young to be properly evaluated. If the United States makes efforts to build coalitions and genuinely respect multilateral processes, this conflict does not need to disrupt U.S.-ASEAN relations. However, the United States is inclined toward unilateral behavior and military solutions. This approach can easily spiral out of control and have ramifications far beyond its ability to manage.

Conclusion

The post–Cold War Southeast Asian security environment is one of uncertainty, and it is impossible to draw strong conclusions about the future shape of regional security. Tensions exist within ASEAN that may eventually lead to intra-ASEAN military conflict. Although such conflict is highly unlikely, it is possible, given that ASEAN does not constitute a "security community." In the immediate post–Cold War period, the ASEAN states focused on keeping the United States engaged in the Asia Pacific. They considered the United States crucial to regional stability. After September 11th, however, the shape of U.S. military involvement in Southeast Asia is much more uncertain and complex. It seems more likely that the United States will remain strongly engaged in regional security, but perhaps no longer as a stabilizing influence. The U.S. war on terrorism has the potential, if it is mishandled, to introduce new and complex tensions into intra-ASEAN relations, as well as into the international security environment. China's intentions and actions in the region remain opaque. In general, China has conducted its relations with ASEAN with restraint. However, its conduct in the South China Sea continues to raise questions about its long-term behavior. The real possibility of growing tensions between the United

States and China also complicates the regional security picture. The ASEAN states must find a way to walk a line between these two potential adversaries.

Notes

1. Ganesan, 1999: 23–24.

2. For an overview of ASEAN's general security concerns, see Chalmers, 1997: 36–56.

3. This discussion draws on the following sources: Mack and Ball, 1992: 197–208; Klare, 1997: 18–61; Hinds and Sprague, 1996: 22–24; Klare, 1993; Selin, 1994a; Selin, 1994b; Nagara, 1995; Wattanayagorn and Ball, 1995; Acharya, 1994; Singh, 1993; Mak, 1995; Mak, 1994; Karp, 1990; Wattanayagorn, 1995; and Anwar, 1993a.

4. Acharya, 1994: 11–16. Acharya bases his assessments on data from the Stockholm International Peace Research Institute (SIPRI) and the International Institute for Stategic Studies (IISS). He notes that there is sometimes a considerable discrepancy in the data between these two institutes. SIPRI pegs ASEAN defense expenditures as increasing by 7.4 percent in constant U.S. dollars between 1987–1991. IISS found a higher rate of increase, 14.4 percent.

5. Assessments of current ASEAN defense procurements are based on the following sources: International Institute for Strategic Studies (1997): 164–198; (1998): 165–201; (1999): 171–209; and (2000): 178–218.

6. Anwar, 1993a: 19.

7. Ibid.: 16–17.

8. "If Nanny Retires," 1990: 38; Buszynski, 1990: 259–260.

9. Acharya, 1994: 27–28.

10. Singh emphasizes intra-ASEAN tensions as the single most important factor accounting for the ASEAN arms buildup. Singh, 1993: 212–213.

11. Acharya, 1995a: 181.

12. Ganesan, 1995: 793. I interviewed a Malaysian government official who made it clear that Malaysia is keenly aware of Singaporean military acquisitions and vice versa. Over the years, Singaporean-Malaysian relations have been strained by a number of incidents. See Acharya, 1994: 29, and Selin, 1994a: 56.

13. Acharya, 1994: 30.

14. Mak, 1994: 24.

15. Mak quotes a report on the Argentine performance against the British during the Falklands/Malvinas War by Rear Admiral James Linder. Despite possessing the most sophisticated weaponry available, Argentina lost the conflict, according to Linder, because of "maintenance and personnel training deficiencies as well as inadequate logistical and communications capabilities" Mak, 1994:21.

16. See Acharya, 1990. Singh argues that military cooperation only occurs in nonsensitive areas. Singh, 1993: 213.

17. Acharya, 1995a: 180.

18. See Ganesan, 1995: 789–790, and Mak, 1995: 305–311. For a completely opposite point of view, see Nagara, 1995: 186–206.

19. This discussion of intra-ASEAN post–Cold War tensions is based primarily on Ganesan, 1999. See also Morrison, 1999; Baker and Morrison, 2000; and McNally and Morrison, 2001.

20. McNally and Morrison, 2001: 151.

21. Solomon and Drennan, 2001; Paal, 2000.

22. Huxley, 1993: 21. For a comprehensive account of U.S.-ASEAN security relations through the end of the Cold War, see Alagappa, 1989.

23. Alagappa, 1989: 24; Acharya, 1993: 57–58.

24. The "San Francisco system" consists of bilateral security treaties, all signed in San Francisco. These treaties are the Mutual Security Treaty with Japan; the Mutual Defence Treaty with the Philippines; and the Australia–New Zealand–U.S. Accord. All of these were signed in 1951. South Korea (1953) Taiwan (1954, abrogated when the United States and China normalized relations), and Thailand (1962, the Rusk-Thanat communique) were later added to the system. See Stuart and Tow, 1995: 4–5, and Green and Self, 1996: 38.

25. Lasater, 1996.

26. The Bush plan essentially called for the United States to deploy forces rapidly into areas of regional conflicts then support these forces with reserves in situations of protracted conflict. Outside analysts concluded that the actual budgetary and force allocations needed to make this strategy work were not available. Stuart and Tow, 1995: 10–11.

27. Pollack, 1996; Moffett, 1995: 15. For indications of uncertainty about America's policies toward Asia, see "Innocents Abroad," 1996: 2, and "America's Chinese Puzzle," 1996: 35–36.

28. Quoted in Stuart and Tow, 1995: 12.

29. Ibid.: 17–20.

30. "Asia's Flagging Alliance," 1996; "America and Japan," 1996.

31. Holloway, 1995: 16.

32. Singapore refrained from normalizing its relations with China out of deference to Indonesia. See Bert, 1993: 320–321.

33. See Hu, 1995: 117–135; Glaser, 1993; Denoon and Frieman, 1996: 422–439; Garrett and Glaser, 1994: 13–34; Wang, 1999: 21–46; and Deng, 1999: 47–72.

34. Hu, 1995: 119.

35. Chen Qimao, 1993: 241–245; Garrett and Glaser, 1994: 17.

36. Cheng, 1999: 182.

37. Shambaugh, 1999–2000: 63.

38. Wang, 1999: 73–96.

39. In terms of purchasing power parity, the GDP of the ASEAN countries (excluding Cambodia) was about 60 percent that of Japan in 1995; in terms of foreign trade, ASEAN was 82 percent of Japan's. Cheng, 1999: 184.

40. Ibid.: 186.

41. Hu, 1995: 121.

42. Shambaugh, 1999–2000.

43. Deng, 1999.

44. Glaser notes that some younger-generation Chinese specialists on Japan see increased Japanese involvement in regional and global issues as possibly beneficial to Chinese interests; they do not believe that a more prominent Japan necessarily means a remilitarized Japan. Glaser, 1993: 257.

45. Christensen, 1999.

46. Shambaugh, 1999–2000: 69.

47. Kristof, 1998.

48. Shambaugh, 1999–2000: 61–63; Cheung, 1999.

49. Glaser, 1993: 259–261; Bert, 1993: 319, 322–323; Shambaugh, 1992: 98.

50. Roy, 1996. See also Lampton, 1998, and Nye, 1997–1998.

51. Roy, 1996: 761.

52. Ibid.: 761–762. The view that China's growing power will naturally lead it toward hegemonic behavior is widely held by analysts. See Dibb, 1995; Wortzel, 1994; and Roy, 1993.

53. Roy, 1996: 762–763; Chen Qimao, 1993; Deng and Wang, 1999; Ross, 1997.

54. The notable exception has been the case of Vietnam, which was under Chinese direct rule for over 1000 years, from 111 B.C. to A.D. 949. See Amer, 1993: 314–315, and Chin, 1993: 10. Roy cites Chen Jian as arguing that the only real examples of Chinese expansionism were when non-Chinese Mongols occupied the Chinese throne. Roy, 1996: 763. At the same time, Roy himself interprets Chinese history as indicating that China "was an assertive and domineering power, forcing its weaker neighbors to accept Chinese guidance and to pay tribute." Roy, 1993: 182.

55. See Chang Pao-Min, 1987.

56. Roy, 1996: 764; Chen, 1993: 245–246; Nagara, 1995; Yuan, 1995: 74–79; Denoon and Frieman, 1996: 426–427.

57. Yuan, 1995.

58. Acharya and Evans, 1994: 15. The figure of $12 billion is cited by Gerald Segal and taken from the *IISS Military Balance*.

59. Bernstein and Munro, 1997: 25.

60. See "Soft Border, Soft Wars," 1995: 28.

61. Quoted in Chanda, 1995: 24.

62. Ibid.

63. Sheng, 1995.

64. Roy, 1994: 157. Joseph Nye argues that China already is best characterized as "soft authoritarian," though he sees this as part of a gradual movement towards a more peaceful democratic China. Nye, 1997–1998.

65. F. Wang, 1999: 35.

66. Segal, 1995: 61–62.

67. Segal, 1994; Economy, 1999; Hornik, 1994.

68. For the purposes of this discussion, we will only focus upon the conflict over the Spratly Islands. The Paracel and Pratas island groups in the South China Sea are also under dispute but are under the effective control of China and Taiwan, respectively. Chang Pao-Min, 1990: 20.

69. Ibid.

70. See L. Lee, 1995; Valencia, 1995; Khoo, 1993; Gallagher, 1994; Chen Jie, 1994: 893–903; Guan, 2000; Furtado, 1999; and Samuels, 1982.

71. "Treacherous Shoals," 1992: 15. For a detailed account of this encounter, see Chang Pao-Min, 1990: 25–27.

72. The Philippines refers to the area of the Spratlys that it claims as "Kalayaan" (Freedomland). Kalayaan is an administrative district of Palawan province. Khoo, 1993: 194.

73. Snyder, 1995: 1; Chanda, Tiglao, and McBeth, 1995; Chanda, 1995: 24–28.

74. "Treacherous Shoals," 1992: 16.

75. Ibid.; Valencia, 1995: 10–11.

76. China may be modifying the basis of its claim from that of historical waters to "one based on Chinese sovereignty over islands and their adjacent waters." However, most of the features in the Spratly Islands do not meet the UNCLOS definition of "islands" and, therefore, do not possess territorial waters or EEZs. Snyder, 1995: 7–8.

77. Chen Jie, 1994: 893. Chalmers Johnson explicitly rejects Chen's assertion, arguing that the Chinese claim to the Spratlys "has not been embedded in the Chinese

national psyche for much longer than a decade, if at all. However, China's claim of sovereignty over the South China Sea has become a fact of life, and China's nationalism would make it very hard to back down or compromise." Johnson, 1997: 23.

78. Valencia, 1995: 12.

79. Valencia states that China and Taiwan's claims to the South China Sea are "in no way" supported by modern international law or the UNCLOS and are increasingly subject to criticism and ridicule. Ibid.: 23. Gallagher says that the only independent confirmation of China's claim to the Spratlys is from 1867, when a British ship encountered Chinese fishermen in the area. Gallagher, 1994: 171.

80. Buszynski, 1992: 836.

81. Taiwan has been as uncompromising as China on the question of the South China Sea. Taiwan and China have, on occasion, cooperated against other claimants in the region. Valencia, 1995: 39–42. For a critical account of Taiwan's strategies toward its claims in the South China Sea, see Yu, 1990.

82. Until 2001, these talks were financially supported by the Canadian International Development Agency (CIDA). See Snyder, 1995: 18, 21, 26–27.

83. For a positive evaluation of these workshops, see Townsend-Gault, 1994, and Djalal and Townsend-Gault, 1999.

84. Furtado, 1999: 387.

85. L. Lee, 1995: 538–539; Nguyen, 1996: 15–16.

86. Ibid.: 15. The ASEAN states confronted China, "informally over dinner," on the eve of the Hangzhou meeting. ASEAN closed ranks and presented a united front in opposition to Chinese actions. This united response both surprised and disconcerted the Chinese. Leifer, 1996: 38.

87. Baja, cited in Guan, 2000: 210; Thayer, 1999. According to Thayer, the embassies of Malaysia, Singapore, Thailand, and Vietnam asked the Philippines to clarify Baja's remarks.

88. McNally and Morrison, 2001: 135; Thayer, 2001.

89. Chanda notes, for example, that none of the other states that have disputes with China over the Spratlys were willing to comment for his article on Beijing's actions regarding Mischief Reef. See Chanda, 1995: 27–28.

90. Cossa, 2000: 10.

91. Shambaugh, 1992: 89, 101–105; Roy, 1994: 166.

92. Chang Pao-Min, 1987.

93. The colonial powers used Chinese immigrants to serve "middleman" functions between the colonial administration and the indigenous people. The Chinese made a profit out of these interactions, contributing to communal tensions. Ibid.: 184.

94. Roy, 1996: 766.

95. Roy cites senior Southeast Asian leaders, such as Lee Kuan Yew and Goh Chok Tong of Singapore as supporting this view. In Roy, 1994: 155, he also cites Lee as expressing sympathy for China in the face of Western political pressure. Prime Minister Mahathir of Malaysia is quoted as seeing the "threat from China as (no) worse than the threat from the U.S." Other Asian figures are quoted as being unconcerned about China. These statements may be honest expressions of a lack of concern.

96. This point was made by Bilahari Kausikan, Singapore's ambassador to the UN and Singapore's high commissioner to Canada. Singapore believes in a balance-of-power approach to regional politics but is not confident of the U.S. commitment to Asia. By contrast, China will always be in the region and must be accommodated.

Bilahari Kausikan, presentation as the York Centre for International and Strategic Studies (YCISS), York University, Toronto, Ontario, April 9, 1996.

97. Interview with a high-ranking Indonesian government official, Jakarta, Indonesia, February 20, 1995.

98. Snitwongse, 1995: 523–524.

99. Cossa, 2001; Ferguson, 2001; Glaser, 2001.

100. Breckon, 2001.

5

The Challenge of
the Post–Cold War Era

A SEAN responded to the changing environment of the Asia Pacific by strengthening its institutional structures. It expanded the scope of its activities and its membership and demanded a prominent role in new regional institutions. However, ASEAN's ability to play a leading role in the larger Asia Pacific is uncertain. ASEAN's efforts to manage regional security within the ASEAN Regional Forum (ARF) are limited by ASEAN's own institutional practices and the fact that the major powers of the region have their own distinct agendas to pursue. ASEAN's expansion to include the remaining states of Southeast Asia has undermined its diplomatic clout and internal political cohesion. ASEAN's attempts to create a meaningful ASEAN Free Trade Area (AFTA) may be bearing fruit, but it is still too early to tell. The post–Cold War era is proving to be a challenge to ASEAN's durability.

Institutional Change Within ASEAN

The Singapore Summit of 1992 introduced a number of fundamental changes to ASEAN's basic structure. ASEAN institutionalized its summit meetings. The heads of government now meet every three years, with informal gatherings in the interim.[1] The ASEAN Secretariat was also reformed. The secretary-general of the ASEAN Secretariat was renamed the secretary-general of ASEAN and given ministerial (as opposed to the previous ambassadorial) status. The appointment is for five years, and can be renewed. The secretary-general's new responsibilities were to initiate, advise, coordinate and implement ASEAN activities. The reorganized secretariat was composed of one deputy secretary-general, four bureau directors (the bureaus are General Affairs, Economic Cooperation, Functional Cooperation, and Economic Research), eleven assistant directors, and eight senior officers.

The Economic Research Bureau was another new instrument, designed to provide the secretariat with advice on the implementation of ASEAN activities. ASEAN instituted an ASEAN Cooperation Unit (ACU) to assist in the development of ASEAN programs and projects. The functions of the technical secretariats of the now-defunct economic committees fell to the Economic Cooperation Bureau. ASEAN institutionalized an annual Senior Officials Meeting–Post-Ministerial Conference (SOM-PMC) as part of its effort to increase discussion of regional security initiatives with non-ASEAN governments in the region. Finally, in 1992, an ASEAN Senior Official Meeting that brought together officials from foreign and defense ministries to discuss regional security was also institutionalized. Despite these changes, however, the secretariat remained incapable of independent action. In 1998, in the wake of the Asian economic crisis, it underwent further reform.

The ASEAN Regional Forum

ASEAN created the ASEAN Regional Forum (ARF) in response to numerous strategic considerations and external political pressures. The Cold War imposed a logic on Southeast Asian security affairs that subsumed many local disputes.[2] With its end, there was no clear threat against which Asia Pacific states could organize regional alliances. However, there were numerous smaller disputes that could exacerbate intraregional tensions. Moreover, regional states began to appreciate that "security" encompasses "economic, social, ecological and political factors."[3] Transnational factors such as pollution, crime, and terrorism needed to be addressed on a regional basis. In addition, the security of Southeast Asia and Northeast Asia were clearly connected; conflict in one subregion could easily affect economic prospects in the other. Of greatest concern to ASEAN was how to manage relations between the United States, China, and Japan, and the roles of these powers in the region. ASEAN hoped that the ARF would keep the United States in the region and engage China in a structure that could influence its long-term behavior.

The Creation of the ARF

Soviet president Mikhail Gorbachev first broached the idea of a regional security conference for the Asia Pacific in Vladisvostok in July 1986. Gorbachev suggested a Pacific Ocean Conference, similar to the Helsinki conference. In Krasnoyarsk in September 1988, he presented a seven-point proposal calling for a regional security consultative body. In the years immediately following Gorbachev's initial proposals, as many as seven governments offered suggestions for a multilateral regional security instrument. Gareth Evans, the Australian foreign minister, took up the call in 1989–1990, arguing for a Council for Security and Cooperation in Asia (CSCA) roughly based on the Council for Security and Cooperation in Europe (CSCE). Canadian foreign minister Joe Clark pushed for a similar regional security instrument.

The ASEAN states were initially unreceptive to the idea of a regional security forum. They argued that Asia was too complex and diverse for a CSCE-type arrangement to work. Moreover, they were afraid that another regional organization would detract from ASEAN's preeminence in the region. The ASEAN states also feared that any formal mechanisms could be used by the West to pressure them on issues of human rights and the environment. However, they were more open to the idea of using the ASEAN Post-Ministerial Conferences (ASEAN-PMC) as the venue for extra-ASEAN security consultations. The ASEAN-PMCs had been held since 1978. They immediately followed ASEAN's Annual Ministerial Meetings (AMM) and had been the forum for security dialogue both within ASEAN and between it and its regional "dialogue partners."[4] Using the ASEAN-PMC allowed ASEAN to control the agenda and reduce the risk of being sidelined. Engaging extraregional powers in a security forum ensured ASEAN some level of influence over their actions that it would not otherwise have.

In 1990, Gareth Evans advanced the idea of using the ASEAN-PMC as the basis of a regional security dialogue. The idea was rejected in the course of the general Asian rejection of the CSCA proposal. However, by 1990, track-two initiatives had begun to play a more important role in regional security building. "Track two" refers to the activities of academic and nongovernmental actors. Track-two frameworks bring these groups into contact with governmental officials, acting in an unofficial capacity, to discuss issues that cannot be addressed officially. In Southeast Asia, the most active track-two player was the ASEAN-Institutes of Strategic Studies (ASEAN-ISIS) network, which consisted of think tanks from five ASEAN countries. In May 1990, attendants at the ASEAN-ISIS meeting recommended that the region implement a security dialogue. In June 1991, ASEAN-ISIS published a memorandum entitled *A Time for Initiative: Proposals for the Consideration of the Fourth ASEAN Summit*. The memorandum encouraged ASEAN to play a "central role" in any prospective regional security dialogue mechanism and suggested that the ASEAN-PMC sponsor a conference on "stability and peace in the Asia Pacific."[5] The idea of using the ASEAN-PMC for security dialogue gathered momentum in other track-two meetings. However, ASEAN remained uncommitted.

During the 1991 ASEAN-PMC meeting Japanese foreign minister Taro Nakayama, with support from Australia and Canada, unexpectedly proposed using the ASEAN-PMC as a regional security apparatus. ASEAN's initial reaction to the proposal was "deafening silence," apparently because the Japanese had preempted ASEAN's deliberations on the same question.[6] However, the United States saw an Asian regional security forum as a threat to the U.S. system of bilateral security relations and was hostile to the initiative. ASEAN raised a number of objections to the Japanese initiative, and Japan retreated to its established bilateral security approach when it recognized the strength of U.S. opposition. Nonetheless, ASEAN saw that an Asian multilateral regional security forum was in the making; "[c]onsequently, the ASEAN states decided to claim the process in the hope they could channel rather than resist the momentum."[7] In January 1992, during the Fourth ASEAN Summit in Singapore, the ASEAN ministers approved using the ASEAN-PMC as the avenue for a regional security dialogue. At the July AMM, Singapore, with the backing of Australia and the United States, "recommended expanding the existing ASEAN-PMC dialogue structure."[8]

During 1993, the ARF slowly emerged. There were numerous track-two activities, including meetings between ASEAN-ISIS representatives and ASEAN senior ministers. ASEAN-ISIS provided the ASEAN states with ideas concerning such matters as ASEAN's role in the ARF. At the same time, the new Clinton administration in the United States was more inclined toward multilateralism than its predecessor had been. It envisioned a "New Pacific Community," based around U.S. bilateral security alliances.[9] An ASEAN-based security dialogue could complement the U.S. security structure.

Finally, ASEAN made a formal proposal to establish a regional security dialogue. The Joint Communique of the Twenty-Sixth AMM (July 23–24, 1993) specified the need to "evolve a more predictable and constructive pattern of political and security relationships in the Asia Pacific." At an informal dinner after the ASEAN-PMC, ASEAN, its dialogue partners, and invited guests (China, the European Union, Russia, Papua New Guinea, Vietnam, and Laos) agreed to establish a regular gathering of foreign ministers, to be called the ASEAN Regional Forum, to discuss regional security issues. The ARF was born.

The ARF Meetings

The first working session of the ARF was held in Bangkok in July, 1994. This was preceded by a preparatory meeting of ARF Senior Officials (ARF-SOM) in May 1994. At this meeting, ASEAN resisted Australian and Canadian pressure to speed up the ARF process and institutionalize confidence-building measures. In this, it was supported by China, which supported the informal consensual approach.

The inaugural ARF meeting in Bangkok, was low key and unstructured. There was no formal agenda. Three hours were set aside in which eighteen foreign ministers were each allotted ten minutes to address the topic of "Asia-Pacific Security—Challenges and Opportunities."[10] ASEAN approached the ARF very slowly and tried to make all the participants—especially China—"comfortable" with the process and the other states. The initial discussions focused on the means to achieve the ARF's primary function of encouraging "a predictable and constructive pattern of relationships" through dialogue, and the pace at which they should proceed.[11] ASEAN clearly registered its proprietary role in the ARF.[12] The closed session discussed Cambodia and, briefly, the South China Sea. This last topic was barely tolerated by China, which had earlier rejected any suggestion that the issue be negotiated within the ARF. The participating states agreed to hold the ARF on an annual basis and endorsed the ASEAN Treaty of Amity and Cooperation (TAC) as a "code of conduct" governing state relations.[13]

Between the first and second ARF meetings, the organization took tentative steps toward creating a tangible structure. The ARF held three workshops: a seminar on confidence building in Canberra in November 1994; a seminar on peacekeeping in Brunei in March 1995; and a seminar on preventive diplomacy in Seoul in May 1995. These workshops consisted of government official, academics, and members of regional think tanks and were designed to accommodate Chinese concerns. The seminars produced working reports, which were presented to the next ARF meeting in Brunei.

During this interim period, in February 1995, the Philippines discovered that China had seized and placed markers upon Mischief Reef, part of the Spratly Islands chain. Filipino officials believed the reef had been seized as many as six months before, at around the time of the first ARF meeting. At that meeting, China's foreign minister Qian Qichen had rejected discussing the South China Sea in a multilateral forum, but he had also reiterated China's peaceful intentions in the region. The Mischief Reef incident undermined China's credibility and called into question the ARF's ability to instill a sense of acceptable conduct in its members.

The second working session of the ARF was held in Brunei on August 1, 1995. For this session, ASEAN produced a concept paper, which formally claimed that ASEAN had "undertaken the obligation to be the primary driving force" within the ARF.[14] The concept paper laid out broad guidelines for future ARF meetings. First, "meetings will have no formal agenda and approach sensitive security issues in an oblique and non-confrontational manner," according to the standard ASEAN practice. Second, the paper outlined a three-step process for the development of the ARF: confidence-building measures, followed by preventive diplomacy, followed by conflict resolution. The concept paper promoted the established ASEAN practices of consultation and consensus as the methods of building intra-ARF relations. The paper rejected the idea of an ARF Secretariat, asserting that ASEAN would be the repository of all ARF documents and would provide the necessary support for ARF through the ASEAN Standing Committee. Finally, the paper recommended that the ARF should progress at a pace "comfortable" to all of its participants.

The ARF adopted most of the concept paper's recommendations. Two ARF structures were established to help the chairman of the ARF-SOM make recommendations to the forum concerning the implementation of its proposals. These were the Inter-Sessional Support Group (ISG) on Confidence Building and Inter-Sessional Meetings (ISM) created to address cooperative activities like peacekeeping and search-and-rescue coordination. These structures were designed to appear as though they functioned on an ad hoc basis, in order to accommodate China's opposition to institutionalized ARF activities. The chairs of these intersessional groups are shared by an ASEAN and non-ASEAN state. Indonesia and Japan cochair the ISG on confidence building. Malaysia and Canada cochair an ISM on peacekeeping, and the ISM on search-and-rescue cooperation and coordination is cochaired by Singapore and the United States. The second working session of the ARF was most notable for its more advanced tone. According to Michael Leifer, "The meeting's principal accomplishment was the agreement on norms and procedures that gave the ARF an institutional, if embryonic, identity."[15]

Problems and Prospects

The ARF is only eight years old (1994–2002) and cannot be fairly assessed for effectiveness and significance. Its methods are designed to work over the long term, making short-term evaluations suspect. Nonetheless, a number of analysts have criticized the ARF approach to building regional security. The ARF is important to ASEAN because ASEAN has invested a great deal of its own prestige into the making the ARF "work." The ARF is also the vehicle through which ASEAN hopes to achieve a longtime goal, the ability to shape its own security environment rather than be subject to the machinations of the great powers.

The ARF has produced some tangible results. Most observers agree that the ARF serves a useful purpose simply by providing a regular meeting place for the states of the region to discuss issues and tensions that may arise between them. The ARF's intersessional meetings, workshops, and annual meetings have encouraged progress in some areas of conflict. The 1995 Brunei meeting provided the United States and China with an opportunity to informally address and defuse the immediate causes of bilateral tensions between the two states.[16] To an extent, the ARF successfully engaged China in a discussion of the Spratly Islands dispute. China had kept the South China Sea issue off the official agenda of the ARF's Bangkok meeting in 1994. The chairman's statement at the end of the 1995 meeting, however, called for all disputant states to find a peaceful resolution to the Spratlys issue and abide by relevant international treaties and conventions, especially the 1992 ASEAN Manila Declaration. However, as discussed in Chapter 5, China has refused to permit any substantive discussions of the Spratlys conflict within the ARF.

Security issues have arisen during the course of the ARF's brief history that have demonstrated its limited ability to address, let alone resolve, conflict. Taiwan is not included in the ARF, and the ASEAN states have washed their hands of the Taiwan issue, at least at the official level. Taiwan, however, has the potential to be a major flashpoint between the United States and China, and it does have larger implications for the region if it proves indicative of China's willingness to use force. In March 1996, China and the United States found themselves in an extremely tense situation over Taiwan. The ARF was incapable of affecting the standoff.

The conflict between North and South Korea is another area of tension the ARF was unprepared to confront. In August 2000, North Korea finally joined the ARF. It did so after internal political changes in both Koreas led to conciliatory diplomatic initiatives, which, in turn, led to a significant alleviation of tensions between the two. The ARF played no role in bringing about this regional détente, though it may play a meaningful role in helping to maintain it. The ARF was also incapable of addressing the Indonesian-backed campaign of violence against East Timor in 1999 and was ineffectual in dealing with some of the Asia Pacific's nontraditional security issues, such as the problem of the regional haze caused by forest fires in Indonesia.

ASEAN does not expect the ARF to deal with these issues. The ARF is meant to build transparency and confidence between participating states. It is not meant to address contentious issues. The ARF augments, but does not replace, existing security arrangements. This approach is supported by Japan and China and is the most logical and consistent extension of the "ASEAN way" to the larger Asia-Pacific region. To many other ARF members, however, the organization's approach to regional security issues underlines problems with the ARF. The ARF is, therefore, faced with a critical issue of moving quickly and effectively enough to ensure the interest and commitment of its more impatient—mainly Western—members while maintaining the gradual pace and nonintrusive methods that will keep its Asian participants, particularly China, engaged. On the surface, ASEAN is ideally suited to play this delicate balancing act. However, some of the central principles around which ASEAN has constructed the ARF are fundamentally flawed.

The ARF is modeled upon the ASEAN methods of consultation and consensus building, which ASEAN believes can be applied to the larger region. According to ASEAN's concept paper on the ARF:

ASEAN has a pivotal role to play in the ARF. It has a demonstrable record of enhancing regional cooperation in the most diverse sub-region in the Asia Pacific. It has also fostered habits of cooperation and provided the catalyst for encouraging regional cooperation in the wider Asia Pacific region. The annual ASEAN Ministerial Meetings have contributed significantly to the positive regional environment today. There would be great hope for the Asia Pacific if the whole region could emulate ASEAN's record of enhancing the peace and prosperity of its participants.[17]

To reinforce this point, Jose T. Almonte claims,

ASEAN's experience during the past three decades proves that the plural multi-ethnic communities of East Asia can be united—despite the lack of an overarching civilization similar to that which facilitated the unification of Europe after the Second World War. The basic lesson ASEAN teaches is that differences or even disputes should not stop countries from promoting mutually beneficial relationships—because the very act of sitting down together can begin to build mutual trust and confidence. And this is no small accomplishment since, in societies without mutual trust, any individual player's refusal to cooperate for mutual benefit can be a rational recourse.[18]

Sitting down and talking can build trust and confidence. However, the ASEAN approach assumes that mutually beneficial interests can be found between states, which may not always be the case. Massive disparities in economic and military power, for example, may create a situation where one nation is able to assert its will on others with very little cost to itself. Moreover, the ASEAN approach assumes that misunderstanding and a lack of trust underlie most disputes, problems that can be alleviated through communication. Again, this is not necessarily true. Many conflicts arise from competition over resources and advantage. These are issues of competing interest and can only be resolved when states agree to compromise on those interests. Building confidence, in itself, will not cause a redefinition of interests.

The ASEAN states assert that the actual process of interaction accounts for the success of the ASEAN way. If the states of the ARF agree to work together, they argue, the process of interaction will bring about cooperative behavior. Confidence-building measures will create trust between states and eventually give rise to preventive diplomacy followed by genuine conflict management. This process has supposedly been demonstrated within the ASEAN context, and ASEAN is extending its example of security community building to the Asia-Pacific region. However, ASEAN's argument does not accurately reflect the emergence and efficacy of the ASEAN way. The context within which ASEAN developed is more fundamental to understanding the success of the ASEAN way than the process. The ASEAN states had an incentive to make the ASEAN way work because they were weak states, of similar ideological disposition, threatened by much more powerful external actors and forces, existing in an uncertain and potentially hostile international environment. They learned to work around their various disputes because doing so was more beneficial than allowing such disputes to undermine whatever security and influence they might create by working together. ASEAN contributes to the reduction in regional tensions by facilitating contact between its members, but its members continue to define their national self-interests in fairly narrow terms.

In addition, the dominant powers of the ARF begin their interactions from very different positions than the original ASEAN states were in. The United States and China are not weak powers that can be forced to cooperate out of a fear of external threats. For these great powers, global and regional interests and aspirations are considerations that may well moderate their willingness to cooperate. Their incentive to make the ASEAN way work is not the same as for the ASEAN countries.

Some of the security challenges facing the Asia Pacific are not amenable to the ARF's focus on constructing a regional identity to manage conflict and dependence on the ASEAN method of consensus building. According to John Garafano, "On the most fundamental level, the wide variety of threats to stability—in their origins, intensity, and likely maturation—decreases the likelihood that an essentially unitary approach to security can successfully manage all of them. Looking more closely at the kinds of hard decisions and choices that are necessary to solve some of these conflicts, one can conclude that identity-building by itself will not address such realities."[19] If the ARF cannot actually resolve conflicts, it will appear irrelevant to many of its most important members.

The ARF's commitment to consensus building leads to other problems. The more states that are involved in a negotiation, the greater the chances of either failure or that negotiated agreements are less effective than they could be. Some ARF supporters argue that ASEAN's economic success is a testament to the validity of the ARF's methods in the security realm.[20] However, ASEAN's contribution to the economic success of its members was minimal and peripheral. Moreover, ASEAN has survived by avoiding the discussion of security issues precisely because these issues are so different in nature from economic issues. This method of interaction also assumes that the most difficult issues facing states should be deferred while less contentious issues are settled. This follows directly from the ASEAN experience, where cooperating around issues of conflict made it possible to defuse the issues over the long run, as in the dispute between the Philippines and Malaysia over Sabah. However, these developments occurred because the ASEAN countries decided that there was too much at risk to not cooperate. A similar dynamic might be at work in the Asia-Pacific region, but this is not certain.

The ARF's contention that transparency is a valid foundation for confidence building is also questionable. As noted in the discussion of the reasons for ASEAN's weapon purchases in Chapter 4, state weakness is often at the heart of military buildups. Transparency may actually make a state feel more insecure by exposing its weaknesses to its neighbors.

These kinds of concerns have led some analysts to call for smaller regional organizations that can focus more explicitly on difficult issues, rather than a large body that may not be able to give different issues the time and attention they deserve.[21] In theory, such extra-ARF activity would not detract from the ARF. The ARF is meant to complement existing security arrangements. In practice, however, the more security activity that takes place outside the ARF, the more irrelevant the organization will appear, and the less influence ASEAN will have over the regional security environment. Others have argued for more flexibility within the ARF by allowing smaller groups to develop, under the auspices of the ARF, which would directly address contentious issues. However, promoting active conflict resolution within the ARF at this time pushes the organization beyond what it can sustain. Even ASEAN has not reached the point where it can resolve disputes between its members. Given the many divergent security and political interests of its member states, the undemanding ARF approach may be the only way that so many different states can coexist under one regional banner.

Robyn Lim argues that the ARF can make no meaningful contribution to the security of the Asia Pacific and, in fact, serves as an instrument through which China can exert regional influence while undermining the stabilizing effect of U.S. power. Lim sees China as an aggressive power, willing to use force to achieve its ends, which is manipulating the ARF to its advantage. Security relations in the Asia Pacific will revolve around China, Japan, Russia, and the United States. Regional security will ultimately depend upon the choices that China makes, "whether it chooses to integrate peacefully into a new regional order, or whether it opts to assert hegemony on the basis of size, centrality and history."[22]

The fate of the ARF will significantly affect ASEAN's development. ASEAN has invested an enormous amount of its prestige in the ARF and has shaped the organization according to its own methods and objectives. If the regional states ultimately judge it to be a failure, ASEAN's standing will decline. Its methods will be deemed ineffective beyond the Southeast Asian context, undermining its ability to be an independent and meaningful entity. Under such circumstances, it cannot assume that its own members would remain loyal to the vision of ASEAN as a player in the regional security environment.

ASEAN will also have considerable difficulty holding on to its dominant role in the ARF. From its inception, the non-ASEAN states have expressed the view that the "ASEAN Regional Forum" is only a transitional phase before the ARF becomes the "Asian Regional Forum." This view is still strongly held by the Western powers and Japan.[23] Australia has never been happy about ASEAN's proprietorial claim to the ARF and is uncomfortable with ASEAN's slow pace of institutional development. Some non-ASEAN actors have complained of being treated like "second-class citizens" within the ARF.[24]

On the other hand, for the great powers, there were a number of advantages to following ASEAN's lead in the creation of the ARF. It was easier to utilize ASEAN, a proven institution, than to build a new structure. Moreover, as an Asian organization, ASEAN had a much better chance of getting China to the multilateral table than any Western-inspired institution. China continues to support ASEAN's leadership role in the ARF, and while it is generally suspicious of multilateral institutions, it favors ASEAN's slow and incremental approach to building regional relations. However, the importance of the ARF to the larger powers should not be exaggerated. In large measure, China joined the ARF to avoid being left out. The United States continues to put its greatest efforts in its bilateral relationships.

These points being made, it is important to give the ARF its due. Alistair Johnston has argued that there is compelling evidence to support the view that Chinese officials are being socialized to a vision of the Asia Pacific that is conducive to regional cooperation. He argues that the ARF, despite its low level of institutionalization, is evolving into a more structured organization, allowing China to become much more comfortable with the concepts and ideas of regional multilateralism. In this assessment, the ARF has worked very much as envisioned by its most optimistic supporters. The reasons for China's loosening attitude, however, are largely attributable to the small group of policymakers in the Comprehensive Division of the Asia Department of the PRC Foreign Ministry. These eight to ten overworked officials are China's representatives to the ARF. As they have become more comfortable with the formal and informal processes associated with regional multilateralism, they have started to see China's security interests as positively tied to the regional structures and have done their best to move the country in a multilateral direction. While particular Chinese officials may support creeping multilateralism for normative reasons, Chinese leaders tolerate these developments because of concerns about China's international image.[25]

These are positive developments, but they raise questions about the fragility of the ARF process. Even if one group of officials is socialized into the multilateral environment, is this success a strong enough basis to predict that leaders and other officials in other government and military departments, who may be operating under completely different sets of assumptions and motivations, will also be socialized? Probably not. Many individual participants in organizations such as the ARF may be socialized to regional norms and perspectives that are not shared by other political actors within their states.

Given the level of internal dissent, the long-term intentions of most of the larger powers to make the ARF an "Asian Regional Forum," and the questionable applicability of the ASEAN way to the ARF, ASEAN will need to reduce its control of the ARF sometime soon and to accept much larger roles for other states within the institution. China's support of ASEAN's position in the ARF has been important to the endurance of the ASEAN way in the organization, but China's motivations are suspect. It approves of ASEAN multilateralism largely because it is a method of interaction that allows China to block significant progress on various issues, if necessary, and offset U.S. and Japanese political influence. This is the kind of division that could undermine the ARF. However, accepting a loss of status in the ARF may seriously weaken ASEAN's internal cohesion, which is strongly linked to ASEAN's effectiveness as a regional player.

The ARF may represent a nontraditional, diplomatic approach toward managing a traditional security problem, in this case the emergence of a rising, revisionist power in China. The ARF is the new regional institution that is most directly concerned with integrating China into the larger region through a process of socialization. Whether or not China is susceptible to this kind of approach is uncertain. The ARF can help to maintain stability in a system characterized by a stable balance of power; however, it cannot help to create such a balance.[26] The ARF has been made possible because the great powers themselves could not agree on a way to manage their own relations. For similar reasons, ASEAN has enjoyed an undeserved level of regional prominence on issues of security.

The ASEAN leaders' attitudes and statements regarding the ARF indicate that they believe the organization can be more central to the management of regional security than is realistic. However, the ASEAN states have also quietly pursued policies that promote traditional balance-of-power relationships. ASEAN hopes that the ARF can serve as the basis for genuine confidence building and conflict management in the Asia Pacific. However, its members are not prepared to put all of their hopes in this one option. The ARF will only be successful if it can meet the needs of its most powerful members. In the short term, ASEAN may be able to affect the ARF agenda, but it cannot control that agenda without accommodating the demands of the more powerful states. Inevitably, and probably very quickly, the ARF will slip beyond ASEAN's control; indeed, it must if it is to make any difference in the region. ASEAN can continue to play a significant role in the ARF, but it must recognize that its role is not to set the regional security agenda but rather to facilitate contacts between the larger powers. At its best, the ARF can encourage the maintenance of a stable regional environment, but if the larger powers become overtly competitive, the ARF will quickly be irrelevant.[27]

ASEAN's Expansion

ASEAN has expanded rapidly in the post–Cold War period.[28] Vietnam joined ASEAN in 1995. In 1997, Myanmar and Laos were incorporated. Cambodia joined in 1999. Making ASEAN truly representative of all of Southeast Asia has been a stated goal of ASEAN's leaders from the organization's inception. They believe that the larger ASEAN is, the louder and more influential its voice in international economic and security forums can be. An expanded ASEAN has a better chance of being an economic and political counterweight to the large powers of the region, China, Japan, and India. Bringing in mainland Southeast Asia has the potential to increase the ASEAN states' GDP to US $650 billion (in 1995 prices). It increases ASEAN's member-state population and market size from 340 million people to almost 500 million. Finally, by incorporating all of Southeast Asia, ASEAN may be better placed to promote regional peace and stability.[29] However, the incorporation of mainland Southeast Asia has also created enormous problems for the organization, which probably outweigh any advantages associated with expansion.[30]

Vietnam

Vietnam joined ASEAN in July 1995.[31] Vietnam's membership in ASEAN has profound symbolic value. Fear of Vietnam defined ASEAN for much of its institutional history; now ASEAN's main antagonist has joined the fold. The decision to allow Vietnam membership, and to fast-track the applications of the other Southeast Asian states, was pushed by Thailand, which saw itself as the economic hub of mainland Southeast Asia and perceived ASEAN's expansion as an opportunity to increase its own status within ASEAN.[32] The other ASEAN states went along with Thailand's plans because, ironically, they felt that having Vietnam and the other mainland states inside the organization would balance Thailand's influence. However, Vietnam's membership introduces many potentially disruptive factors to ASEAN's internal relations. Vietnam is the traditional competitor to Thailand in Indochina and a major state that could challenge Indonesia's aspirations to regional leadership. Assimilating it into the ASEAN fold will be complicated and take time. For now, Vietnam is content to follow the lead of the other ASEAN states as it tries to adapt to the new demands being placed on its diplomatic service (for example, the need to educate diplomats and officials in English, the language of ASEAN). This could change as Vietnam becomes more self-assured and economically successful.

Myanmar

Myanmar's inclusion in ASEAN has created the most obvious, and perhaps most serious, problems in ASEAN's expansion. Myanmar is an international pariah. Far from enhancing ASEAN's international prestige, Myanmar's inclusion has seriously weakened ASEAN's international standing. The difficulties ASEAN has had in negotiating its membership reveal problems that the organization must address in both its internal and external relations.

In September 1988, Myanmar's military declared martial law and assumed power as the State Law and Order Restoration Council (SLORC), continuing the military's brutal domination of Burmese society.[33] In May 1990, the SLORC organized elections, which were won handily by the National League for Democracy (NLD), an opposition umbrella group led by Aung San Suu Kyi. The new parliament was never convened. Instead, the SLORC announced that the elections had been held to select a constitutional assembly, not a parliament.

In response, the West and Japan imposed various sanctions against Myanmar. By contrast, ASEAN expressed its disapproval of Western "meddling" in Southeast Asian affairs. Thailand initially allowed Burmese refugees to enter its territory, but it later repatriated them and allowed Myanmar's military to use Thai territory to stage attacks on ethnic insurgents in Myanmar. Singapore supplied the SLORC regime with small arms and ammunition; Malaysia was the first ASEAN country to send an ambassador to Rangoon. ASEAN's reaction to the SLORC was primarily motivated by commercial interests. In 1988, Myanmar had opened its economy to foreign investment.[34] Thailand's military engaged in lucrative logging and fishing deals with the SLORC regime. Other ASEAN countries also took advantage of Myanmar's new economic openness. In 1998, more than 50 percent of all foreign direct investment (FDI) in Myanmar originated in ASEAN.[35]

In 1992, Thailand suggested that ASEAN invite Myanmar to attend that year's AMM as an observer. The Muslim ASEAN states objected to this idea because of the SLORC's treatment of Myanmar's Muslim Rohingya people. The SLORC was uninterested in meeting the ASEAN countries in multilateral dialogue, favoring bilateral meetings instead. By 1994, however, relations between the two parties had changed. The SLORC saw participation in ASEAN as a way to end its international isolation and enhance Myanmar's economic development. For ASEAN, concern over China's increasing influence in Myanmar and a belief in the country's economic potential combined to override other objections. In the years that followed, ASEAN frequently responded to Western criticism of its policies toward Myanmar with the assertion that isolating Myanmar would only drive it more deeply into China's embrace. In 1994, China and Myanmar conducted $1.5 billion worth of trade; Chinese engineers were busy improving the country's infrastructure; and Myanmar's military purchased Chinese arms worth $1.4 billion. China was involved in the construction of Myanmarese naval bases, expanding its ability to project power in Asia. Indonesia was concerned both with China's activities in the Andaman Sea and with Thailand's pursuit of unilateral relations with Myanmar and China. Singaporean president Goh Chok Tong visited Myanmar in March 1994, and Malaysia voiced its belief that Myanmar's domestic situation had improved.

In July 1994, Thailand invited Myanmar to attend the annual AMM as its guest. ASEAN made it clear that it wanted Myanmar to join the organization but stipulated that conciliatory gestures on the domestic front were necessary before accession was possible. The SLORC junta granted Aung San Suu Kyi an early release from house arrest in July 1995. This gesture enabled Myanmar to sign the TAC, thereby becoming an official ASEAN observer.

Myanmar applied for full ASEAN membership during the 1995 AMM. At that meeting, ASEAN expressed its commitment to incorporate all of Southeast Asia by 2000, regardless of the economic and political differences between the current ASEAN-Seven and its prospective members. ASEAN answered criticism of its policies toward Myanmar by arguing that it was pursuing "constructive engagement," a policy of quiet diplomacy combined with increased economic relations in an effort to induce the SLORC to reform its internal policies. However, in May 1996, the SLORC regime cracked down on its democratic opposition, detaining more than 250 NLD members. Moreover, Myanmar has strongly rejected the idea that "constructive engagement" was ever meant to influence its domestic politics. Myanmar has defined the term to mean that "ASEAN would like to see Myanmar as an equal" and has consistently rejected calls for democratic reform.[36]

In 1996, Myanmar, Cambodia, and Laos were granted ARF observer status. Malaysia assumed the ASEAN presidency that year, and Prime Minister Mahathir Mohamad used his chairman's prerogative to advance Myanmar's accession date from 2000 to 1997. This decision aggravated some ASEAN members. The U.S. and European governments tried to use the development to include Myanmar among the security issues addressed by the ARF. Some ASEAN members saw this as an opportunity to pursue a "good cop, bad cop" approach to the SLORC. However, ASEAN members were not prepared to coordinate their policies regarding Myanmar. In October 1996, Rangoon launched a new round of domestic repression.

This new SLORC action drove ASEAN and its Western partners further apart. Malaysia's foreign minister, Abdullah Ahmad Badawi, as the chairman of the ASEAN Standing Committee, warned Myanmar that its actions threatened its early accession to ASEAN. Singapore, the Philippines, and Thailand questioned the plan to advance Myanmar's entry to ASEAN. Their reservations were expressed as uncertainty over Myanmar's ability to meet the conditions of the ASEAN Free Trade Area (AFTA), but they actually revolved around Rangoon's domestic conduct. Jakarta and Kuala Lumpur, however, insisted that Cambodia, Laos, and Myanmar join ASEAN in 1997. ASEAN eventually agreed to admit the three new states at the same time, without specifying a date for their accession.

In April 1997, U.S. State Department spokesman Nicholas Burns announced that the United States was "trying to use our influence to make the point that Myanmar should be given a stiff message that it is not welcome [in ASEAN]."[37] This statement created a powerful backlash within ASEAN. The United States softened its rhetoric, acknowledging that ASEAN had the right to choose its own members. However, the damage had been done. Largely as a reaction against the perception that the West was trying to bully it and intrude on its internal affairs, ASEAN voted to admit Myanmar in 1997, as scheduled. The vote may have reinforced ASEAN's independence, but it also severely damaged its international standing.[38]

Europe deeply opposed ASEAN's decision to admit Myanmar. In Singapore in February 1997, the Myanmar problem came up during a meeting of the European and ASEAN foreign ministers. This meeting was in preparation for the 1998 Asia-Europe Summit Meeting (ASEM). In 1996, the European Union (EU) had imposed visa restrictions on members of the SLORC regime, and it was unclear that ASEAN membership would automatically confer on Myanmar the right to participate in ASEM. A meeting of the ASEAN-EU Joint Cooperation conference, scheduled for November 1997, was postponed indefinitely. ASEAN wished to admit Myanmar and Laos as observers; the EU objected on the grounds that neither state had signed the 1980 ASEAN-EU cooperation treaty, and Myanmar would not be invited to do so. As a compromise, the EU proposed that Myanmar and Laos be allowed a "passive presence" at the meeting. The ASEAN-Seven refused to accept this arrangement. In 1998, Thailand, in an effort to reconvene the Joint Cooperation Conference, accepted the "passive presence" proposal, but Rangoon refused to go along. As early as 1996, the issue of Myanmar had created tensions between ASEAN and Europe, with some ASEAN members suggesting that the EU be excluded from the ARF as retaliation for its "interference" on the Myanmar question. By 1998, however, ASEAN's willingness and ability to alienate Europe over Myanmar had declined in the aftermath of the Asian economic crisis.

Cambodia

The Cambodian elections of May 1993 were the culmination of the Paris peace process. The elections resulted in the winning party, the Front Uni pour un Cambodge Independent, Neutre et Pacifique (FUNCINPEC), and the runner up, the Cambodian People's Party (CPP), forming a coalition government, which also included elements of the nationalist right. Prince Norodom Ranariddh, the leader of FUNCINPEC, and Hun Sen, the CPP leader, were appointed co-premiers. In 1993, Singapore was Cambodia's top trading partner, followed by Indonesia and Vietnam. ASEAN business interests quickly established relations with the new royal government. Both FUNCINPEC and the CPP were happy to assist ASEAN businesses in getting licenses to exploit timber, textile manufacturing, and tourism, and they may even have facilitated illegal trade in weapons, drugs, and prostitution.

ASEAN did not move to assume peacekeeping or stabilization duties in Cambodia after the 1993 UN pullout for a number of reasons. The ASEAN members had little experience in peacekeeping. More importantly, ASEAN members' interests in Cambodia were divided. Different ASEAN countries had favored different factions within Cambodia, and some business interests were better served by a disintegrating Cambodia than one with a strong government. Other pressures, however, pushed ASEAN toward favoring Cambodia's stability. ASEAN's organizational interests were not served by having a member state on the verge of collapse. Strategic concerns about the development of a regional power vacuum were also relevant. ASEAN itself could even be divided by its members' involvement in Cambodia's domestic affairs once ASEAN admitted Cambodia, if the country did not have a strong central government.

Tension between the Cambodian co-premiers developed in 1996, when both parties cultivated ties with other Cambodian factions, including segments of the Khmer Rouge (KR). Violence between the opposing political camps flared in 1997. On July 5, Hun Sen seized control of Phnom Penh, at the cost of sixty lives. Prince Ranariddh was driven into exile, and heavy fighting erupted in Cambodia's northern provinces. ASEAN called a special foreign ministers' meeting for July 10. ASEAN had been set to admit Cambodia in 1997. Over Vietnam's objections, ASEAN decided to suspend Cambodia's accession to membership indefinitely. ASEAN continued to recognize Ranariddh as co-premier and proposed that a caretaker government oversee the planned 1998 elections; however, Hun Sen, alluding to the established ASEAN practice of nonintervention, bluntly told the organization to stay out of Cambodia's internal affairs. However, ASEAN had to play an active role in the Cambodian situation, given Thailand's strategic concerns and the ASEAN members' reluctance to participate in Western sanctions.

ASEAN offered three alternatives to the Cambodian situation: restoring the coalition government, with Ranariddh reinstated as co-premier; having Ranariddh and Hun Sen nominate representatives to head a caretaker government that would exercise power until the UN-supervised elections in 1998; or allowing Ranariddh to nominate a member of FUNCINPEC to work with Hun Sen until the elections. However, the United States and Australia dropped their demands for Ranariddh's reinstatement in response to reports that he had met representatives of the KR. Instead, they called for the maintenance of the coalition government, with a strengthened FUNCINPEC contingent. Thus, Hun Sen found it easier to rebuff ASEAN and downplay the significance of Cambodia's failure to join the organization.

Hun Sen then embarked on a strategy that took full advantage of ASEAN's internal contradictions. Ung Huot, Hun Sen's self-appointed co-premier, attended ASEAN's thirtieth anniversary meeting and offered to accept ASEAN mediation in exchange for immediate Cambodian membership. ASEAN asked for an official letter from Hun Sen explaining his view of where mediation should be directed. Overriding the desires of Malaysia and Vietnam, (as well as Myanmar and Laos) ASEAN voted to keep Cambodia's membership on hold and to take human rights into account when reviewing its membership application.

ASEAN renewed its offer of mediation to Cambodia in August 1997. Cambodia had already written a letter requesting ASEAN's involvement. In Phnom Penh, the ASEAN envoys agreed with Hun Sen's plan to delay Ranariddh's return while providing for the safe return of FUNCINPEC supporters. The ASEAN states now saw Ranariddh as important to the efforts to restore political stability to Cambodia, but they no longer called for his restoration. The organization justified this about-face with the argument that "member states recognize states, not governments," a position that ASEAN had ignored to that point. As further incentive, Hun Sen promised elections in May 1998.

The Asian economic crisis, which started in July 1997, eroded ASEAN's bargaining position with Hun Sen. In January 1998, Cambodia shifted its position yet again. Hun Sen castigated ASEAN for its inability to cope with its own difficulties while lecturing Cambodia on human rights and democracy. He refused to meet the ASEAN delegation. In the end, Japan brokered a truce between Hun Sen's and Ranariddh's forces in March 1998. This arrangement allowed Ranariddh to return to Cambodia to contest the election, after receiving a royal pardon for smuggling arms and conspiring with the KR. ASEAN helped expedite judicial proceedings against Ranariddh and joined the United States and Japan in calling for King Sihanouk's return to Cambodia from his exile in Beijing. However, ASEAN was largely shut out of substantive developments in Cambodia from this point on.

The Cambodian election did not occur without controversy. Ranariddh and his allies threatened to boycott the elections because of intimidation, violence, and a biased supervisory body. The elections of July 26 were marred by violence but accepted by an international community anxious to wash its hands of Cambodia. The CPP received 41.4 percent of the vote; FUNCINPEC took 31.7 percent, with the remaining 14.3 percent going to the party of government-critic Sam Rainsy. The CPP declared itself the winner, though Hun Sen offered to incorporate the other parties in a coalition government. The key ministries would remain under CPP control, however. On September 1, the National Election Committee confirmed the final count, while the supreme court turned away the opposition's claims of irregularities in the election process. On April 30, 1999, ASEAN formally admitted Cambodia to its ranks, fulfilling the dream of ASEAN's founders to incorporate all of Southeast Asia.

ASEAN Expansion—Too Much, Too Fast?

ASEAN admitted the mainland Southeast Asian states for political, economic, and security reasons. It believed that the opportunity for uniting Southeast Asia was highly auspicious in the post–Cold War period and might not present itself again for a long time. ASEAN leaders were afraid that Myanmar's isolationist tendencies would reassert themselves if they did not act quickly. Other political considerations also played a role. President Suharto and Prime Minister Mahathir saw their political careers winding down and wanted the unification of Southeast Asia as part of their legacies. Perhaps most importantly, ASEAN believed that its international voice would be far louder, and its economic appeal greatly enhanced, if it could present a united front to the world. In the short term, however, ASEAN's international prestige and legitimacy were severely compromised by its decision to admit Myanmar and by its contradictory approach to domestic upheaval in Myanmar and Cambodia. The situations in those two countries also raised uncomfortable questions about human rights and political stability in the established ASEAN countries, as well as new questions about the ASEAN way.

ASEAN gambled that its economic and political importance would eventually force other states to accommodate its newest members on its terms. This may have been a miscalculation. Normally, Western countries do not allow human rights concerns to stand in the way of business. Individual ASEAN countries would not have allowed solidarity with Myanmar to damage their economic interests, either. However, the existence of ASEAN, the organization, changed these calculations. So long as the West could punish ASEAN without threatening its economic relationships with individual ASEAN states, the stalemate over Myanmar could continue indefinitely, at considerable cost to ASEAN's international prestige. Eventually, this situation would have offset the economic benefits of its expansion. Whatever the final outcome of this situation may have been, however, the Asian economic crisis undermined ASEAN's bargaining position. ASEAN found itself in conflict with its most important allies over its new members at a time when its members were most in need of external assistance. These vulnerabilities increased pressure on ASEAN and added weight to calls that it must reform its practices to allow for greater intervention in its members' domestic affairs.

If ASEAN's political motives for expansion backfired, its security calculations were also questionable. One major security consideration motivating ASEAN's expansion was its desire to bring all of Southeast Asia under one set of rules for conflict management. With the states of Cambodia, Laos, Myanmar, and Vietnam part of ASEAN, all of Southeast Asia, ostensibly, accepts an approach to intra-ASEAN conflict that should secure the stability of the region. Other security considerations have more uncertain implications. ASEAN incorporated Myanmar, in part, to prevent Rangoon from being pulled more deeply into Beijing's orbit. However, if various ASEAN countries became involved in a conflict with China over the Spratly Islands, for example, would Myanmar maintain ASEAN solidarity? The answer to that question would almost certainly be "no." Myanmar and China are too closely linked, both economically and militarily, for Myanmar to endanger that relationship for the sake of ASEAN solidarity. Vietnam falls on the other side of the equation from Myanmar in regard to China. Vietnam's relations with China are quite amicable at the moment, but this may change if the situation concerning the Spratly Islands heats up. Vietnam joined ASEAN counting on ASEAN's support in any conflict it has with China. Yet, events in 1997 demonstrated that ASEAN is not prepared to offer the kind of support that Vietnam expects. On the question of China, the new members have added further weight on both sides to the preexisting fault lines in ASEAN.[39]

For the ASEAN-Six, the economic rationale for expansion included creating a larger market for intra-ASEAN trade through AFTA; facilitating investment in Vietnam, Cambodia, Myanmar, and Laos; improving ASEAN's appeal as a target of foreign investment; and furthering overall economic cooperation in Southeast Asia. In theory, expansion enables the ASEAN-Six to help their businesses stay internationally competitive by creating access to cheaper raw materials and production locations. To the new members, the economic benefits of inclusion in ASEAN were numerous. They hoped for increased investment from the ASEAN-Six, as well as improved export opportunities and more development assistance. Throughout the 1990s, ASEAN investment in mainland Southeast Asia increased considerably. Vietnam and Myanmar's major trading partner is Singapore, while Thailand is the major trading partner to Laos and Cambodia. By contrast, the economic significance of the four new members to the old ASEAN-Six is far more limited. Foreign investment from the ASEAN-Six into the new member states is relatively small in absolute terms, though it is a significant share of their FDI. Nonetheless, the ASEAN-Six are much more important to the new members for economic development than vice versa. These economic imbalances create the possibility of the more developed ASEAN countries cementing an unequal and exploitative relationship with the newer and weaker members, creating a situation more conducive toward ASEAN division than unity.

Economically, the expansion of ASEAN is most valuable to the ASEAN-Six because it makes AFTA more appealing as an investment community. However, the inclusion of new members also complicates and prolongs the AFTA process. The new members have been given extensions beyond 2003 to complete their tariff reductions under AFTA. Vietnam is expected to meet AFTA requirements in 2006, Myanmar and Laos in 2008. There is a general concern among observers that the new ASEAN states will use their influence to slow regional integration and liberalization.

A major concern is how well prepared the new ASEAN states are for AFTA and how well they understand what belonging to ASEAN and AFTA may require. The new members have been reluctant to grant most-favored-nation (MFN) status to fellow members, to produce lists of goods for the common effective preferential tarriff (CEPT) program, or to meet deadlines for tariff reductions on goods traded within ASEAN and remove nontariff barriers. Short-term adjustment costs to the the new ASEAN states will include a significant drop in government revenues due to reduced tariffs, the inability to develop and protect infant and state-owned industries, and industry adjustment, possibly causing worker dislocation, in economies where unemployment and underemployment are already very high and social welfare nets are lacking. The technical capabilities needed to fully implement AFTA, such as computerization and trained staff, are lacking in the new member states, which will add to the considerable pressures on government resources created by the AFTA process. These factors will result in a certain loss of sovereignty for the new members. Taking these considerations together, it is not clear that the new ASEAN states will completely accept the compromises inherent in joining ASEAN.

There are potential economic benefits available to Cambodia, Laos, Vietnam, and Myanmar in joining ASEAN, which may be enough to bring about their compliance and cooperation in AFTA and ASEAN. For example, most of them will gain easier access to world markets as part of an economic bloc. They will not have to negotiate access individually. However, many of the benefits are only possibilities and may vary from state to state. Myanmar, for example, has poorly developed infrastructure and offers cheap labor as its greatest comparative advantage, which is not a great advantage in a highly mobile international labor market. Moreover, the appeal of ASEAN has waned somewhat in the aftermath of the Asian economic crisis.

The commitment of the new member states to the ASEAN community is weak. To the extent that it does exist, an ASEAN community took more than thirty years to develop. The new members cannot feel part of this community. Vietnam was only recently ASEAN's primary threat; it remains a major power and potential challenger to ASEAN's established order. Cambodia has clearly demonstrated that its commitment to ASEAN is shallow. There is no reason to believe that Myanmar or Laos have any commitment to ASEAN beyond the advantages that membership affords them. In addition, if ASEAN's informal processes of interaction are based upon Malay cultural practices, then the incorporation of the Buddhist mainland into ASEAN is sure to strain internal relations. A division between mainland and maritime Southeast Asia may develop.

The decision to widen ASEAN was strongly related to the competition between Thailand and Indonesia for regional leadership. Thailand saw mainland Southeast Asia as a region in which it could exercise considerable political and economic influence. Since 1988, with its rapprochement with Vietnam (at the expense of ASEAN unity) Thailand has directed its foreign policy away from the Malay archipelago toward mainland Southeast Asia. Bringing Vietnam, in particular, into ASEAN was an effort on the part of the other ASEAN states to keep Thailand from monopolizing the mainland. Thailand's special relationship with China has also worried Jakarta. However, Thailand hoped that the new members would be more willing to follow its lead within ASEAN. Recent events have compromised this objective. In 1997, the recently reelected government of Thailand was faced with the problem of refugees from the wars in Myanmar and Cambodia. These events, combined with its own desire to establish its democratic credentials with the West, prompted Thailand to call for reforms in the ASEAN way to allow the right to comment on members' domestic policies that have regional effects. Thailand was supported by the Philippines, but the Thai initiative was soundly rejected by the other ASEAN countries. The new ASEAN countries opposed any attempt to make ASEAN a more intrusive regime. These countries were attracted to ASEAN by the promise of exercising international influence without having to be answerable for their domestic conduct. Thailand's initiatives undermined its leadership ambitions with the new members. Thailand's actions also indicated the potential volatility of intra-ASEAN relations as some member states become more democratic and responsive to civil society.

The inclusion of the new states requires ASEAN to be even more flexible and informal in its decisionmaking practices, in order to accommodate the new members' cultural, political, and economic differences. At the same time, however, there are pressures from within for ASEAN to become a more formal and coherent unit in order to deal with emerging economic and political issues. These demands are already in tension, challenging ASEAN's ability to evolve.[40] The addition of the new member states means that ASEAN must accommodate four more states with different interests and perspectives. This is sure to slow the decisionmaking process and add to the tensions within ASEAN.

Regional Economic Initiatives

As discussed in Chapter 2, ASEAN has a history of unimpressive and failed economic initiatives. In the post–Cold War period, however, ASEAN's efforts to reconstruct itself as an economically oriented institution took on a new urgency. Attempting to broaden its economic contacts, ASEAN has engaged in trade relationships with the Asia-Pacific Economic Cooperation forum (APEC), and it has tried to construct its own structure, the Asian Free Trade Area (AFTA). However, ASEAN's relationships with APEC has been ambivalent, and it has attempted to control APEC's capacity to intrude on national economic sovereignty. AFTA shows some important signs of evolving into a meaningful regional economic agreement, but it will not change the ASEAN states' dependence on outside markets.

ASEAN and APEC

APEC was proposed by Australian prime minister R. J. Hawke in January 1989.[41] Though Australia played a key role in creating APEC, the initiative for the organization actually originated in Japan. The Japanese Ministry of International Trade and Industry, concerned about the region's economic dependence on the United States, quietly orchestrated APEC's emergence.[42] APEC's first meeting was held in Canberra in November 1989. The inaugural meeting was attended by twelve countries: the six ASEAN states, Australia, the United States, Canada, Japan, New Zealand, and South Korea.[43]

Many observers were skeptical about the practical utility of APEC.[44] Some critics of APEC argued that the process of economic liberalization underway in East Asia is driven by private sector activities. Agreements between governments cannot significantly contribute to this process. Other critics argued that the low level of economic cooperation and institutional development in the Asia Pacific, combined with the immense regional diversity, means that APEC rests on a dubious political and economic foundation.[45]

The strongest criticism of APEC is that its organizational rules ensure that it cannot grow into an effective regime. APEC's first principle is "open regionalism." This concept extends the benefits of trade liberalization in any APEC country to all other states, including nonmembers, regardless of whether or not they reciprocate. APEC's second principle is that it is a consensual, voluntary body that operates without binding rules. This principle reflects the concern of Asian states that they not be forced into unwanted commitments. Critics argue that, combined, these rules encourage "free riders," states that, unbound by any need to reciprocate, will take advantage of the liberalizing efforts of other states without implementing similar reforms themselves. When this happens, the liberalizing states will lose their incentives to continue reforms, and the entire APEC process will fail. Supporters of APEC claim that states in the region are liberalizing their economies unilaterally and are clearly not concerned with questions of reciprocity. If this is the case, however, then APEC appears unnecessary to the liberalization process. APEC is a market-driven institution in a region supposedly committed to free trade. As a result, there should be little to negotiate between states. Thus, APEC can only be a weak institution.[46]

ASEAN and APEC: Competitive or Complementary?

From the outset, ASEAN has been wary of APEC. In 1990, ASEAN laid out the Kuching Consensus, the principles under which it would participate in APEC. The consensus agreement stressed the need for ASEAN to remain a coherent, independent body within APEC and the need for APEC to be a nonbinding, consultative body that could not impinge on the sovereignty of its members, would respect economic and political differences, and would promote international trade. ASEAN envisioned APEC as a mechanism designed to provide information and facilitate dialogue between its members. ASEAN officials subsequently indicated that they will accept the gradual institutionalization of APEC. Nonetheless, ASEAN remains committed to an APEC that practices open regionalism and is voluntary and consensual in nature. ASEAN agrees that APEC should promote regional economic liberalization but rejects any attempts to make such measures binding.[47] As John Ravenhill points out, ASEAN's approach guarantees that APEC will go nowhere quickly. Using Early Voluntary Sectoral Liberalization (EVSL) as an example, he argues,[48]

> The failure of the [EVSL] program highlighted the lack of any mechanism in APEC for dealing with trade liberalization in sensitive sectors. As APEC moves towards its deadlines for complete freeing of trade, political sensitivities will be heightened. Governments . . . will leave liberalization in the most difficult sectors until last—agriculture in East Asia, textiles in most Western countries. A voluntary, unilateral approach to trade liberalization will not produce the desired outcomes. But the APEC framework lacks an incentive structure conducive to negotiated liberalization. The EVSL debacle . . . cast doubt on APEC's overall capacity to deliver on its free trade agenda.[49]

ASEAN has resisted strengthening APEC for a number of reasons. ASEAN fears that APEC could evolve to challenge ASEAN's status in the

Asia Pacific or dilute ASEAN's character by engaging its members in a wider institutional forum. ASEAN won a preeminent role in APEC by insisting that an ASEAN state host the APEC Ministerial Conferences every other year. ASEAN hoped that assuming such a role in APEC would enable it to maintain its regional profile and influence APEC's development. However, ASEAN lacks both the unity and economic clout to dictate terms to the much larger APEC economies. Since 1993, divergent economic interests between the ASEAN states have made it difficult for the organization to maintain a common position within APEC.

The ASEAN states fear that a strongly institutionalized APEC would be dominated by the United States, which would use APEC to further its own economic interests, at the expense of weaker members. ASEAN worries that the enormous disparities in income, technology, and skill levels between APEC states could lead to dependency, increased tensions, and a north-south divide within APEC. Moreover, the ASEAN countries accept the argument that economic liberalization is proceeding at its own pace within the region and do not believe that a binding APEC is a necessary institutional structure. Finally, and most importantly, the ASEAN countries, and Asian states more generally, see APEC as a regional confidence-building measure. Its value lies in its facilitation of contacts between the major regional states and its potential to improve relationships, not in its economic initiatives.

The West has a very different view of APEC. Western states, notably the United States, expect tangible economic benefits from APEC. Without those benefits, they will likely lose interest in APEC. The disagreement between Western and Asian states over APEC also reflects fundamentally different views of the appropriate relationship between the state and private sector. Western states expect APEC to promote a neoliberal economic approach, which limits states' roles in the operation of markets. By contrast, Asian members of APEC believe that states play a legitimate role in shaping economic development. Asia's economic relations are based on social networks, as opposed to the "firm based," legalistic economies of the West.[50]

If APEC remains a loose, consultative structure, as ASEAN wants, it will probably lose the commitment of the West. If APEC is essentially irrelevant, as some critics argue, this may not matter; ASEAN will still reap the rewards of gradual regional economic liberalization without having to face APEC's challenge to its own institutional standing. Under such conditions, APEC would neither help nor hinder ASEAN's own development. If, however, APEC becomes an effective instrument of economic integration in the larger region, it will challenge ASEAN's preeminent regional role. It will also exacerbate tensions within ASEAN, as different members states pursue their individual economic interests with the outside world.

ASEAN and AFTA

At the 1991 ASEAN Economic Ministers' Meeting, Thailand proposed that ASEAN create an ASEAN free trade area for manufactures, to be established within fifteen years.[51] The AFTA agreement was endorsed at the January 1992 ASEAN summit in Singapore. AFTA has the potential to transform ASEAN from a loosely knit organization to an institutionalized economic regime. ASEAN hopes that AFTA will attract more foreign investment to the region, to take advantage of the improved economies of scale, and offset the trade-diverting effects of other trade blocs and regional groupings. The ASEAN states intend AFTA to create a "training ground" for ASEAN businesspeople, who will learn to compete with each other before moving into the international marketplace. AFTA is not designed to increase intra-ASEAN trade, though this would be one of its effects. ASEAN economic success is dependent on an open world economy, and ASEAN is committed to preserving that system.[52]

ASEAN decided to pursue AFTA for four distinct reasons. The first was to provide ASEAN with a new purpose. With the end of the Cold War and the Cambodian conflict, AFTA provided an important focus for ASEAN's activities and demonstrated that ASEAN remained relevant. Second, in 1992, the ASEAN states were deeply concerned about the growth of economic regionalism elsewhere in the world, as well as the possibilities that the Uruguay Round of the General Agreement of Tariffs and Trade (GATT) might fail and that APEC would undermine ASEAN's trade efforts. ASEAN hoped that AFTA would provide its members with more leverage and a louder voice in international economic negotiations and with regional trade partners.

Third, attitudes toward trade liberalization within ASEAN changed throughout the 1980s and 1990s. Liberal reformers appeared within the protectionist ASEAN states. Indonesia, Malaysia, and Thailand had experienced trade liberalization during the 1980s, which had created economic growth and industrial diversification.[53] Despite divisions between export-oriented economic sectors and other sectors inclined toward protectionism, the trend was toward an intellectual consensus within ASEAN states on the benefits of trade liberalization. Other factors reinforced the move toward greater liberalization. The 1985 Plaza Accord encouraged Japanese companies to invest abroad, and they targeted Southeast Asia. Other foreign business followed Japan's lead into the region. Between 1987 and 1991, over $42 billion in foreign investment flowed into Southeast Asia, $16 billion of it from Japan.[54] This influx of capital supported the liberal reform policies of the traditionally protectionist ASEAN states and increased the ranks of the business and political leaders supporting the policy transformation. It also fundamentally altered the nature of intra-ASEAN trade. In 1980, 28.2

percent of intra-ASEAN trade was in manufactured goods; by 1990, manufactures accounted for 61.3 percent of intra-ASEAN trade.[55] Much of this was trade between industry affiliates located in different ASEAN countries. The ASEAN countries recognized their interest in making it easier for multinational corporations to establish themselves on a regional basis.

Fourth, ASEAN was worried that international trade and investment would be diverted from its members and toward China and other global regions. (See Table 6.1 for an indication of China's investment diversion effect.) ASEAN hoped that AFTA would make its members more attractive and offset such a possibility. Averting trade diversion was the "primary economic purpose" behind AFTA.[56] In 1986, ASEAN had rejected the Philippines' proposal for creating a free trade area. Just five years later, however, the regional states had come to depend upon FDI-led economic growth. The ASEAN states realized that Southeast Asia, as a region, could attract more foreign investment than any individual ASEAN country. AFTA was not designed as a regional trading bloc but a regional investment area.

AFTA was officially launched in January 1992. It called for the reduction of tariffs on all intra-ASEAN trade in manufactures, processed agricultural products, and capital goods to a 0–5 percent range within fifteen years, starting in 1993. The ASEAN states also agreed to remove nontariff barriers. Raw materials and unprocessed agricultural products were not considered in the agreement. The details of the initial AFTA agreement were sketchy, and were developed during 1992. An ASEAN content of at least 40 percent was necessary for a product to qualify for preferential treatment. AFTA would be implemented through a CEPT, which was divided into three categories: fast track, normal track, and exclusion list. Fifteen product groups were placed on the fast track. Those with current tariffs below 20 percent would be reduced to 0–5 percent by 1998. Those with tariffs above 20 percent would be reduced to 0–5 percent by 2003. Most goods were on the normal track. Those with tariffs above 20 percent were scheduled to

Table 5.1   Foreign Direct Investment in China, Singapore, and Southeast Asia[a] (in U.S.$ millions)

	1988	1989	1990	1991	1992	1993	1988–1993
China	3,194	3,393	3,487	4,366	11,156	26,000	51,596
Singapore	3,655	2,887	5,575	4,888	6,730	6,829	30,564
Southeast Asia	3,336	4,688	6,399	8,038	8,590	8,739	39,790

a. Southeast Asia includes Indonesia, Malaysia, Philippines, and Thailand
Source: Joseph L.H. Tan, "Introductory Overview: AFTA in the Changing International Economy." In Joseph L. H. Tan, ed., *AFTA in the Changing International Economy* (Singapore: Institute of Southeast Asian Studies, 1996), 3.

have those tariffs reduced to 0–5 percent by 2008, phased in over three stages. Goods with tariffs below 20 percent would have their tariff rates reduced to 0–5 percent by 2003.

The exclusion list contained items not subject to AFTA. Agricultural products were excluded, and governments could add items to the list as they deemed necessary. Two types of exclusion were allowed, general exceptions and temporary exemptions. General exceptions were permitted when a state felt that restricting an import was necessary to protect national security, public morals, human, animal or plant life, or to protect articles of cultural significance. The agreement allowed temporary exemptions of products deemed "sensitive" to the development of domestic industries. These temporary exclusions were subject to review after eight years. If the products remained exempted, the other ASEAN states were entitled to penalize the relevant exports of the restricting state. In contrast to the earlier Preferential Trading Agreements (PTA), the CEPT covered all manufactured items except those specifically excluded.

AFTA's Implementation

Only seven months passed between Thailand's first proposing AFTA and the signing of the agreement in 1992. The initiative moved so quickly that domestic opposition to it within the ASEAN states could not mobilize. A number of factors gave AFTA its initial push. The initiative was sponsored by Thailand's prime minister, Anand Panyarachun, and his high level of support meant that AFTA needed to be addresssed by the other ASEAN leaders, meaning that bureaucratic opposition at lower levels was not able to form. The ASEAN leaders liked AFTA because it accorded with policies they were already adopting and because the 1992 ASEAN Summit was only the fourth meeting of ASEAN leaders in the organization's history, so it needed a major initiative as its focus. None of the ASEAN states provided much opportunity for business to object to AFTA. The initial AFTA agreement was only twelve pages long, an indication of the speed with which it was cobbled together. This short document was little more than a general statement of the intention to create a free trade area. This lack of specificity contributed to regional skepticism about AFTA.

In its first year, AFTA experienced a number of setbacks. In Thailand, the Anand government lost power and was replaced by the government of Chuan Leekpai after the elections of September 1992. The Chuan government was more open to Thai business interests and traditional economic nationalism. Thailand adopted a cautious approach to AFTA, and AFTA lost its influential sponsorship. Nationalist elements in all the ASEAN bureaucracies delayed the AFTA implementation process, for which they were often responsible. Also, the industries that would be detrimentally affected by AFTA—petrochemicals in Thailand and Malaysia and textiles, iron, and steel in the Philippines, among others—asked for government protection from AFTA. They doubted their ability to compete with their more developed counterparts in other ASEAN countries, notably Singapore. In Indonesia, protected businesses pressed for a rethinking of AFTA. Thailand, the Philippines, and Indonesia were permitted to pursue a more gradual program of tariff reductions under AFTA, while Malaysia and Singapore promised to begin cuts on January 1, 1993. However, Malaysia was unhappy with the staggered approach to AFTA, which placed its own industries at a disadvantage. The AFTA process ground to a halt. On January 1, 1993, only Singapore began implementing tariff cuts.

Supporters of AFTA were also being heard by the ASEAN governments. The growth of the export-oriented sectors in the ASEAN countries provided a counterweight to the nationalist and protectionist elements. These new and developing sectors of the regional economy threw their weight behind AFTA. The Japanese government pushed its ASEAN counterparts to adopt economic policies that would facilitate intra-industry trade in the region. Regional think tanks supported economic liberalization. The ASEAN governments were encouraged by the fact that foreign investors were attracted to regional stock markets, which could serve as a potential source of foreign capital. Total levels of FDI in Southeast Asia were dropping, and global capital investment could provide the foreign funds on which the region was becoming increasingly dependent.

From 1992 onward, a number of international trading agreements became active. The Uruguay Round of GATT, completed in 1993, called for larger tariff cuts in a shorter period of time than AFTA, increasing the pressure on AFTA to compete. The North American Free Trade Agreement (NAFTA), signed in 1992, came into effect in 1994. Southeast Asia feared that NAFTA would be a significant source of trade diversion. The implementation of the EU's Single European Act helped convince ASEAN that Southeast Asia could not afford to be left behind in a world of developing trade blocs. Even though AFTA was not a trade bloc in the same sense as NAFTA or the EU, the ASEAN states saw it as a credible response to the growth of economic regionalism elsewhere.

The most important factor contributing to the development of AFTA was China's emergence as a major competitor to the ASEAN countries for FDI. ASEAN countries widely perceived China as the reason for the decline in FDI to Southeast Asia in 1992.[57] China was providing low-cost manufactured goods at more competitive prices than the ASEAN countries. Its enormous potential consumer market also attracted foreign investment.

In 1993 and 1994, ASEAN governments addressed the concerns of the domestic interests adversely affected by AFTA. Thailand provided an 8 billion baht (U.S.$320 million) fund to provide improvement loans and support to AFTA-affected industries. In other ASEAN countries, industries successfully lobbied for the implementation of nontariff barriers or placement on the AFTA exclusion list. These side deals were made even as the ASEAN states accelerated regional liberalization.

By October 1993, senior ASEAN officials had developed a plan to relaunch and strengthen AFTA. Five of the six ASEAN countries committed to beginning AFTA tariff cuts on January 1, 1994, thereby eschewing the staggered implementation process in favor of a common start date. The date for AFTA's completion was moved to 2003, from the original 2008. The ASEAN countries agreed to begin implementing accelerated tariff reductions by January 1, 1996. Fast-track items were to have their tariffs reduced to 0–5 percent by 2000, while normal-track reductions were to be completed by 2003. Procedures governing the temporary exclusion list strengthened. AFTA's scope was expanded as unprocessed agricultural goods were brought into the CEPT mechanism, though a number of exclusions were still permitted. This was a significant step forward for AFTA, given the power and prominence of the agricultural communities in most ASEAN states. ASEAN established a working group to determine how to include as many agricultural goods as possible under AFTA, while keeping the list of "sensitive" excluded products as short as possible. The AFTA-Plus program helped facilitate the removal of nontariff barriers. Other issue areas, like services, investment and industrial production were included under AFTA auspices. Finally, the ASEAN countries agreed to establish a disputes settlement mechanism (DSM), designed to address all disputes arising from intra-ASEAN economic cooperation. These measures were formally adopted by the ASEAN leaders at their fifth summit, in Bangkok in December 1995.

Difficulties implementing AFTA persisted, but the political pressure to see AFTA to fruition meant that it made progress. Overall economic growth in the ASEAN countries blunted AFTA's adverse impact on the domestic economies. AFTA improved ASEAN's economic growth, albeit only marginally, and the various side deals that ASEAN countries arranged with AFTA-disadvantaged industries prevented serious domestic opposition. AFTA was an arrangement that the ASEAN countries could pursue with minimal political cost.

From 1996 to 1997, senior officials refined the agreements signed in December 1995. They met to negotiate AFTA's application to services, investment, and industrial production. The protocol on the DSM was adopted in November 1996. Negotiations for the Framework Agreement on Services began. The framework aims to eliminate discriminatory measures and market access limitations among ASEAN members. Article IV of the framework agreement requires AFTA members to commit to measures that exceed their obligations in the General Agreement on Trade in Services

(GATS), while specifically denying the benefits of AFTA to service providers from non-ASEAN countries. Though it has no specific deadline, a first round of negotiations began in December 1996 and ended in 1998. At the time of this writing, a second round of negotiations is ongoing. The first phase of negotiations elicited general commitments from the ASEAN countries, but the second phase is dealing with explicit details. Progress has been slow. To speed the negotiations, ASEAN adopted a temporary exclusion list and a sensitive list, which allow governments to exempt some service sectors while making progress in other areas. In 1995, the ASEAN leaders also agreed to implement an ASEAN Investment Area (AIA), to make the region even more attractive to foreign investment. The AIA was officially launched in October 1998, during the Asian economic crisis, as a symbol of Southeast Asia's commitment to international trade.

When it was first created, AFTA was criticized for two major weaknesses, the lack of specificity of its provisions and its weak institutional structures and capabilities. By 1997 and the start of the economic crisis, however, AFTA had added considerable substance to its basic provisions. AFTA's survival and gradual development into a meaningful economic institution may be a triumph of the ASEAN way. The ASEAN way has allowed AFTA to develop in a manner that is sensitive to the needs and interests of its members. According to Richard Stubbs,

> The strategy of developing a vaguely worded statement, which did not violate any of the participants' basic interests and, therefore, to which all participants could agree, allowed AFTA to move forward at a pace with which all governments felt comfortable. The key was to allow decision-makers to square the obligations they accrued in signing the agreement with their commitments to their personal networks of business interests at home. Musjawarah and mufakat, or "consensus" and "consultation" were the watchwords. AFTA could not advance without all signatories being satisfied that their interests were being safeguarded.[58]

The revamped ASEAN Secretariat is supposed to oversee AFTA, but it remains underfunded and understaffed. Critics argue that the secretariat cannot deal effectively with the complex questions raised by regional integration.[59] Most of AFTA's administrative work is done by the ASEAN secretariats within member states. ASEAN's reluctance to institutionalize AFTA reflects its familiar concerns with maintaining and protecting the sovereignty of its members. This semi-institutionalized approach to AFTA, however, may be appropriate to the ASEAN context. The limited institutional capacity of key ASEAN states means that they would have difficulty in implementing a binding legal arrangement. It is easier for weak states to withdraw from the economy than to attempt to regulate parts of it. For now, the ASEAN states appear content either to work around economic disputes or, in extreme cases, to allow disputes to be resolved by the World Trade Organization (WTO). This approach is consistent with the ASEAN way and seems to contribute to the durability of AFTA.

While AFTA is making halting progress, however, there are legitimate questions about the extent to which it can affect regional economic integration. Even if AFTA's primary purpose is to attract foreign investment, its success will ultimately be measured by the increased level of intra-ASEAN trade. The volume and value of intra-ASEAN trade has increased markedly in recent years, as intraindustry trade has grown within the region. Nonetheless, intra-ASEAN trade remains a relatively small percentage of overall ASEAN trade. It hovered at around 20 percent of total ASEAN trade for most of the 1990s. In 1995, it was 23 percent.[60] Most intra-ASEAN trade is between Singapore and other Southeast Asian states. When goods transshipped through Singapore are factored out, intra-ASEAN trade falls to about 12 percent of total trade.[61] When Singapore is factored out altogether, intra-ASEAN trade falls to around 5 percent. Because Singapore is a free trade area, most exports from ASEAN states already enjoy duty-free access to Singaporean markets. Thus, AFTA's provisions will have virtually no

Table 5.2   Percentage of Singapore's Trade with Major Partners, 1991 and 1997

	1991	1997
To Japan	8.7	7.1
From Japan	21.3	16.9
To ASEAN-4	23.2	25.5
From ASEAN-4	19.2	21.9
To ASEAN-7	23.7	27.4
From ASEAN-7	19.3	22.4
To United States	19.7	18.5
From United States	15.9	16.9
To EU	14.6	13.9
From EU	13.0	13.9

ASEAN-4 = Brunei, Malaysia, Philippines, Thailand
ASEAN-7 = Brunei, Indonesia, Malaysia, Myanmar, Philippines, Thailand, Vietnam
Source: Vera Simone, *The Asian Pacific*, 2d ed. (New York: Longman, 2001), 387.

Table 5.3   Percentage of Total Exports Between ASEAN-Six, Excluding Singapore, 1991 and 1997

	Brunei	Malaysia	Philippines	Thailand	Indonesia
1991	13.25	5.87	4.38	3.58	2.70
1997	4.55	6.98	5.18	8.04	5.93

Source: Vera Simone, *The Asian Pacific*, 2d ed. (New York: Longman, 2001), 387.

effect on the bulk of intra-ASEAN trade. The vast majority of the ASEAN countries trade is with states outside of Southeast Asia. Even if AFTA goes exactly as planned, by 2003 it will only cover 12–15 percent of ASEAN's total trade, precisely because most of Southeast Asia's trade is with non-ASEAN members.[62] By contrast, around 40 percent of NAFTA trade is conducted between member states; for the EU, intraregional trade is around 70 percent.[63] Under the best conditions, AFTA can be of only limited significance to its members. Other economic arrangements and organizations will necessarily attract more of the individual members' time and attention. While AFTA may be important as an institutional focus for ASEAN's activities in the future, it is not enough to make the organization a paramount economic actor.[64]

There is the possibility that the incentives favoring AFTA are not sufficient to overcome other concerns. Because the trade benefits of AFTA are quite small, ASEAN states may be more inclined toward entering larger, nondiscriminatory trade arrangements that allow for selective liberalization. This may allow them to accommodate domestic economic concerns for a longer period of time.[65] Alternatively, different ASEAN states may be tempted to enter discriminatory arrangements with more important, extraregional trading partners. Singapore has expressed an interest in joining NAFTA; has signed bilateral trade agreements with Australia, Canada, Chile, Japan, Mexico, New Zealand, South Korea, and the United States; and is negotiating more comprehensive deals with most of those nations. Its activities may compromise ASEAN's economic aspirations by detracting from the commitment to AFTA.[66] Even as AFTA is making halting but significant progress toward becoming the basis of a viable economic grouping, other economic interests and the external orientation of the ASEAN economies are limiting AFTA's ability to serve as an anchor for ASEAN's activities in the coming century.

Conclusion

With the resolution of the Cambodian conflict and the end of the "communist threat" to Southeast Asia, ASEAN was bereft of a clear goal on which to focus its energies. It reformed its structures to strengthen its organizational capacity. It expanded its activities and membership. However, there are numerous difficulties associated with these new endeavors. While it is too early to tell how these various intiatives will play out, it appears that ASEAN's reach is exceeding its grasp. The ARF plays a useful role in promoting regional contacts. However, it is inadequate as an instrument to *create* peaceful relations between its members. ASEAN's expansion to include the rest of Southeast Asia has weakened ASEAN rather than strengthening it as intended.

ASEAN's newest initiatives in the economic sphere hold the greatest promise. AFTA has the potential to increase economic linkages between the ASEAN countries and to turn the organization into a functional organization that serves a clear and mutually beneficial purpose to its members. AFTA is meant to attract foreign investment so that the ASEAN countries can successfully continue to export goods to the rest of the world. This process may cause the ASEAN economies to become more integrated, and it should help fuel the continuing emergence of a consumer-oriented middle class in the ASEAN states. If and when the ASEAN countries create a burgeoning and consumer-driven middle class, their economies will begin to export their products to one another. At that point, AFTA could become the linchpin for ASEAN's activities, and a whole new range of possibilities for regional integration will appear. This success is dependent on the ASEAN states' continuing economic development, however, and is a long-term, best-case scenario. There are many ways for such a scenario to be derailed. For now, AFTA is a useful mechanism, but only of middling economic importance to its participants. Even if AFTA proved to be wildly successful, the relatively small levels of intra-ASEAN trade mean that it could not be the most important economic institution in which the ASEAN countries participated. A successful AFTA will increase intra-ASEAN trade, given time. However, the entire direction and nature of the ASEAN economies would need to change before AFTA could emerge as a meaningful counterpart to the EU or NAFTA. In the meantime, other trade arrangements have the potential to be of far greater economic importance than ASEAN to the ASEAN states.

A number of common factors underpin ASEAN's post–Cold War initiatives. First, most of the organization's intiatives are, once again, motivated by external threats and considerations. The ARF was pushed by ASEAN's fear that a regional security institution would develop which would detract from its own institutional primacy. AFTA was pushed by the emergence of APEC, NAFTA, and other international economic developments. One important factor affecting Myanmar's admission was ASEAN's fear that Myanmar would fall under Beijing's control.

ASEAN's intiatives have also been motivated by a need to find a focus for its activities. Keeping ASEAN alive appears to be a good in itself, a belief based on the perception that the ASEAN countries exercise far greater international influence as part of a group than as separate states. ASEAN's international influence is an important part of its appeal to its members. How far the member states are willing to go to maintain ASEAN's international influence, however, is a difficult question. Many observers have suggested that ASEAN can no longer practice its principles of nonintervention in a globalized world, one where domestic events can have regional consequences. In these circumstances, ASEAN needs to become the forum in which its members can resolve their differences amicably. The principle of nonintervention, even the structure of the ASEAN way, needs to be reformed to accommodate these new realities. Domestic disputes leading to regional tensions will occur, whether ASEAN chooses to address them or not; it is better that these disputes be resolved within an established framework. According to Kay Moller, "Either interference becomes legitimate, or the association will become increasingly meaningless."[67] However, this kind of argument misunderstands ASEAN's fundamental nature. ASEAN is about promoting the sovereignty of its member states. The ASEAN countries need to be convinced that allowing interference in their domestic affairs from other member states will have the overall effect of enhancing their sovereignty. If they cannot be convinced of this, then they should calculate whether maintaining ASEAN's relevance on the international stage is more beneficial to them than permitting the organization to interfere in their domestic affairs. ASEAN was created to codify the principle that its members would not interfere in each other's domestic affairs. Allowing intervention means more than just reforming ASEAN's practices. It also involves reforming the fundamental norms and logic that form the organization's foundation. Yet, without the willingness to allow ASEAN to become a more interventionary body, it will fade into irrelevance and will lose its appeal to its members. ASEAN is caught in a difficult situation: reform is necessary to maintain its relevance, yet its members are largely unwilling to accept the necessary reforms.

Notes

1. Chin, 1995: 433–435.

2. The following account of the origins and implications of the ARF is based primarily upon Acharya, 1993: 59–64; Antolik, 1994; Leifer, 1996, 1999; Findlay, 1994; Simon, 1998; Ortuoste, 2000; Ortuoste, 1999; Garofano, 1999; R. Lim, 1998; Ba, 1997; Almonte, 1997–1998; Caballero-Anthony, 1998; Johnston, 1999; Foot, 1998; Harding, 1997: 1; Narine, 1998; Narine, 1997; Sundararaman, 1998; Oldham and Wettlaufer, 2000: 9–10; Thayer, 2000; and Dosch, 1997.

3. Oruoste, 1999: 44.

4. ASEAN's "dialogue partners" at the time were Australia, Canada, New Zealand, Japan, the United States, and the European Community. At present, the dialogue partners include these states plus the European Union, Russia, and China.

5. Ortuoste, 2000: Annex-10.

6. Ibid.: Annex-14.

7. Antolik, 1994: 120. See also Findlay, 1994: 142.

8. Leifer, 1996: 21.

9. Lasater, 1996.

10. The eighteen founding members of the ARF were the six ASEAN states (Brunei, Indonesia, Malaysia, the Philippines, Singapore, and Thailand), ASEAN's

dialogue partners (Australia, Canada, the European Union, Japan, South Korea, New Zealand, and the United States), and China, Laos, Papua New Guinea, Russia, and Vietnam. Findlay, 1994: 143.

11. Singaporean foreign minister Wong Kan Seng, quoted in Findlay, 1994: 31.

12. The chairman, Thai foreign minister Prasong Soonsiri, explicitly linked the emergence of the ARF to the ASEAN-PMCs and ASEAN initiatives. Singaporean foreign minister Shanmugam Jayakumar stated that the ASEAN process of development would provide valuable lessons for ASEAN for when it would "steer the ARF in subsequent years." Thailand's deputy foreign minister Surin Pitsuwan also stated that "ASEAN will always have the driver's seat." Leifer, 1996: 33, 36.

13. Ibid.: 34–35.

14. See *ASEAN Regional Forum: A Concept Paper,* "Political and Security Cooperation, Political Documents."

15. Leifer, 1996: 44.

16. Hiebert, 1995.

17. Introduction, pt. 3 in *The ASEAN Regional Forum: A Concept Paper.*

18. Almonte, 1997–1998: 81.

19. Garofano, 1999: 75.

20. Ibid.: 85.

21. Acharya, 1993: 62–63.

22. R. Lim, 1998: 116.

23. Vatikiotis, 1995: 23; Leifer, 1996: 41.

24. Leifer, 1996: 26–27, 35, 41.

25. Johnston, 1999: 315.

26. Leifer, 1996.

27. Sheldon Simon predicted that in the future, the ASEAN states' security cooperation will focus on intra-ASEAN bilateral relations and further subregionalization, which will downgrade the importance of ASEAN. While this may be the most practical way for ASEAN to advance its security interests, it does not appear to be the direction in which ASEAN is growing. However, ASEAN may eventually conclude that its ability to affect the larger regional security environment is limited and return to the more circumscribed role recommended by Simon. See Simon, 1992.

28. This section draws on the following: Australian Department of Foreign Affairs and Trade (DFAT), 1997; Kraft, 2000; Cribb, 1998; Moller, 1998; Amer, 1999; and Leifer, 1996: 47–48.

29. Australian DFAT, 1997: 309. Figures are from ibid.: 309–310.

30. This discussion will not consider ASEAN's incorporation of Laos, mostly because Laos' admission to ASEAN entailed very few difficulties.

31. Hiebert and Schwartz, 1995: 23–24.

32. Schwartz, 1994: 24.

33. SLORC changed its name to the State Peace and Development Council (SPDC) in late 1997. Since this change falls on the edge of the period addressed in this book, I shall continue to refer to it as SLORC.

34. McCarthy, 2000.

35. Moller, 1998: 1088–1089.

36. Myanmar's foreign minister, Ohn Gyaw, cited in Kraft, 2000: 463–464.

37. Vatikiotis, 1997:14–15.

38. ASEAN's incorporation of Myanmar may not have been solely a knee-jerk reaction to Western intervention. ASEAN was concerned about the effect of Myanmar's domestic policies on the organization's larger interests, and, in June

1997, ASEAN may have received assurances from SLORC that it would act on these concerns. By that time, U.S. efforts to placate ASEAN may have created the impression that U.S. policy on Myanmar had softened. ASEAN may have interpreted U.S. statements as encouraging it to admit Myanmar then apply pressure on the SLORC for domestic reform.

39. For a discussion of the issues involved in incorporating Vietnam into ASEAN, see Leifer, 1993: 269–279; Thayer, 1995: 47–61; Hoang, 1994.

40. Interviews with Dr. Panitan Wattanayagorn, Bangkok, Thailand, January 16, 1995; M. Rajaretnam, Singapore, February 10, 1995; and Dr. Emmanuel Lallana, Manila, Philippines, March 29, 1995.

41. Crone, 1992. A good description an analysis of the history and nature of economic cooperation in the Pacific region is found in Higgott, Cooper, and Bonnor, 1990. This discussion also utilizes Drysdale and Elek, 1997, and Hellman and Pyle, 1997: 203–208.

42. Krauss, 2000.

43. Initially, neither the United States nor Canada was invited. The United States made known that it wanted an invitation and was offered one; Canada had to lobby actively for an invitation. Rudner, 1995: 8–9; Baker, 1998: 167–169.

44. Narine, 1999: 364–365.

45. MacIntyre, 1997: 235.

46. Aggarwal, 1993: 1034.

47. Soesastro, 1995a: 484–485; Kahler, 2000.

48. The EVSL program was meant to allow some APEC states to proceed with liberalization more rapidly than others on a voluntary basis. It failed when Japan adamantly refused to discuss politically sensitive economic areas, demonstrating significant political tensions with APEC. See Wesley, 2001.

49. Ravenhill, 2000: 325.

50. Gallant and Stubbs, 1997; Stubbs, 1995.

51. See Ravenhill, 1995; Soesastro, 1995b; Stubbs, 2000; Bowles, 1997: 219–233; Bowles and Maclean, 1996; Luhulima, 1994; Nesadurai, 2001; ASEAN Secretariat, 1997; Tan, 1996; Menon, 1996; and Chia, 1998.

52. Arif, 1996: 209, 218.

53. Singapore and Brunei are already free trade regimes.

54. Stubbs, 2000: 303.

55. Bowles, 1997: 223.

56. Ibid.: 224.

57. In 1988, FDI going into Southeast Asia (the ASEAN 4, not including Singapore) came to U.S. $3.3 billion; FDI going into China totaled $3.1 billion. By 1993, FDI going into the ASEAN 4 was $8.7 billion; for China, the figure was $26 billion. Tan, 1996: 3.

58. Stubbs, 2000: 313.

59. Ravenhill, 1995: 860–861.

60. Australian DFAT, 1997: 310.

61. Oxley, cited in Australian DFAT, 1997: 310. Other estimates have put intra-ASEAN trade without Singapore at as low as 5% of total trade.

62. Ibid.: 327.

63. Ravenhill, 1995: 862.

64. Using a complex economic model, Innwon Park concludes that AFTA will improve the welfare of the ASEAN states by the following percentages of national income: Indonesia, 0.6%; Malaysia, 1.6%; the Philippines, 0.7%; Thailand, 1.3%.

For Singapore, the improvement is a negligible 0.1% because it is already a free trade regime. (Park does not include Brunei.) See Park, 1995: 141.

65. Ibid.: 389.

66. "Singapore's Trade Initiatives," 2000.

67. Moller, 1998: 1104.

6

The East Asian Economic Crisis

Beginning in May 1997, East Asia was caught in the grip of a financial crisis, involving the radical devaluation of most of the region's currencies and accompanied by economic upheaval and political instability, particularly in Indonesia. The crisis lasted for almost two years. The region is still experiencing the political and economic consequences.[1]

Like other regional organizations, ASEAN was helpless in the face of the worst economic downturn in East Asia's modern history. This fact shattered ASEAN's credibility as a regional leader and an economic regime, and it raised dangerous questions about ASEAN's methods of operation and cast doubt on its viability as a regional institution in a globalizing world. At the same time, however, the events of the crisis exposed serious divisions and tensions between East Asia and the Western world, particularly the United States. These tensions may have created new opportunities for ASEAN's future development. However, this possibility remains remote and is beset by considerable political complications. Even if ASEAN does become the focus for a new set of regional structures, its role will be quite different than what it has traditionally envisioned for itself.

Analysts have debated whether the crisis was a reaction to domestic structural inadequacies within East Asia or the result of unstable international forces. The answer is somewhere between these two poles: the crisis was caused by investor panic, but poor regulatory regimes within the ASEAN states (and other East Asian countries) made them vulnerable to that panic. The crisis also indicated significant instability within the world financial system.

The Crisis

There remains considerable debate over how to explain the East Asian economic crisis. The view of the "Washington establishment" and the

International Monetary Fund (IMF) is that the crisis was created by structural deficiencies in the Asian economies. Crony capitalism, weak corporate governance, poor standards of disclosure, lack of transparency, and other fundamental flaws inherent in "Asian capitalism" led to economic collapse. These factors distorted the ability of markets to function effectively. The solution to this problem is to implement fundamental structural reforms in Asia that would force Asian states to adopt Anglo-American economic models. Supporters of this position also argue that "moral hazard" played a role in creating the crisis. Investors, foreign and domestic, believed that their investments were protected by implicit guarantees from local governments and international financial institutions. This encouraged them to indulge in sloppy credit analysis and make poor business decisions. When it became apparent that Asian governments could not guarantee foreign investments, lenders responded by pulling their money out of East Asia, forcing the crisis.

A second, alternative explanation for the crisis is that it was the result of an investor panic. According to this view, the affected Asian states were experiencing trade difficulties, but their economic fundamentals remained sound. There was no change in economic indicators in the period before the crisis that could account for the extremity of the international crisis in confidence that afflicted the region in 1997. Therefore, the crisis was a symptom of fundamental instability in the international financial architecture. To prevent future crises, mechanisms need to be in place to control unstable markets and provide public money to reassure jittery investors. While financial panic may have been the proximate cause of the crisis, the real culprit was a failure of banking regulation, at both the national and international levels. East Asia opened itself to the free flow of international capital while lacking the proper instruments needed to regulate and control that capital. The Asian countries adopted the wrong domestic policies, but their greatest mistake was in allowing excessive financial liberalization, something they were encouraged to do by many of the same Western states and Western-based financial institutions that pinned responsibility for the economic collapse solidly on Asian business practices.

The weight of the evidence most strongly supports the second argument. Indeed, the Asian economic crisis was a repeat of other banking crises that occurred in the previous two decades in other parts of the world. Even so, structural deficiencies within the affected Asian economies and political systems were important contributing factors to the crisis, even if they were not the major causes. The following analysis presents an historical overview of the circumstances that led to the crisis, the events of the crisis itself, and the IMF's response to the economic upheaval.[2] The focus of the analysis is primarily upon Southeast Asia, but it is important to consider the effects of the crisis on some of the other East Asian states, particularly

South Korea. Understanding the crisis and its political consequences requires tracing its effects on the wider region.

Factors Leading to the Crisis

Even before the accelerated financial deregulation of the 1990s, central banks in the affected Southeast Asian states lacked the autonomy to supervise properly their domestic financial sectors and to enforce prudential norms. Without a strong supervisory regime, commercial banking and financial companies in much of Southeast Asia were characterized by significant undercapitalization, weak credit appraisal, and inadequate loan loss provisions. In the early 1990s, Indonesia, Thailand, Malaysia, and the Philippines, under pressure from international and domestic interests, undertook a process of financial liberalization and deregulation, which resulted in the creation of numerous new financial institutions. As this deregulation occurred, the governments paid little attention to the new kinds of financial regulation that would be necessary to monitor the flow of capital. Moreover, these states lacked financial expertise needed to undertake the necessary regulation. Deregulation enabled inexperienced private domestic banks and businesses to borrow dollar-denominated loans from foreign lenders, at rates of interest lower than at home. The preexistent weaknesses of the domestic financial sectors were exacerbated by the processes of financial liberalization, the accompanying inflows of foreign capital, and the incursion of more experienced and sophisticated foreign banks and financial actors into domestic markets. The fragile Southeast Asian financial sectors collapsed when, in the mid-1990s, they were exposed to the shocks of export slowdowns, declines in export prices, and steep increases in interest rates. Inadequate legal frameworks also increased the chances of bank failure, making it difficult for banks to work out debt recovery and recover collateral guarantees from delinquent borrowers.

The move toward deregulation and liberalization affected states with strong governing structures as well. In South Korea, the government of Kim Young Sam came to power in 1993, promising to deregulate the financial sector, partially to facilitate South Korea's acceptance into the Organization for Economic Cooperation and Development (OECD). The South Korean government gradually abandoned its traditional role in coordinating industrial investment, relaxed its monitoring of foreign borrowing, and accepted the monetarist position that controlling inflation is the primary objective of macroeconomic policy.

Even as East Asian states were opening themselves up to the inflow of foreign capital, more of that capital was becoming available. In the late 1980s, overinvestment in Japan created stock market and real estate bubbles. These bubbles were exacerbated by the Japanese government's attempts to stimulate domestic demand.[3] The Japanese economic bubble burst in the late 1980s, causing a general economic downturn in the early 1990s. Japanese banks were saddled with billions of dollars in nonperforming loans to Japanese businesses and real estate interests. The Japanese central bank followed an expansionary monetary policy, pumping money into the economy in an attempt to restore consumer confidence and promote spending. Consumers did not respond, however, and continued depositing their money into banks. Liquidity in the system increased. Japanese banks utilized these capital resources to increase the loans they were making to Asian countries. Rather than cleaning up their bad loans, the Japanese banks hoped that they could make profits elsewhere in Asia that would enable them to outgrow, or alleviate, their own financial woes. Thus, Japanese credit became easily available to other Asian businesses.[4] In the United States, a powerful economy combined with low interest rates meant that enormous amounts of cash were available for overseas investment. In Europe, as in Japan, an economic downturn, combined with expansionary monetary policies meant to stimulate consumer spending, added to the excess liquidity in the world system. U.S., European, and Japanese financial institutions were attracted to the high profit margins and booming economies of Southeast Asia. Interest rates in the region were high and the relative risks of investment low, given that the local currencies were pegged to the U.S. dollar. With this excess liquidity and low inflation at home, foreign lenders were prepared to lend money to Southeast Asian businesses at rates lower than what they could get domestically, and local businesses were prepared to borrow abroad.

Much of the finance flowing into Southeast Asia during this period was in the form of short-term loans.[5] Interest rates on short-term loans were lower than for long-term credit. To lower borrowing costs, banks and corporations preferred loans in foreign currencies and short maturities. The implicit agreement between borrowers and lenders was that these loans would be continually rolled over so long as borrowers consistently serviced them. These short-term loans represented long-term credit at cheaper rates of interest. These financial interactions created a self-reinforcing confidence in the health of the recipient economies; neither investors, borrowers, nor governments paid attention to financial supervision.

The Southeast Asian economies—with the notable exception of Singapore—had pegged their currencies to the U.S. dollar, or to a basket of currencies in which the U.S. dollar was disproportionately weighted. Much of the borrowing and lending in Southeast Asia was premised on the expectation that the fixed currency rates would hold. Fixed currency rates encouraged lenders to lend without bothering to "hedge" their loans.[6] The fixed-rate policy was beneficial to Southeast Asia when the U.S. dollar was relatively weak, but by 1995 the dollar had started to rise in value, and it pulled up the Asian currencies with it, affecting the competitiveness of

Southeast Asian exports in the world economy. During the same period, the relative decline in the value of the yen helped to undercut ASEAN's high-value-added exports.

More controversial is the effect of the devaluation of the Chinese yuan on East Asian exports. According to many analysts, the 1990 and, especially, 1994 devaluations of the yuan squeezed Southeast Asia's low-value-added exports.[7] China gained market share in the United States and Japan at the expense of Southeast Asia. However, some analysts argue that the evidence supporting this claim is unconvincing. Even before the 1994 unification of China's dual exchange rate system, most transactions between China and the outside world were conducted at the depreciated market rate, meaning that the yuan devaluation was not a significant factor contributing to the crisis.[8]

The main ASEAN countries (excepting Singapore) had been running economically sustainable current account deficits for several years. By 1996, the four Southeast Asian countries ran current account deficits of between 4 and 8 percent of GNP, with Thailand's deficit being the highest. The influx of foreign capital and FDI into Southeast Asia, combined with the fixed-rate regime, created inflationary pressures. Under the fixed-rate exchange system, central banks were required to purchase foreign exchange with local currency, causing an oversupply of local currency. This dynamic fueled annual inflation of about 6 percent in Southeast Asia, even as inflation in the United States and Japan decreased.

Between 1993 and 1996, investors and fund managers from the United States, Japan, and Europe pumped enough money into Thailand, Indonesia, and Malaysia to make all three economies red hot. By the end of 1996, European banks had lent $318 billion to the countries of East Asia. Japanese banks had lent $260 billion; U.S. banks $46 billion.[9] With so many foreign and domestic banks willing to lend, many Asian companies found it easy to expand, without regulatory oversight. Investors' belief that regional governments were providing an implicit guarantee to support any investments contributed to the general financial carelessness. The level of foreign debt grew accordingly. By mid-1997 private foreign debt in Indonesia reached $65 billion; in Thailand, debt to foreign banks went from $29 billion in 1993 to $69 billion in 1997 (see Table 6.1).[10]

Much of the investment in Asia during this period was in speculative real estate, such as golf resorts, condominiums, and office towers. Private actors invested in real estate because they expected inflation to grow, as foreign currency continued to pour in and the domestic money supply continued to expand. Under these conditions, property was the best hedge. In 1996, the general slowdown in world trade affected East Asian exports. Considerable industrial capacity (in industries such as steel, semiconductors, electronics, and assembly) had built up in East Asia, and much of it became idle. Additional investment in manufacturing contributed to a global oversupply of East Asian products. Despite the economic downturn, international capital continued to flow into the region, accelerating investment in speculative activities. With notable national variations, these conditions applied across Southeast Asia. Under these circumstances, a significant number of business failures were inevitable, resulting in a large number of nonperforming loans. The crisis was the result.

The Asian Crisis Begins

The East Asian economic crisis began in earnest in May 1997, with the attack of foreign currency speculators on Thailand's currency, the baht. Signs of the impending crisis had appeared much earlier, however, coming in mid-1996, with the collapse of the Bangkok Bank of Commerce, which was rescued by the government. The bank had lent large sums of money to corrupt politicians, leading observers to suspect a political fix and revealing the weakness of Thailand's banking regulatory sector. In February 1997, Somprasong Land became the first Thai real estate company to default on a Eurobond. This indicated that the flow of foreign funds into Thailand had created a real estate bubble that was about to burst. Also in February, Finance One, Thailand's largest finance company, revealed that it was in trouble by seeking to merge with a commercial bank. These developments indicated that the Thai economy was less sound than it seemed. Foreign banks began calling in loans and currency speculators began their attack on the baht. Japanese officials hinted that they might raise interest rates to combat the decline of the yen, exacerbating the situation. Though this threat never materialized, it combined with investors' concerns over the state of the baht and created uncertainty about the safety of investments predicated on currency stability. Investors, uncertain of Thailand's ability to defend the value of the baht, began selling local currencies.

The Thai government was unable to sustain the baht's peg of twenty-five baht to one U.S. dollar, and, on July 2, 1997, it allowed the baht to float on international currency markets. The currency rapidly declined in value. The collapse of the baht meant that the considerable foreign loans managed by local banks could no longer be readily financed. Business debts increased in value and became more difficult to service. Currency traders next turned their attention to Indonesia and Malaysia, hoping to provoke similar currency devaluations. Foreign investors began to reconsider the financial circumstances of the other regional states. They decided that many of the problems that they had previously overlooked in Thailand—crony capitalism, poor banking regulation, and a lack of transparency—were also present in Malaysia and Indonesia. Investors and rating agencies, which had previously focused on macroeconomic indicators (budget deficits, debt-GDP ratios,

Table 6.1   Foreign Debt in East Asia, 1992–1997

	South Korea		Thailand		Malaysia		Indonesia		Philippines	
	Total (U.S.$ billion)	Short-term (%)	Total (U.S.$ billion)	Short-term (%)	Total (U.S.$ billion)	Short-term (%)	Total (U.S.$ billion)	Short-term (%)	Total (U.S.$ billion)	Short-term (%)
1992	44.2	—	41.8	35.2	20.0	18.2	88.0	20.5	33.0	15.9
1993	47.2	46.3	52.7	43.0	26.1	26.6	89.2	20.2	35.9	14.0
1994	56.9	53.5	65.6	44.5	29.3	21.1	107.8	18.0	40.0	14.3
1995	78.4	57.8	83.2	49.4	34.3	21.2	124.4	20.9	39.4	13.4
1996	102.0	58.2	90.8	41.4	39.8	27.8	129.6	25.0	41.2	19.3
1997	154.4	44.3	100.8	n.a.	42.7	23.9	131.2	n.a.	45.4	n.a.

Source: Helen E. S. Nesadurai, "In Defence of National Economic Autonomy? Malaysia's Response to the Financial Crisis." *The Pacific Review* 13, 1: 77.

Table 6.2   Capital Flows to Indonesia, Malaysia, Philippines, South Korea, and Thailand (U.S.$ billions)

	1995	1996	1997	1998	1999	2000e	2000f
Net external financing	98.1	118.6	39.5	−15.2	−4.9	−1.2	−6.8
Net private flows	94.2	119.5	4.9	−38.7	−5.2	−3.8	1.9
Equity investment, net	15.5	16.8	5.2	16.8	30.1	15.6	13.6
Direct investment, net	4.4	4.8	6.8	12.3	14.6	9.5	9.0
Portfolio investment, net	11.0	12.0	−1.7	4.5	15.4	6.1	4.6
Private creditors, net	78.7	102.7	−0.3	−55.5	−35.3	−19.3	−11.7
Commercial bank credit, net	64.9	69.6	−17.4	−48.8	−29.3	−15.3	−5.8
Nonbank credit, net	13.8	33.2	17.2	−6.7	−6.0	−4.1	−5.9
Net official flows	3.9	−0.9	34.6	23.5	0.2	2.6	−8.6
International financial institutions	−0.5	−1.9	22.7	19.7	−4.6	2.5	−7.9
Bilateral creditors	4.4	1.0	11.9	3.8	4.9	0.1	−0.8

Source: Asian Development Bank, 2001: 19.
Notes: e = estimate, f = forecast

etc.), began looking at microeconomic factors, such as the amount of short-term dollar debt and debt-equity ratios in Southeast Asian corporate sectors. Investors began applying Western prudential standards to East Asian borrowers. Japanese banks, struggling with bad-debt problems at home, began calling in loans. Most Southeast Asian currencies suddenly looked vulnerable. All of the economies had substantial short-term dollar debt that would be difficult to service if the pegged currencies collapsed. Investors began selling off local currencies en masse. Malaysia soon joined Thailand in floating its currency, the ringgit.

Indonesia then startled investors by floating its currency, the rupiah. Investors, worried that a competitive devaluation might be beginning in Southeast Asia, began unloading local currency as quickly as possible, creating the very currency devaluations they feared. In August 1997, the IMF announced a rescue package for Thailand. The United States, however, contributed virtually nothing to the package. In part, its inaction was due to U.S. Congressional restrictions on financial aid implemented after the earlier Mexican crisis. However, the United States did not view the support of Thailand as a major national interest. Japan contributed only $4 billion to the rescue package. Investors interpreted the IMF response as indicating a lack of international interest in supporting Thailand. In addition, the IMF package required structural changes that were unrelated to Thailand's immediate problems, causing observers to believe that the country's economic situation was worse than expected. These developments deepened the crisis by inflaming investor anxieties.

In mid-October, Taiwan depreciated its currency by 12 percent. Again, investors were shocked because of Taiwan's massive foreign-exchange reserves, which could presumably have insulated it against any attacks on its currency. Investors feared that Taiwan's devaluation would cause a competitive devaluation in Hong Kong or South Korea. This led to a selling of the Hong Kong dollar and Korean won. These moves did not appear economically rational, given the strengths of the respective economies. Hong Kong, as part of China, was running an enormous current account surplus.[11] The South Korean economy appeared very strong, with low inflation and unemployment, very manageable debt, and 8 percent growth in GDP. Its published debt-to-GDP ratio was only 30 percent, and its current account deficit was shrinking. Nonetheless, the Hong Kong stock market lost 10 percent of its value, though its currency peg held; South Korea soon found itself experiencing the most dramatic economic decline in the region, outside of Indonesia.

At this point, Indonesia was experiencing massive currency depreciation and was the object of an IMF bailout. This time, the United States made a significant contribution to the bailout. The legal restrictions limiting U.S. financial support had lapsed, and the importance of the crisis to U.S. interests was now clearer to Congress. Japan and Singapore also helped to support the rupiah. These measures helped investor confidence, but that confidence was soon shaken by reports that President Suharto's health was in decline. Wealthy Indonesians began selling rupiah and relocating their money offshore, further damaging the currency.

In South Korea, investors focused on the structure of the country's foreign debt. They estimated that short-term debt stood at $110 billion, three times South Korea's official foreign reserves. Rumors circulated that the government was concealing the true extent of the country's debt. Driven by what was now a full-fledged regional panic, investors rushed to the exits, causing a massive decline in the value of the won. Korean banks began selling their holdings of foreign securities, including Russian and Latin

American bonds, in order to boost their liquidity, thereby spreading the crisis beyond Asia. Because Japanese banks had lent heavily to Korean corporations and Japan competed with Korea in some major industries, investors saw the yen as vulnerable to a devaluation of the won. These observations fueled fears that Hong Kong and Taiwan would engage in competitive currency devaluation, leading to a further withdrawal of investor funds from East Asia.

The Domestic Responses

Though all were affected, not all East Asian economies were devastated by the crisis. Domestic political and economic arrangements are critical to explaining the divergent effects of the crisis.[12] Of the original ASEAN members, Singapore and the Philippines were the least affected by the economic downturn. In the case of the Philippines, its relatively small exposure to the international economy and low levels of foreign investment insulated it from the economic collapse. It experienced much milder shocks its ASEAN neighbors because it had a much shorter distance to fall once the crisis hit. Though it is cold comfort, in this instance, the Philippines' long and frustrating history of economic underdevelopment and institutional weakness insulated it from the crisis.[13]

By contrast, Singapore was highly exposed to the international economy, yet it suffered least of the ASEAN countries. Indeed, Singapore attracted regional capital looking for a safe haven as the crisis wore on. Lim argues that Singapore's durability was due to its managed-float exchange rate regime. Unlike its neighbors, Singapore floated its dollar against a weighted basket of foreign currencies, including the U.S. dollar, the Japanese yen, and the Malaysian ringgit. This system allowed for a gradual readjustment in the Singaporean dollar as these other currencies shifted in value and limited the loss of competitiveness in Singapore's export sectors. Singapore also acted earlier in 1996 to deflate a property bubble that had started to build. This situation caused some economic discomfort when the crisis hit, but was manageable due to the government's preemptive measures. Singapore responded to the crisis by *increasing* the liberalization of its financial sector. This move reaffirmed its commitment to open markets, the free flow of capital, and global economic integration. However, these moves should not be interpreted as an endorsement of unfettered liberalism and the marketplace. Singapore's continuing openness to the world economy and its decision to liberalize its financial sector further was only possible because "the state's heavy intervention in the land, labor, and capital markets provide many potential policy levers—such as large accumulated budget and current account surpluses—with which it can adjust the economy to cyclic downturns and external shocks like the . . . crisis.

. . . Strong domestic controls are the flip side of the world's most open economy."[14]

In Thailand and Indonesia, the nature of state institutions interacted with global forces and events to shape the crisis.[15] In Thailand, the weaknesses of the democratically elected government made it impossible for the state to act decisively once the crisis began. The structure of Thailand's political system required governing political parties to cobble together broad-based coalitions in order to form a government, making it difficult for the government to implement any meaningful economic reform. All parties in the government had gained power through the financial contributions of Thai business and financial interests, which would have been damaged by any radical reform. These same political factions used government resources to prop up insolvent banks. This type of political interference eroded international and domestic confidence in the Thai economy. If the government had been able to implement extensive reforms, the crisis may not have exploded across the region. Thailand's political paralysis and governmental impotence forced dramatic constitutional changes in the latter part of 1997, a direct result of the economic crisis.

When the crisis hit Indonesia, most analysts believed that it could withstand the storm far better than Thailand. Indonesia's basic economic indicators were stronger than Thailand's, and it possessed a government capable of decisive action. Indeed, the Suharto regime had dealt with economic crises in the past and had demonstrated a willingness to act even when governmental cronies were affected. Thus, despite Indonesia's reputation as a bastion of crony capitalism, there was a reasonable expectation that the government would move to restore investor confidence. Initially, President Suharto's government did act as foreign investors expected: it cut back on government spending and projects, even some linked to the president's children and cronies; opened up the economy to more foreign investment; and took other measures meant to display its willingness to make hard choices. When it became apparent that these measures were not enough to protect the rupiah from the regional contagion, Indonesia went to the IMF for help and, on October 31, 1997, signed a $23 billion (soon to rise to $38 billion) bailout package. This, too, was seen as a positive development and further indication of Indonesia's willingness to do what was necessary to restore investor confidence.

Throughout November 1997, as part of the IMF package, the government announced the elimination of some import monopolies, closed sixteen small banks, reduced tariffs, and opened the wholesale and distribution sectors to foreign investment. Indonesia also began to review some of its strategic industrial plans. Again, many of these measures affected crony businesses. Even as the government was moving forward on these initiatives, however, President Suharto began sending mixed signals. He quietly signed a decree permitting the resumption of eight large-scale projects that he had suspended, as well as seven projects that were subject to review. All of these projects were connected to Suharto's children or cronies, and some projects made little economic sense under the best of conditions. These developments highlighted the fact that Suharto was the only important player in Indonesia. If he changed his mind, no one could operate as a check on his decisions.

From this point on, investors began receiving confused signals from Indonesia, which shook their confidence in the Suharto regime. Suharto's children and cronies began fighting back against the government, suggesting in some cases that incoming international funds would be used to rescue insolvent businesses, a measure strictly prohibited under the terms of the IMF agreement. At the same time, the Indonesian government attempted to implement the reforms it had agreed upon with the IMF, with varying levels of success. Foreigners and Indonesians alike were unclear as to what path Suharto was following. The situation worsened as reports of Suharto's declining health reached the press.

By the end of 1997, the rupiah had declined by 54 percent from its previous value. In January 1998, the Indonesian government introduced a budget that was based on highly unrealistic assumptions about Indonesia's near-term economic performance. Foreigners also misunderstood the budget as being expansionary. The situation led to suggestions by the IMF that it might not continue to support Indonesia, and the rupiah continued its free fall. The international response to the budget caused various international leaders to pressure Suharto to comply with a revamped and even more severe IMF rescue package. He finally agreed to do so, but by this time his credibility with international investors was gone. When the crisis began, the rupiah was pegged to the U.S. dollar at approximately 2,400 to 1; during January 1998, it fell to an all-time low of more than 17,000 to 1. The Indonesian economy ground to a halt as businesses proved unable to service their foreign debts with the massively devalued rupiah. Solvent businesses were denied international lines of credit. Imports and exports stopped flowing through the Indonesian economy. Unemployment grew and tens of millions of Indonesians fell below the poverty line.

The political structure of Indonesia contributed to investor uncertainty and loss of confidence in the economy. If Suharto had acted consistently, his regime may have survived. In any case, too much was riding on the decisions and actions of one man. However, the situation is not quite this simple. It is also possible that any government in Indonesia would have faced similar problems so long as it relied upon the guidance of the IMF. As discussed below, the IMF implemented policies that turned the Asian economic downturn into a full-fledged crisis. At least part of Suharto's unwillingness to follow IMF prescriptions reflects his realization that the IMF plan was not working. At a certain point, it is impossible to distinguish if the IMF plan did not work because of Suharto's behavior or because of its inherent flaws. However, the evidence that the IMF did not know what it was doing in Indonesia, or in the Asian crisis more generally, must be taken into account. The Indonesian case also illustrates the uncertainty in interpreting the causes of the crisis. Exactly why Indonesia was hit by the crisis still remains unclear.

The case of South Korea illustrates some of the key debates on the nature of the economic downturn.[16] The reasons for South Korea's economic collapse are particular to the state itself, though some commonalities with Southeast Asia, particularly financial liberalization in the early 1990s, are apparent. Some analysts argue that the South Korean system was an accident waiting to happen. Meredith Woo-Cumings argues that South Korea was caught between "a highly effective bureaucracy that sought to regulate the corporate sector and a political ruling group that, relying on the financial support of big business, ended up circumventing the best efforts of the bureaucrats. . . . In the end, it took a massive banking and corporate crisis and the institution of a democratic regime to break this logjam."[17]

Others argue that the charges of systemic corruption in the Korean system are vastly overblown. Chang Ha-Joon claims that the regular flow of money from business to politicians and bureaucrats under the established Korean system rarely related to projects in the main manufacturing sectors; these were insulated from conventional politics. It was only under the Kim Young Sam government that these processes began to break down and specific Korean *chaebol* (business conglomerates) began to enjoy special relationships with the government. Under Kim, the process of financial liberalization, begun in the early 1990s, accelerated considerably. The state opened its borders to capital from foreign banks, making it easier for *chaebol* to establish both financial relationships with outside actors and banks of their own. The government, as a result, began to lose its traditional control over the banking sector, which it had utilized as leverage against the *chaebol* in the past.[18] Deregulation, as in Southeast Asia, was not accompanied by sufficient government oversight. In South Korea this inadequacy was not the result of weak state capacity but a deliberate policy decision, based on an acceptance of Western market ideology. Political liberalization made it easier for business to affect political actors, thereby circumventing the regulatory function of the state. From this perspective, South Korea quickly went from being a strong, well-regulated state to a comparatively weak state, with a politically constrained bureaucracy. Again, financial liberalization and a failure to implement strong regulations directly account for the effects of the crisis.

Malaysia's response to the crisis was determined by its domestic politics.[19] Malaysia was in the unique position of having a relatively low level of foreign debt. This enabled it to avoid the ministrations of the IMF. The ruling elite in Malaysia, led by Prime Minister Mahathir Mohamed, defined the economic crisis as caused by foreigners. It generally refused to accept that Malaysian economic policies contributed to the situation. A more pressing concern for the Malaysian government, however, was its need to maintain existing economic arrangements. The government of Malaysia (United Malays National Organisation, UMNO) followed economic policies designed to promote an ethnic-Malay business class. The economic crisis had the potential to undermine those economic advances by forcing the government to alter policies that had accorded advantages to Malays. Moreover, allowing Malay-owned companies to fail ran the risk of alienating UMNO's ethnic support.

In its initial reactions to the crisis, the government blamed the unfolding events on the actions of foreign currency traders and Western interests. Mahathir went as far as to suggest a "conspiracy" directed against Muslim and Asian states by a Western world that did not want Asians to succeed and challenge Western dominance. Mahathir's comments hurt the performance of the Malaysian ringgit and stock exchange, as foreign investors pulled their funds out of the country. These investors disapproved of the government's decision not to implement IMF-like policies; they were also concerned about the possibility of government action to restrain investors' freedom of movement. In the second stage of its response, the government did attempt to implement austerity measures and contractionary policies similar to what the IMF had done in other states. Deputy Premier Anwar Ibrahim supported these policies. Prime Minister Mahathir was temporarily silenced by his inability to stop the ringgit's slide. These developments reflected deeper and growing political divisions within UMNO itself. In mid-1998, the Malaysian government reversed itself again. Mahathir resumed direct control of government economic policy, abandoning the contractionary approach and implementing expansionary fiscal and monetary policies. A certain amount of liberalization was included in the new package, in the form of greater allowances for foreign ownership of Malaysian assets. However, in August–September 1998, Malaysia introduced capital controls that effectively cut its connections to international financial and capital markets.

The Malaysian government targeted short-term capital flows in implementing currency controls. The controls effectively withdrew the ringgit from the international currency trading system. They required exporters to sell their foreign exchange to the central bank at a specified rate. The bank then sold foreign exchange to foreigners for approved payments, primarily imports and debt services. The ringgit remained convertible on the current account but not the capital account, which prevented the purchase of foreign exchange for speculative purposes. Residents were forbidden to transfer ringgits to foreign accounts and were allowed to leave the country with only limited foreign exchange for the purpose of travel. Nonresidents could only convert ringgits into foreign currencies with the approval of the central bank, and those selling Malaysian securities would have to hold the security for twelve months before they could convert ringgits into foreign exchange. People with offshore accounts were given from September 1–October 1 to repatriate their ringgits. After that, repatriation became illegal. This rule ensured that, rather than generating capital flight, the Malaysian measures actually produced a short-term capital inflow. Overall, these measures stabilized the Malaysian economy, shielded it from the worst effects of the crisis, and helped push the country toward the best and fastest economic recovery among the ASEAN states.[20]

Causes of the Asian Economic Crisis

The debate over what caused the Asian crisis remains unresolved. The answer has important implications for how to address future crises. It is clear that dubious domestic economic policies contributed to the weakening of the affected Asian economies. In the end, however, the argument that the crisis was caused by weakly regulated banking systems and exacerbated by financial panic is the most sustainable. The operation of an unstable and unaccountable international financial system encouraged these conditions.

Was the crisis a case of the market suddenly penalizing Asian states for faulty economic policies? There is no doubt that some vulnerabilities were shared by the affected Asian states of South Korea, Thailand, Malaysia, and Indonesia. Sharply slowing export growth, sizable current account deficits, heavy foreign borrowing, and declining social profitability of investment were factors in each of these economies. However, the strengths of the Asian economies still far outweighed their weaknesses. Inflation was low; governments were running small deficits or surpluses; GDP growth rates were high; and the countries enjoyed high investments and savings rates.

The argument that rising current account deficits were the direct cause of the crisis has attracted considerable attention. It is, at best, an incomplete explanation. Current account deficits in Asia were used to finance industrial inputs and capital goods, not unproductive consumer goods, as in Latin America.[21] Excluding Thailand and Malaysia, the other affected Asian countries were running relatively low current account deficits. Moreover, there was no evidence to suggest that Thailand, or any other Asian state, was incapable of making enough export earnings to continue servicing its foreign debts. The situation in Asia was sustainable for the foreseeable future. Thus, the argument focusing exclusively on Asian vulnerabilities appears to be a post facto rationalization of investor behavior.

The moral hazard argument assumes that local governments and international actors, such as the IMF, indirectly encouraged bad investment by guaranteeing foreign loans. The risk to lenders was reduced by the belief that any failed investments would be reimbursed by an outside party. There is weight to this argument. Banks and other lenders in East Asia were operating with uncertainty about the quality of their prospective borrowers. Under these conditions, economists expect banks to ration their credit. In Southeast Asia, however, the risk-averse behavior of banks broke down due, in part, to implicit deposit guarantees from local governments and stable exchange rates. Moral hazard also appeared at the corporate and international levels. The pressure to maintain high growth rates across Southeast Asia resulted in public guarantees to favored and important private projects. In some cases, governments directly controlled, subsidized, or directed credit toward selected firms and industries. International banks also allowed their risk management capabilities to fall by the wayside when dealing with East Asia. The continuing economic dynamism in East Asia made bankers complacent about the possibility of economic downturn. In part, these financial institutions believed that the IMF or other forms of multilateral support would cover their investments.

The moral hazard argument, however, does not apply to all the affected states. As Robert Wade demonstrates, South Korea did not have a history of bailing out failed companies.[22] It had supported individual chaebol affiliates, but it always punished the parties involved by removing their managerial powers or replacing them altogether. This approach should have curbed moral hazard on the part of businesses, at least. Wade argues that the tendency of investors and businesses to lend recklessly was driven by the high growth rates of the Asian economies. Because of the incentives of the financial system, the costs of missing out on popular investment opportunities were too high. Investors were encouraged to follow the crowd. Indeed, "lack of transparency" was not as large a problem in Asia as some commentators have asserted; signals that there might be growing economic difficulties were available in public records and indicated in commentaries by the Bank of International Settlements. However, bankers and investors decided to ignore the warning signs.

The Asian countries had economic difficulties, but there was no reason to believe that they could not continue servicing their debts in the period preceding the crisis. The vulnerabilities in the Asian economies contributed to the crisis once it started. The crisis was mostly the result of investor panic. The same incentives that impelled bankers and investors to rush into Asia to invest also caused them to rush for the exits once the region began experiencing economic shocks. The Asian economic weaknesses served to exacerbate and, to a large degree, rationalize herdlike behavior. This response caused an economic crisis far beyond what was merited by any "objective" measure of Asian economic fitness. The situation was worsened by the fact that there are a relatively small number of fund managers in the Western world—perhaps as few as one hundred—who actually manage the hedge-fund capital going into emerging Asian economies. These few are under enormous pressure to perform well in environments of limited information and are particularly inclined toward herd behavior.[23]

Financial liberalization and the lack of state capacity to monitor financial transactions are at the heart of the Asian crisis. The states that best weathered the economic storm were least exposed to the flow of international "hot money," possessed strong states capable of effectively managing and controlling the flow of finance, or both. Of the major Asian trading states, Taiwan was least affected by the crisis.[24] Taiwan financed most of its development through domestic savings and had very little exposure to foreign portfolio investment or borrowing. Taiwan's central bank, the Central Bank of China (CBC), and its Ministry of Finance created a tightly regulated financial system that included strict limits on foreign investment. During the crisis, the CBC took measures to control and penalize currency traders. The government followed an expansionary fiscal policy designed to provide liquidity for Taiwanese businesses in distress. Taiwan's concern with national security prompted it to move cautiously on questions of financial deregulation. Nonetheless, along with Singapore, it is an excellent example of the need for strongly regulated financial markets in Asia.

Robert Wade has developed an argument in which Asian economic development has been based upon a model that is not amenable to Western financial and cultural practices, the high-debt Asian developmental model.[25] Wade argues that the high savings rates in Asian countries facilitated the Asian developmental state. Asian households save a high percentage of their incomes, which are deposited in banks. Banks have to lend, so they lend to firms seeking investment capital. Large Asian companies have financed much of their growth through bank borrowing, in contrast to the U.S. model of business where companies rely upon issuing stocks to attract capital. Relying on bank loans, Asian companies carry relatively high debt-to-equity ratios, in contrast to Western or Latin American firms, which enabled them to invest far more than they could have earned or financed through equity alone, allowing for the region's rapid economic expansion. Corporate sectors with high debt loads, however, are vulnerable to shocks that can reduce cash flow or increase fixed payment obligations, such as currency devaluations or a rise in interest rates. The high-debt model encourages and relies upon close linkages between bankers and business. It also usually involves significant government direction and participation.

The model created "revenue-maximizing and non-risk averse" firms.[26] Firms were willing to accept lesser rates of profit as long as they could meet their total revenue objectives and expand their market shares. The close relationship between firms, banks, and government necessary to sustain the model is the basis of the "crony capitalism" practiced in many Asian countries. Significantly, this model requires a closed or partially closed capital account in the home country. This prevents capital from being easily moved in and out of the country, thereby protecting the corporate sector from systemic shocks and allowing it to maintain high levels of investment. The opening of the capital account in most Asian states undermined this model. With access to foreign capital and willing lenders, Asian companies exposed themselves to banks and investors who did not appreciate or understand the value and logic of the high-debt model.

Initially, international investors were unconcerned with questions of debt-servicing capabilities and the relatively shallow technological and skill capacities of many Asian firms. While this information may have been available, investors were swept along by the economic opportunities in Asia. The success of the Asian model, however, was contingent on the continuing ability of export-oriented firms to maximize revenue and market-share expansion in the global economy. Their ability was compromised by the economic slowdown in Japan; the resulting industrial overcapacity; rising interest rates, which affected debt servicing obligations; and other factors associated with the recession of the mid-1990s. When faced with the economic shocks of 1997, international investors reconsidered the levels of debt of the companies in which they were invested, compared these to the debt-equity ratios of Western companies, and began calling in loans or withdrawing their funds.

The upshot of Wade's argument is that Asian capitalism requires a particular relationship between banks and business. By allowing enormous foreign investment into the Asian states, the "high-debt" model countries undermined their own model of development. Western investors, from a different cultural and financial background, were not willing to take the short-term risks or make the long-term commitments necessary to sustain the high-debt approach.

Besides the opening of the capital account, the retreat of governments from economic management also helped to weaken the Asian development model. Opening the capital account was part of a general Asian acceptance of the Western ideological commitment to minimal government intervention and financial sector liberalization. As noted above, South Korea essentially abandoned its industrial policy to join the OECD. Firms were able to pursue their private objectives of maximizing revenue and market share without a government agency acting to oversee their activities and promote broader social and policy goals. Even in states lacking the capacity to provide strong government oversight, the basic acceptance of the neoliberal agenda meant that governments were complacent about opening their economies to the operations of the international capital market. In Malaysia and

Indonesia, governments pulled back from overseeing their economies. In Thailand, the desire to establish itself as a regional financial center increased the level of financial sector liberalization without the necessary strengthening of central bank capabilities.

We need to be careful in applying the "high debt model" to all of East Asia. There is no single model of Asian development. However, there is a strong Asian consensus that governments have a legitimate role to play in the management of regional economies, and there are several distinctive forms of Asian capitalism that "bear little resemblance to either stylised Anglo-American economic theory or corporate activity in North America, Britain, Australia or New Zealand."[27] Governments' abilities to fulfill this interventionary role vary from state to state. The high-debt model was clearly at work in Japan and Korea. State capacity in Southeast Asian countries, however, varied considerably as did their ability to implement this model. Nonetheless, Southeast Asia has a strong tradition of state intervention and organization of the economy.[28] Singapore's development was initiated and organized through state-run industry and careful government regulation designed to take advantage of foreign investment and technology. As noted above, Malaysia implemented economic policies designed to address political and ethnic tensions between Malays and ethnic Chinese. The government created state-run industries and undertook initiatives such as Malaysia's Multimedia Super Corridor (MSC), meant to make Malaysia a regional information technology powerhouse, attract high-tech foreign investment, and boost the skills level of Malaysian workers.[29] Indonesia has a history of strong economic nationalism. The government encouraged state industry in important areas and attempted to develop indigenous industry behind protective trade barriers.[30] Despite their experiments with financial deregulation and liberalization, East Asian countries remain ideologically disposed toward interventionist government policies.[31]

The origins of the Asian Crisis are found at the micro level of firm behavior. Resolving the problem, however, required that governments act to restructure their banking sectors in the long term but restore credit flows in the short term. This did not happen. The Asian banking crisis made it impossible for solvent companies to continue operating. As a result, the financial crisis became a full-scale economic crisis. The proper response to the situation was for Asian states to take over distressed assets from banks and replace them with government bonds.[32] A government-led approach to the crisis would have been the fastest way to restore confidence in the banking system. Active and interventionist states could have quickly alleviated the banking problems, enabling solvent companies to regain access to needed capital rapidly. Governments could have borrowed to finance the recapitalization of banks. These debts would be liquidated in the next phase, which would privatize state assets, including revitalized banks. These were not the measures undertaken by the IMF.

Rajiv Kumar and Bibek Debroy argue that, despite the evident flaws inherent in the Asian model of development, these "should not be used to take away from the central argument that the Asian crisis essentially represented a case of market failure rather than government failure."[33] Misdirection of credit was done by the private sector, not the state. The Asian development model needs reform, but the crisis demonstrates that a strong linkage between the banks, state and the corporate sector is required to reduce systemic risks. The strengths of the Asian model should be maintained and developed.

Measures to calm investors and reassure them that debts would still be manageable under new currency regimes were necessary to deal with the crisis. At the same time, solvent businesses needed liquidity to keep afloat. In facing the crisis, most Asian states were guided by the IMF. The IMF implemented a set of policies that followed its standard operating procedures and turned an economic downturn into a crisis.

Mishandling the Economic Crisis

The IMF took the lead in restructuring the economies of Indonesia, Thailand, and the Philippines. It required that the governments of these countries cut spending, reduce subsidies, and raise interest rates even further to stabilize their currencies. Many observers criticized the IMF reforms as inappropriate for the Asian crisis.[34] Jeffrey Sachs and others argued that the IMF used the same medicine that it employed to deal with financial crises in states where the public sector was out of control. In Asia, the problem was one of private debt, not government overspending. The IMF's insistence that governments cut spending and raise interest rates at a time when the Asian economies actually needed economic stimulus and easier access to credit actually exacerbated the problems, particularly in Indonesia.

The IMF's stabilization programs assumed that the Asian countries' institutional structures needed fundamental reform. The IMF closed financial institutions and enforced strict regulatory standards. In Indonesia, this policy increased investor panic; the abrupt closing of sixteen commercial banks precipitated a run on the whole banking system. The IMF demanded that Thailand, Indonesia, and South Korea implement high real-interest rates and fiscal restriction.[35] This approach was based on the IMF experience in Latin America, where high interest rates were tolerable because corporate debt-to-equity ratios were low, and the high interest rates controlled inflation. In Asia, high real-interest rates devastated private actors who were functioning with high debt loads and low inflationary expectations. Asian businesses, even those that were financially sound, suddenly found needed capital to be prohibitively expensive.

The IMF's policies were partly based on the belief that the primary goal of its reforms should be the return of foreign capital. High interest rates were meant to achieve this goal. A program of recovery, however, must rely on more than just the return of foreign investment. Moreover, the IMF policies drove investors away by making economic recovery more difficult, for the reasons described above. In addition, the IMF's requirement of structural reforms in the middle of the economic downturn exacerbated the problems. The IMF imposed Western standards of financial restructuring, including demands for changes in labor laws to make it easier to fire workers and the removal of regulations on foreign ownership, to allow foreign banks and firms to buy their Asian counterparts. These changes were made when interest rates and levels of indebtedness were high, and they created closures, layoffs, and deflation, and accelerated capital flight. It is also telling that the IMF demanded even greater liberalization of the affected Asian economies when it was increasingly apparent that too much liberalization was the major cause of the economic crisis. A pullback from liberalization would have been the more appropriate strategy. However, the IMF was driven as much by ideological commitments as economic analysis.

Asian governments finally began to turn away from the IMF strategy. They began cutting interest rates and introducing fiscally expansionary policies. South Korea used government funds to buy bad loans and finance bank mergers. The IMF itself began to reverse some of its policies, allowing its Asian patients to run budget surpluses. There is evidence that the IMF was chastened by its experience in Asia and is willing to learn from its mistakes.[36] It eventually allowed its Asian clients to run deficits. Nonetheless, the IMF's initial efforts in Asia seriously damaged its credibility, a reality that has powerful implications for the future.

The IMF''s measures exacerbated the hardship faced by the weakest and poorest segments of the Southeast Asian populace.[37] The IMF was widely perceived in Asia as being most concerned with recovering and protecting the money of wealthy foreign investors and banks. Foreigners, who had been every bit as imprudent as Asians in their choice of investments and the lending of money, were protected at the expense of Asian societies. Some of the IMF's actions were clearly meant to further U.S. economic goals in some of the affected East Asian states, most notably South Korea.

Many Asians now perceive the IMF as a blunt instrument of U.S. policy and, at the least, as uninformed and inexpert in dealing with Asia.[38] These perceptions are not universally held—the government of Singapore clearly favors IMF activities in Asia. Moreover, Mark T. Berger argues that, despite distrust of IMF motives, the failure of APEC and other regional institutions to address the crisis effectively has actually left the IMF in an enhanced position in the Asia Pacific.[39] However, the momentum for some kind of Asian counterpart to the IMF has been growing in the region.

Conclusion

The East Asian economic crisis was the result of a number of factors. At heart, it was a crisis of banking regulation at the national and international levels. Structural weaknesses within the East Asian economies certainly contributed to the crisis, but the magnitude of the economic downturn was far out of proportion to the actual health of the Asian economies. The crisis was an example of growing instability and volatility in the world financial markets.

To the ASEAN countries, the crisis revealed their vulnerability to world markets. ASEAN's own efforts to deal with the crisis were spectacularly unsuccessful, and served mostly to highlight the considerable divisions that still exist between ASEAN's member states. The events of the crisis, and the feelings of powerlessness it engendered in Asia, caused Asian leaders to advocate the establishment of a regional institution capable of protecting Asians' economic interests. ASEAN may be able to play a meaningful role within such an organization. However, other factors beyond ASEAN's control—such as historical rivalries between the regional powers—must first be overcome before an effective regional organization can take shape.

Notes

1. "Asia's Economies," 1999; Goad, 1999a: 67.
2. This analysis is based primarily, though not exclusively, upon Kumar and Debroy, 1999; Wade and Veneroso, 1998a; Wade 1998a, b, c; Eichengreen, 1999; Sachs, 1997; "On the Rocks," 1998; Bank for International Settlements, 1998: 117; Dibb, Hale, and Prince, 1998: 7–11; Bello, 1998a; Jomo 1998a; Montes, 1998; Montes and Popov, 1999; Hill, 1999; Sikorski, 1999.
3. Wade, 1998c: 1538.
4. "Japan's Stumble," 1998: A1, A16; "No Help Here," 1997: 60–61; "Japan Makes a Stand," 1997: 47.
5. This is the "carry trade," where banks and investment houses borrow yen and dollars and invest in short-term financial instruments. Wade, 1998c: 1539.
6. "Unhedged" means that borrowers did not make a contract, through an option or in the forward market, to buy dollars at a specified baht-dollar rate. Such contracts add to their costs, and borrowers had been confident about the stability of the peg. Wade, 1998b: 365.
7. See Higgott, 1998: 3; Wade, 1998c: 1541.
8. Kumar and Debroy, 1999: 9–10; Eichengreen, 1999: 145 n. 2.
9. "Rebuilding Asia," 1998: 47. According to *Business Week,* the distribution of loans is slightly different: Japan lent $263 billion, Europe lent $155 billion, and the United States, $55 billion. "Rescuing Asia," 1997: 118.

10. "On the Rocks," 1998.

11. Lim also suggests that Hong Kong's reversion to Chinese rule on July 1, 1997, had created uncertainty for market actors about how authorities would respond to an overvalued exchange rate. L. Lim, 1999: 104.

12. See Chapters 5–8 in "Part II: National Responses," in Pempel, 1999: 101–201; and Chapters 6–10 in Jomo, 1998: 137–231.

13. Hutchcroft, 1999.

14. L. Lim, 1999: 113. Lim argues that Singapore's policies reflected the government's need to satisfy its electorate. The argument that Singaporean democratic accountability played an important role in accounting for government policy seems stretched in this context and needs a critical evaluation.

15. MacIntyre, 1999a, b, 2001; Lauridsen, 1998; Montes and Abdusalamov, 1998.

16. Demetriades and Fattouh, 1999; Chang Ha-joon, 1998: 222–231; Dills and Gills, 2000; Y. Lee, 2000.

17. Woo-Cumings, 1999: 117.

18. Chang Ha-Joon, 1998: 226–229.

19. Nesadurai, 2000; Jomo, 1998b.

20. Wade, 1998b: 368–369.

21. Kumar and Debroy, 1999: 3.

22. Wade, 1998a: 5–6.

23. Winters, 1999: 93.

24. Chu, 1999.

25. Wade and Veneroso, 1998a.

26. Kumar and Debroy, 1999: 14.

27. Beeson, 2000: 353.

28. Rodan, Hewison, and Robison, 1997; Jomo, 1997; Vogel, 1991.

29. Welsh, 2000.

30. Murphy, 2000.

31. Stubbs, 1998.

32. Kumar and Debroy, 1999: 18.

33. Ibid.: 19.

34. Sachs, 1997. For further criticism of the IMF, see "Bah Humbug," 1998: 5; "New Illness," 1997: 65–66; Vatikiotis, 1998; Tripathi, 1998: 65; Dibb, Hale, and Prince, 1998: 11–13.

35. The IMF approach to Asia was actually formulated by the U.S. Treasury secretary, Robert Rubin, and his deputy, Lawrence Summers. They looked at Thailand, imagined that its problems were the same as Mexico's, and imposed the same solutions. See Wessel and Davis, 1999.

36. For evidence of IMF learning, see Goad, 1999b: 86. Shalendra Sharma strongly defends the IMF's role and actions in the crisis. See Sharma, 1998.

37. "Austerity Overdose," 1998: 21; "Soft Targets," 1998: 20.

38. Preston, 1998: 256; Beeson, 1999; Higgott, 1998: 17–18, 22.

39. Berger, 1999.

7

Responding to the Crisis

A SEAN failed to deal effectively with the economic crisis. ASEAN also failed to manage other regional issues that arose during the course of the crisis. These failures have cast doubt on ASEAN's ability to respond to new regional imperatives. The actions of the International Monetary Fund (IMF) and the United States created a demand within Asia for an Asian financial institution. ASEAN may have a meaningful role to play in shaping such an institution, but there are considerable economic and political obstacles to be overcome before any regional financial institution can become a reality. The divergent economic policies and different levels of development of the ASEAN states prevent the organization from taking a coherent and coordinated position on regional financial reform. The problems inherent in creating a regional financial regime are presently too great for Asian states to overcome.

Dealing with the Economic Crisis

ASEAN's organizational efforts to respond to the economic crisis were limited.[1] ASEAN failed to utilize mechanisms that were already in place, such as an existing ASEAN currency swap agreement. In May 1997, several Asian central banks intervened to help prop up the Thai baht against currency speculators. However, this intervention was not an ASEAN initiative, and the involved banks used funds provided by the Bank of Thailand, not their own resources. ASEAN did make attempts to address crisis-related issues as they occurred. ASEAN met in Hanoi in December 1998 and adopted the Hanoi Plan of Action and an associated Statement on Bold Measures. They intended the Hanoi Plan to be implemented over six years, from 1999 to 2004. Some of the concrete measures introduced by the Hanoi Plan included an acceleration of AFTA, moving the implementation date for the six original signatories from 2003 to 2002; implementation of the framework agreement on an ASEAN Investment Area (AIA), meant to attract foreign investment; and liberalization of trade in services.[2] Whether or not these measures will become reality, however, is the larger question. ASEAN has a marked history of making grand declarations, but follow-up has been much more difficult.

The ASEAN Secretariat was further reformed. Before 1999, the total number of secretariat positions was sixty-four; after Hanoi, this was increased to ninety-nine. There are two deputy secretaries-general (DSGs). A second DSG had been added in 1997. One DSG is tasked with ensuring the efficient management of the secretariat; the other assists the secretary-general in policy matters. The current secretary-general, Rodolfo Severino, has promoted ASEAN's institutional development and has assumed a more active political role. However, the secretariat remains underfunded, understaffed, and largely incapable of handling its increasing responsibilities.[3]

A special ASEAN finance ministers' meeting in Manila, in November 1997, first proposed the idea of an ASEAN Surveillance Process (ASP).[4] The meeting also produced the Manila Framework Agreement, which was subsequently endorsed at the 1997 Vancouver APEC meeting. This agreement called for, among other things, the creation of a regional surveillance process that would complement the global surveillance of the IMF. At the second ASEAN finance ministers meeting in Jakarta on February 28, 1998, the ministers agreed to establish the ASP "within the general framework of the IMF and with the assistance of the Asian Development Bank."[5] The exact role of the IMF in this process was never clarified and remains unclear. For ASEAN, the ASP is a revolutionary idea, given its potential to infringe upon the sovereignty of its members.

During the period of the crisis, the ASP never really developed. In the crisis aftermath, the process has begun to operate, though its effectiveness is questionable. The broad overall objectives of the ASP are as follows:

1. to assist ASEAN members in spotting a potential crisis and responding to it accordingly;
2. to assess the vulnerability of ASEAN members to financial disruptions and crises;
3. to improve the coordination of ASEAN members' economic policies through the dissemination of sound practices that meet international standards; and
4. to promote a "peer monitoring" environment among ASEAN members through a review of potentially vulnerable sectors.[6]

The ASP involves biannual information-exchange meetings between central bank and finance officials from the ASEAN states. This exchange enables ASEAN states to develop appropriate collective and individual responses to economic difficulties. Beyond monitoring various economic indicators, such as exchange rates and macroeconomic aggregates, the ASP is intended to provide information on members' current and proposed sectoral and social policies. The Asian Development Bank Regional Economic Monitoring Unit (ADB-REMU) has agreed to provide training and technical support to the ASEAN countries during the formative period of the ASP. Under this agreement, for a period of two years, the ADB provides technical training in finance to ASEAN officials at the ASEAN Technical Support Unit (ASTSU) based at ADB headquarters in Manila. The ASTSU provides support to the ASEAN Surveillance Coordinating Unit (ASCU) based at the ASEAN Secretariat in Jakarta.[7]

"Peer review" is different than oversight by international surveillance agencies, which might be unduly influenced by external actors, particularly the United States. Supporters argue that peer review is more collegial and, therefore, more likely to encourage adherence to basic principles and to aid in the harmonization of interests. Nonetheless, any credible surveillance mechanism would need to offer honest exchanges of views on member states' economic management, which might easily be construed as a violation of state sovereignty and the ASEAN way.

There are numerous difficulties with the surveillance process. There is no consensus within ASEAN on the causes of the crisis. It is difficult to prevent future crises through a monitoring mechanism if the involved parties cannot agree on what caused the last crisis. There is not a consensus as to what should be monitored—macro or micro economic indicators, and which ones? There is the problem of inadequate state capacity. Despite the efforts of the ADB and a recently established IMF-Singapore Training Institute, many Southeast Asian officials lack the technical expertise and ability to deal with the increasingly complex economic and financial problems of a globalized economy. Even if the expertise was in place, most ASEAN countries do not have access to the information necessary to make a monitoring mechanism work effectively. In part, this lack of information is due to private-sector obstructionism. If monitoring included private-sector debt, which, given the 1997 crisis, would seem necessary, states would have to extract information from highly secretive private-sector actors, who are afraid of competitors gaining access to their data. Even if this information could be gathered, authorities might be unwilling to share it with the monitors. There is a powerful culture of secrecy around economic data within ASEAN that will be difficult to overcome.

In 1998, ASEAN secretary-general Rudolfo Severino claimed that the two factors proving to be an impediment to an effective ASP were the ASEAN Secretariat's institutional limitations in managing the surveillance process and the reluctance of ASEAN countries to share economic information with one another. One of the arguments for the ASP was that it would be better able to extract information from its participants than the IMF, but this does not appear to be the case.

During the crisis, ASEAN members set forth a number of proposals to deal with the crisis as a group. One suggestion was to conduct intra-ASEAN trade in the Singaporean dollar, the strongest ASEAN currency. However, the proposal was rejected because of the realization that such trade was too small to counteract significantly the effects of currencies devalued in relation to the U.S. dollar.[8] ASEAN countries are dependent upon economic interaction with the outside world. The suggestion to use the Singaporean dollar was replaced by a move to use local currencies for local trade. In the end, however, only the central banks of Malaysia and the Philippines signed a bilateral trade payment arrangement to try and reduce their countries' dependence on the U.S. dollar.

ASEAN suggested measures to address questions of social safety nets and the construction of "ASEAN as a caring society."[9] On October 30, 1998, the ASEAN Secretariat announced the creation of an ASEAN Action Plan on Social Safety Nets. However, initiatives designed to address the domestic social welfare concerns of member states run the risk of compromising ASEAN's principle of nonintervention. Many of the measures that ASEAN has proposed in the wake of the crisis are either too complicated to implement or require a level of coordination and cohesion that ASEAN has deliberately avoided in the past.

At the Third ASEAN Informal Summit in Manila, November 28, 1999, Prime Minister Chuan Leekpai of Thailand suggested that ASEAN create an "ASEAN Troika" to deal with pressing regional matters. ASEAN had created a troika in 1997 to represent its interests in dealing with Cambodia. That troika consisted of the Philippines, Thailand, and Indonesia. Chuan proposed a pared-down instrument that would allow ASEAN to address issues of regional peace and stability more effectively. The ASEAN heads of state agreed, and the proposal was formally adopted by the meeting of the ASEAN foreign ministers on July 24, 2000. The troika is composed of the past, present and future chairs of the ASEAN Standing Committee, that is, the foreign ministers of the three ASEAN states involved in the rotation of the chair. The purpose of the troika "is to enable ASEAN to address in a timely manner urgent and important regional political and security issues and situations of common concern likely to disturb regional peace and harmony. By helping ASEAN to be more responsive to the growing interdependence between the countries of Southeast Asia, the ASEAN Troika would serve to elevate ASEAN cooperation to a higher plane and further serve to enhance ASEAN's unity and solidarity, as well as its overall effectiveness."[10]

However, the troika is not designed to fulfill these principles. It is not a decisionmaking body, and it cannot take on tasks that are not explicitly assigned to it by the ASEAN foreign ministers: "In carrying out its tasks the ASEAN Troika shall refrain from addressing issues that constitute the internal affairs of ASEAN member countries."[11] The troika can only be activated with the approval of all ten ASEAN foreign ministers. Given these limitations, the troika is of little value. Once again, ASEAN has placed the principle of nonintervention well before the possibility of collective action on regional issues.[12]

ASEAN generally avoided a surge of protectionist economic nationalism during the course of the crisis. The crisis furthered ASEAN's institutional development by providing an impetus to AFTA. During the height of events, Singapore proposed accelerating the implementation of AFTA, but Indonesia rejected this suggestion. In October 1998, the ASEAN economic ministers agreed to accelerate tariff reductions by three years. This decision was reversed at the Hanoi Summit three months later, but the summit did advance AFTA by one year, calling for its implementation among the leading ASEAN states by 2002, rather than 2003. AFTA is, slowly, becoming a more institutionalized and effective regime, and it is important that it was not derailed by the crisis. Though AFTA's progress has occurred in fits and starts, this is not an atypical way for international trading agreements to take shape. The ASEAN states have shown a willingness to negotiate binding agreements under AFTA. Individual ASEAN countries continue to demand special dispensations for some of their local industries, but AFTA continues slowly to bring intra-ASEAN trade under its auspices.[13]

By mid-1998, the crisis had begun to provoke bilateral conflicts between the ASEAN states. Singapore, Malaysia, and Indonesia, in particular, were at odds, exchanging barbs and insults that sometimes carried racist overtones. The rise of the Habibie government in Indonesia caused Singapore to withhold U.S.$5 billion in loans that it had agreed to extend to Indonesia. It cited a lack of reforms within Indonesia as the reason for its change of heart. Malaysia and Singapore became embroiled in territorial disputes, as well as conflicts directly related to the crisis. In 1998, Malaysia forced the closure of the Central Limit Order Book (CLOB), a facility in Singapore that traded Malaysian shares. Malaysia claimed that the CLOB undermined the growth of the Malaysian stock exchange. Nearly 90 percent of the CLOB's shareholders were Singaporean, and its forced closure caused panic selling, which resulted in severe losses for many investors. Malaysia's capital controls, though not directed at Singapore, followed Malaysian complaints that high interest rates offered by Singaporean banks for Malaysian ringgit were pulling capital out of Malaysia. Malaysia and Indonesia both accused Singapore of benefiting from their economic distress. Singapore was functioning as a regional safety zone for investors from other Southeast Asian states.

Other ASEAN states were also in conflict. Malaysia-Philippines relations were strained by Malaysia's building structures on reefs in the Spratly

Islands claimed by the Filipinos. Thailand-Myanmar relations were complicated by numerous factors, such as border disputes, refugees, the drug trade,
and the deportation from Thailand of illegal immigrants from Myanmar.

The new ASEAN member states, were also dramatically affected by
the crisis. Though the crisis did not cause the economic devastation wit-
nessed elsewhere in the region, it did change the course of development in
Cambodia, Laos, Myanmar, and Vietnam. In Vietnam, export growth fell
from 38 percent in 1996 to 3 percent in 1998. FDI to Vietnam declined by
60 percent between 1996 and 1998. By late 1997, currencies in the four
countries had been devastated; the Lao kip declined by 80 percent, due to
its link to the Thai baht; the Burmese kyat over 50 percent, and Vietnam's
dong fell about 25 percent between January 1997 and November 1998.[14]
Despite such effects, these countries were not included in the ASEAN
finance ministers' meeting that produced the Manila Framework.

Faced with the severity of the crisis, the new ASEAN member states
pulled back from economic liberalization. Vietnam delayed efforts to liberalize state-owned industry; in Laos, conservative leaders seeking to reduce
the pace of reform were greatly strengthened in post-crisis elections. These
developments emphasize the growing two-tier structure within ASEAN
between the old and new members.

Effects of the Crisis on ASEAN

During the crisis, ASEAN was rendered all but meaningless. Observers
both inside and outside the region expected ASEAN to coordinate a
regional response to the economic downturn and to provide guidance to its
affected member states. Instead, it fell apart. As an organization, it was
unable to influence regional events in any significant way. At the most, it
made pronouncements and attempted to create structures that would prevent future crises, but it could do little to relieve the ongoing economic distress. Even worse was the demonstration of ASEAN disunity. Faced with
crisis, the ASEAN countries struck off on their own, with little regard for
their neighbors.

In many respects, the expectation that ASEAN could have played any
meaningful role in facing the economic crisis betrays a profound misunderstanding of how ASEAN functions and its essential purposes. ASEAN was
never a primarily economic institution, and it has contributed little to its
members' economic success. It is a political regime and works most effectively as Southeast Asia's regional voice to the rest of the world. Nonetheless, the expectation that ASEAN should have done something about the
crisis, and its failure to do anything, deeply compromised its political credibility and the international perception of Southeast Asia as a unified bloc.

This perception, however illusory, was fundamentally important to ASEAN's international prestige. The crisis revealed the extent to which the region has become interdependent, at least in the minds of foreign investors. Whatever ASEAN's original purposes, it must adapt to this more volatile environment if it wishes to remain a relevant regional player.

The crisis weakened ASEAN in three ways. First, it undermined the confidence, born of economic success, which was at the heart of ASEAN's assertiveness on the international stage. Second, ASEAN's inability to respond effectively to the crisis accentuated the weakness of its claims to be a credible economic institution. Third, the economic crisis created problems that ASEAN could not address without violating the ASEAN way. Principles and practices that ensured ASEAN's survival throughout its history now seem to be compromising its viability in a changing regional environment.[15] ASEAN remains unable to agree on how to reform these procedures.

ASEAN's major institutional initiatives in the post–Cold War period have focused on its efforts to expand its activities in the regional security and economic spheres.[16] With both the ARF and APEC, ASEAN demanded and received a level of prominence and influence that its collective abilities did not merit. The ARF is the only Pacific-wide security structure in existence. While its importance should not be exaggerated, the great powers still agreed to follow ASEAN's lead within the forum. This is despite the fact that ASEAN includes no dominant Pacific power, is not a security pact, and its member states, even combined, are no match for the military power of any of the major regional players. ASEAN's collective economic potential, however, and the political and military power that might proceed from that economic potential, was a significant factor in legitimizing ASEAN's claims to a prominent regional role. ASEAN will regain some of its influence as its individual members recover from the crisis. Nonetheless, the memory of ASEAN's organizational disunity during the crisis erodes its regional influence, at least until it proves that it has overcome these obstacles. ASEAN's ability to be a bridge to China is, perhaps, its most powerful claim to continuing dominance in the ARF. In the wake of the crisis, China continues to support ASEAN's role in the ARF. However, ASEAN's stature in the organization is compromised if the legitimacy of its role lies mainly in its political acceptability to a great power and is not reinforced by its independent standing.

ASEAN's prominent role within APEC was justified by an assessment of ASEAN's collective economic potential. Until the crisis, the ASEAN economies were among the most dynamic in the world. Though they were relatively small in comparison to many other individual APEC participants, ASEAN acting as a bloc could constitute a significant economic force, but ASEAN was never able to function as a coherent bloc within APEC. The economic downturn has weakened ASEAN's leading role in APEC. It has also weakened ASEAN's ability to advocate an alternative approach to APEC, one more friendly to Asian views on state and economic relations.[17] This may mean that Asian states' commitment to APEC will decline. It could also indicate a further erosion of the common ground that helps to unite ASEAN. Without demonstrable influence within APEC, many ASEAN members will further question ASEAN's effectiveness and their reasons for remaining committed to the organization.

Before the crisis, ASEAN had expressed its intention to be a prominent regional economic institution. ASEAN was working on the assumption that it only needed to facilitate economic development through mechanisms like AFTA. However, ASEAN cannot claim to be a meaningful economic institution, yet have no ability to affect the worst economic downturn in the region's modern history.[18]

During the crisis, various ASEAN leaders and academics challenged ASEAN's practice of nonintervention. It had become clear that events in one ASEAN country had the potential to dramatically affect neighboring states. Under these circumstances, critics argued, ASEAN needed to have the institutional ability to discuss domestic issues that might have regional effects. In July 1997, the deputy prime minister of Malaysia, Anwar Ibrahim, called for "constructive intervention" within ASEAN. This implied closer cooperation between advanced and less-advanced ASEAN members to promote regional development but not uninvited intervention in the internal affairs of member states. As the economic crisis worsened, however, and other regional problems (such as the haze caused by forest fires in Indonesia) developed, other actors, including Philippine minister of foreign affairs Domingo L. Siazon, Jr., suggested that ASEAN reconsider its principle of nonintervention. In the weeks preceding the July 1998 AMM, Thailand's foreign minister, Dr. Surin Pitsuwan, advanced the concept of "flexible engagement."[19] "Flexible engagement involves publicly commenting on and collectively discussing fellow members' domestic policies when these have either regional implications or adversely affect the disposition of other ASEAN members."[20] Thailand offered three official reasons for its promotion of flexible engagement: "First, flexible engagement was to allow ASEAN to respond to the increasing interdependence faced by the region, as events in one country increasingly affected other countries. Second, flexible engagement was designed to confront new security threats, such as economic disruption and various cross-border security problems. . . . Third, flexible engagement was to enhance the democratization and human rights in ASEAN countries."[21]

When "flexible engagement" was discussed at the July 1998 AMM, however, all of the other ASEAN governments, with the exception of the Philippines, were strongly opposed to the idea. Most of the arguments against the concept focused on its lack of clarity and the considerable uncertainty over how it would be applied. It was not clear which domestic issues would be off-limits to public criticism. ASEAN states feared that making it acceptable for members to criticize each other would lead to mistrust and resentment and renew the kinds of tensions that had permeated the region before ASEAN was formed. Criticism could help destabilize regimes that were already faced with serious internal instability and provide outsiders with the means to divide ASEAN. In the view of most of ASEAN's members, flexible engagement—and any relaxation of the nonintervention principle—would more likely lead to ASEAN's disintegration than its renewal. However, Thailand did not leave the July 1998 AMM completely empty-handed. The ASEAN foreign ministers made a commitment to practice "enhanced interaction." This made it acceptable for individual ASEAN states to comment on their neighbors' domestic activities if those activities affected regional concerns. However, ASEAN itself would not intervene in members' domestic affairs.

Enhanced interaction was tested almost immediately. In Malaysia, the arrest and imprisonment of Anwar Ibrahim on charges of "unnatural sex and corruption" evoked powerful reactions across the region. Though Thailand was highly restrained in its reaction to the situation, presidents Joseph Estrada of the Philippines and B. J. Habibie of Indonesia, both of whom had personal relationships with Anwar, openly criticized Malaysia's actions. The Malaysian government made it clear that it would tolerate quiet, private expressions of concern from its ASEAN allies over Anwar's plight, but it would not tolerate public condemnation. Malaysia struck back at Habibie in Indonesia by questioning the legitimacy of his government. It raised the possibility of blocking Filipino and Indonesian workers from employment in Malaysia. It canceled security exercises with the Philippines' military and even suggested it might support Muslim insurgency in the Philippines. These outbreaks of intraregional hostility were exactly the kind of situations that ASEAN was created to prevent. The ASEAN leaders who had rejected reforming the ASEAN way because of fears about the tensions that reform could evoke were proven correct.

At the pre-APEC Business Summit in Kuala Lumpur, November 1998, U.S. Vice President Al Gore delivered a speech that condemned Malaysia's actions around the Anwar affair. To the ASEAN states, Gore's speech displayed a lack of respect for the region and smacked of intimidation. The U.S. intervention forced the ASEAN states to rally around the ASEAN way and set back the tentative efforts at reform. It seemed to the ASEAN states that enhanced interaction was actually reducing ASEAN's international political relevance by revealing internal tensions, which in turn undermined the unity essential to ASEAN's international standing. The future of enhanced interaction appears doubtful.

The Regional Haze and East Timor

Even as ASEAN proved ineffective in addressing the economic crisis, other regional events eroded ASEAN's credibility and standing in the international community. The problems of the regional haze and the challenge of East Timor presented ASEAN with local crises that, once again, it seemed unable to handle because of its fundamental norms and practices. In both cases, the need to respect Indonesia's sovereignty and its position in Southeast Asia kept ASEAN from coordinating effective responses to issues that the organization should have managed.

The Regional Haze

Throughout 1997–1998, Southeast Asia experienced the environmental disaster of "regional haze."[22] Large parts of Indonesia and Malaysia, and all of Singapore and Brunei, were covered in smoke resulting from forest fires. Most of these fires were burning in Indonesia, though parts of eastern Malaysia contributed to the general problem. Previous episodes of regional haze had occurred in 1982–1983, 1987, 1991, and 1994. The 1997–1998 experience, however, was of a far higher magnitude than anything that had come before. During this period, the total land area consumed by fire in Southeast Asia was around 8 million hectares, or an area twice the size of Taiwan.[23] The haze had potentially devastating health consequences. The Malaysian Air Pollutant Index (MAPI) and the Pollutants Standards Index (PSI, used in Singapore) both designate readings of over 100 to be "unhealthy" and those over 300 to be "hazardous." Readings of over 100 were common for Singapore and much of Malaysia during the haze period. In East Malaysia the situation was much worse. In October 1997, a reading of 849 was recorded in Kuching, Sarawak. As Kuching was hundreds of kilometers from the nearest fire, which implies that readings of over 1000 must have been common in Indonesian Kalimantan, the source of most of the haze, during the fire season. In February 1998, researchers estimated that the measurable, overall economic costs of the fires came to U.S.$4.5 billion.[24]

Large commercial interests in Indonesia caused the fires by using logging techniques that increased the likelihood of fire. These logged areas were sometimes converted to timber or palm plantations, which involved clearing by burning, a practice that often spiraled out of control. In addition, peat swamps were drained for rice production. When these caught fire, the peat proved both particularly toxic and difficult to extinguish. The Indonesian government lacked the physical resources to manage the forest fires. More important, however, was the government's lack of enforcement capability and the political protection afforded to the responsible commercial interests by President Suharto and his family. Indonesian laws regulating and punishing the use of fire to clear land did exist. Attempts to enforce these laws against powerful and well-connected business interests proved fruitless, however, as government departments found themselves overruled or blocked by presidential influence. In East Malaysia, similar dynamics were at work as politically well-connected parties were granted access to timber resources and allowed to ignore inconvenient regulations by powerful protectors.

Following the 1994 incidents of haze, ASEAN environment ministers met in June 1995 and agreed to a Cooperation Plan on Transboundary Pollution. This plan laid out general policies and strategies at the national and regional levels to deal with atmospheric and other forms of transboundary pollution. These proposed measures included, among other things, plans to increase national abilities to deal with forest fires, to share knowledge and technology on preventing and mitigating forest fires, and to build a regional mechanism to coordinate cooperation in fire fighting. The cooperation plan also discussed seeking assistance from outside actors, as necessary, to deal with regional fires.

The ideas and principles behind the cooperation plan were sound, but as with so many ASEAN initiatives, there was little implementation. The fires of 1997–1998 demonstrated the lack of follow-up on the plan. Singapore provided Indonesia with satellite imaging to detect fires and "hot spots," but this was the extent of cooperation based around the plan. In general, the affected states tried to deal with the haze through bilateral and emergency arrangements. The ASEAN environment ministers met in December 1997 and agreed to a Regional Haze Action Plan wherein, once again, ASEAN members agreed to various prevention and monitoring mechanisms and committed to strengthening regional fire-fighting capabilities. In April 1998, the action plan agreed to establish fire-fighting organizations in Indonesia. Despite these efforts, "Doubt . . . remains on the ability of ASEAN as an organization to supply the omissions of the Indonesian national system. This is primarily because of the ASEAN norm for nonintervention in the domestic affairs of member states and the dominant role that Indonesia plays in the grouping. The relative weakness of central institutions in ASEAN is another major factor."[25]

Indonesia was not prepared to put regional interests (or even the health and well-being of its own citizens) ahead of the economic interests of its ruling elite. Domestic politics trumped any effective regional action. This inability to act effectively in the face of a major problem compromised ASEAN's international image and prestige. According to James Cotton,

> It would not be an overstatement to maintain that the haze has been among Southeast Asia's biggest internal challenges if not since the era of "confrontation" then since Vietnam's invasion of Cambodia in 1979. While the

1997 financial crisis has had a greater impact, its causes have been partly external, and increasingly it is viewed as a product of the globalization of finance . . . The haze has posed a challenge to every aspect of ASEAN's character and modalities. Mutual solidarity on the part of governments and a preference for indirect diplomacy have collapsed in the face of the seriousness of the problem. Action plans and ministerial meetings did not prove efficacious, with the Indonesian government incapable of policing its own regulations.[26]

The haze helped fuel the drive for flexible engagement and other calls for reform in the ASEAN way. As we have seen, these calls made little headway.

East Timor

Indonesia invaded and annexed East Timor in 1975. From that time, East Timor became the victim of military brutality and human rights violations on a massive scale. Almost one-third of East Timor's population died under Indonesian occupation before the territory gained its independence in 1999.[27] During this period, the ASEAN countries generally supported Indonesia's claims to East Timor, treating the issue, in accordance with ASEAN norms, as an internal Indonesian matter.[28] ASEAN's silence also reflected its members' unwillingness to antagonize Indonesia. In 1997, B. J. Habibie replaced Suharto as president of Indonesia. President Habibie announced that Indonesia was willing to allow East Timorese to vote on whether they wished to remain in Indonesia or establish an independent state. A UN-supervised referendum on this issue was held on August 30, 1999. Despite massive intimidation from Indonesian-backed militias and the military, Timorese voted overwhelmingly in favor of independence.[29] This result sparked an orgy of killing by the militias, who also forced refugees into West Timor. The situation attracted international condemnation and eventually led the Indonesian government to accept the intervention of a UN peacekeeping force.

The events of 1999 created dilemmas for ASEAN.[30] It continued to support Indonesia's control of East Timor for several reasons. ASEAN was afraid independence for East Timor would instigate the disintegration of Indonesia by encouraging other dissatisfied groups to push for independence. This could cause refugee outflows to neighboring states and spark regional instability. Another concern was that a successful insurgency in East Timor might encourage separatist movements in other ASEAN states. A weakened Indonesia would hobble ASEAN. In addition, ASEAN suspected that Western states were using human rights concerns as a pretext for unilateral armed intervention in the affairs of developing world countries. The 1999 NATO action against Yugoslavia had set the precedent that regimes would be held responsible for gross human rights violations.

ASEAN was bothered by the question of who would determine when the use of force against a sovereign state was justified. Malaysian prime minister Mahathir was most vocal in expressing such concerns and in castigating the West for its hypocritical application of these principles, but his views were widely accepted in the region (and in much of the developing world): "Southeast Asians generally believe that humanitarian intervention could subvert the region's dominant non-intervention norm, weakening political and social cohesion and allowing the West to call into question the legitimacy of governments and regimes not of their liking."[31]

ASEAN states were unhappy that UN intervention was authorized under Chapter VII of the UN Charter, which allowed the International Force for East Timor (INTERFET) and later the UN Transitional Authority in East Timor (UNTAET) to use force to fulfill their mandates. ASEAN regarded these measures as an insult to Indonesia, which had not yet formally ceded its claim to sovereignty over East Timor when INTERFET was deployed.

The ASEAN states were also concerned with the practical difficulties of undertaking a peacekeeping mission in East Timor. With the exception of Malaysia, the ASEAN countries had little experience with UN peacekeeping. Singapore and Thailand worried about a domestic political backlash if their troops were killed. The ASEAN countries worried about the consequences for ASEAN if their troops exchanged fire with Indonesian-backed militias or Indonesian troops. Finally, they worried about the expense of participating in an armed intervention when the effects of the economic crisis were still being felt. Some Southeast Asian states made their participation in INTERFET conditional on financial support from Australia and Japan.[32]

The Indonesian government encouraged substantial ASEAN participation in INTERFET because it wanted to minimize Australian influence. This formal request from Indonesia removed some of the political barriers to ASEAN's involvement in the peacekeeping force. ASEAN did end up making a substantial contribution to the INTERFET force. Of the 9,900 troops deployed, around 2,500 were from ASEAN, and the deputy commander was from Thailand. Malaysia pushed hard to have a Malaysian appointed as UNTAET force commander, but the East Timorese regarded Malaysia as too sympathetic to Indonesia and expressed their strong opposition to a Malaysian commander.

In the short term, ASEAN's perceived inability to act on East Timor confirmed the view of many Western states that "ASEAN is chronically incapable of taking meaningful action even when its own interests are directly engaged."[33] Many Western states saw East Timor as ASEAN's opportunity to demonstrate that it can manage regional security problems and that it did not need external actors playing security roles in the region. Yet, ASEAN was divided over East Timor. Myanmar, unsurprisingly, opposed any external intervention in East Timor, and Vietnam was unenthusiastic about the UN's regional role. Debate within ASEAN focused around the interpretation of noninterference in the context of East Timor. Thailand and the Philippines, the ASEAN states most willing to modify the principle of nonintervention, also made the largest contributions to the UN operations in East Timor. Thailand contributed 1,580 personnel, including 1,230 troops. The Philippines committed 600 personnel, though no ground troops. However, the Philippines also voted against a UN Human Rights Commission resolution to launch an international inquiry into the East Timor situation (the resolution still passed), justifying its vote by claiming to follow the ASEAN policy of noninterference.[34] In Thailand, the deputy foreign minister, Sukhumband Paribatra, defended Thailand's active role, arguing, "It is not necessary to be under the ASEAN banner to help restore peace in East Timor. We are a good UN member and a good neighbour of Indonesia."[35] However, many Thais criticized the government for acting too quickly, and feared that Thailand would bear the brunt of worsened relations with Indonesia if the situation in East Timor deteriorated.

ASEAN's paralysis over East Timor further reduced ASEAN's credibility as the leading force in the ARF. The East Timor situation created the impression that external powers, such as Australia, were required to enforce regional security. The situation may also have encouraged China to test its influence in the region.[36] At least in part, ASEAN's indecision in East Timor reflected a concern with Indonesian sensibilities. However, ASEAN's unwillingness to condemn Indonesian brutality in East Timor undermined its authority to lead the peacekeeping force that was, eventually, sent into the region.[37]

East Timor illustrates the dilemmas of intervention for ASEAN. Allowing intervention into one ASEAN state invites intervention into all. No ASEAN member can afford to tolerate such a precedent. Yet, ASEAN's international influence is linked to its international image as an effective and united regional organization. The more that perception is shaken, the weaker ASEAN becomes. ASEAN may become involved in an internal conflict if it is invited to by a member state, but this entails its own risks. ASEAN's ability to broker peace between a member state's government and insurgent factions is tainted by its inherent tendency to favor the state's position. It is almost inconceivable that ASEAN would forcefully intervene to build peace within a member state. Even its ability to launch a diplomatic intervention in the affairs of member states is very limited.

The Aftermath of the Economic Crisis

The most disruptive phase of the Asian economic crisis ended in 1999. The affected economies of Southeast Asia are now regaining their economic health, though their recovery may be fragile, and an economic divide between Northeast and Southeast Asia may be developing. Whatever the final outcome, the crisis of 1997–1999 will have long-term effects on ASEAN. The crisis highlighted the limits of ASEAN's institutional effectiveness and intra-ASEAN cooperation. However, it may have created some new opportunities for ASEAN's future development.[38]

The most crucial question facing ASEAN in the aftermath of the economic crisis is, can ASEAN reform itself to become a more effective regional institution? The experience with enhanced interaction indicates that the answer is probably "no." ASEAN's members are not prepared to allow the organization or their fellow members to interfere in domestic political and economic decisions. Permitting such intervention is more likely to delegitimize and destabilize the organization than to renew it. Most ASEAN states are engaged in the process of state building and remain determined to keep a firm grip on the instruments of sovereignty. This determination puts them in an untenable situation. Economic and political globalization is challenging the ability of states to function as traditional sovereign entities and introducing disintegrative tendencies into Southeast Asia. The need for a regional organization that can give its members an effective regional voice has never been greater, yet ASEAN appears politically incapable of rising to this challenge.

Part of the difficulty in reforming ASEAN is that it is not certain that implementing extensive reform would actually result in a more effective ASEAN. ASEAN's members might be willing to sacrifice sovereignty if they knew that doing so would meaningfully increase their ability to shape and control the detrimental effects of global forces on the region. Yet, it does not appear that any reform of ASEAN could be so influential. Could a more unified ASEAN have been much more effective during the economic crisis? Probably not. Even as a group, ASEAN lacks the economic resources to influence significantly the international forces affecting the region. The major Asian states that do possess the resources potentially to defend against international economic forces are non-ASEAN states.

ASEAN's efforts to reassert its regional role are being tested by events in Indonesia. So long as Indonesia remains internally focused, ASEAN is handicapped in its activities.[39] Moreover, Indonesia will not allow ASEAN to address the issue of its creeping internal instability. Given the significance of Indonesia's domestic political situation to the region as a whole, keeping this topic off the table will reinforce ASEAN's traditional approach to sovereignty and make it very difficult to discuss any other domestic problem with regional consequences in the future.[40]

The crisis exacerbated the already considerable tensions within ASEAN between its newest members and some of the older members. Tensions between Myanmar and Thailand over questions of Myanmar drug-trafficking and refugees has led to Thai support for Myanmar's insurgents, exactly the kind of activity that ASEAN was created to prevent. The inclusion of Vietnam, Myanmar, and Cambodia in ASEAN would have created adaptive difficulties for the institution under the best of conditions. ASEAN's weakened condition further undermines the willingness of its newest members to accord with its rules.

ASEAN emerged from the Asian economic crisis as a seriously crippled institution. It went from projecting an international image of regional cohesion and effectiveness to one of impotence and irrelevance. ASEAN was never designed to deal with economic crises, and it could not have done so under the best of conditions. However, the crisis created a demand in Asia for new institutional structures, and ASEAN may play a role in meeting that demand.

Regional Financial Architecture and ASEAN Plus Three

After their experience with the Asian crisis, East Asian states have decided that the Western powers, particularly the United States, are unreliable allies at best. According to Fred Bergsten, East Asians recognize that their welfare is linked to their continued access to globalized trade and capital markets. They do not reject existing multilateral institutions but want to work within the framework of existing bodies. However, East Asians now have the measure of the limits of those institutions. They recognize their region's strengths and now want their own institutions in order to supplement existing structures and to ensure that they will never again be dependent on outsiders.[41] Richard Higgott and Nicola Phillips argue that the crisis has given rise to a significant resistance to the international neoliberal project in Asia. While Asians have continued to embrace international free trade, they are now far more wary of unfettered financial liberalization.[42] They are resisting efforts to force them to adopt Western modes of economic and social organization, and they are calling for reform of the international financial architecture.[43]

During the early stages of the crisis, Japan proposed the creation of an Asian Monetary Fund (AMF).[44] The initiative originated with Japan's vice finance minister of international affairs, Eisuke Sakakibara. In 1996, Japanese banks had $265 billion in outstanding loans to East Asian states. Thus, Japan had a strong interest in preventing a regional economic meltdown. The proposed AMF was to be capitalized to the amount of $100 billion, with half of its reserves coming from Japan and the remaining $50 billion from other regional powers, such as Taiwan, Singapore, Hong Kong, and the PRC. These economies all had huge balance of payment surpluses and foreign exchange reserves of almost $800 billion, collectively. The proposed AMF would build on Asia's savings surplus, foreign-exchange reserves, and net-creditor status to finance the debt of the crisis-affected countries. Given that this debt amounted to around $300 billion dollars, the region possessed more than adequate resources to deal with the problem effectively.[45]

The IMF and the U.S. government vociferously opposed the AMF idea. They argued that two rival monetary funds would create "moral hazard" problems by allowing countries access to bailouts even if they did not implement painful structural reforms. The IMF wanted to protect its own status as the primary international institution charged with managing the world economy. Given U.S. dominance in the IMF, this goal was also in the U.S. interest. The U.S. Treasury did not want an AMF that might reduce its ability to force adjustments on Asia and impede the liberalization of trade and finance. The United States was determined that its influence in Asia not be challenged and that Japan, correspondingly, not be a challenger. Kristen Nordhaug also suggests that the United States wanted to ensure that Asian states and private banks, which had been investing heavily in U.S. Treasury bills, not divert their resources to finance a regional mechanism: "If regional banks, led by the Bank of Japan had sold out from their huge holdings of Treasuries to finance this costly operation, the interest rates on Treasuries and long-term interest rates would probably have soared and halted the U.S. economic upturn."[46]

The U.S. and IMF opposition was enough to kill the original AMF proposal, with the support of China and even South Korea, which were afraid of Japanese regional ambitions. The United States managed to protect its coveted role as world economic leader. According to Larry Summers, "U.S. economic leadership is crucial to avoid a descent into the kind of regionalism and protectionism that we saw in the periods between the first and second world wars."[47] Japan was humiliated by the U.S. reaction to its initiative and pulled back from further efforts at regional leadership. In November 1997, Asian finance officials met in Manila and worked out the Manila Framework, which stipulated that any bailout mechanism can only complement the IMF's supervisory role. The meeting called for a new "framework for regional cooperation," though it did not endorse the idea of an Asian rescue fund.

The United States could celebrate its defeat of the AMF proposal only for a short time. The inability of the IMF to halt the crisis and the growing evidence that it was applying the wrong medicine to the wrong problem created considerable resentment within Asia. It became apparent that the AMF proposal might have been enough to forestall the economic downturn from becoming the full-scale crisis that it did. A significant demonstration of Asian resolve to deal with the economic upheaval early in the crisis may have prevented the subsequent investor panic that exacerbated the problem. The U.S. refusal to donate money to Thailand when the crisis began also undermined its position in Asia and bred regional resentment. In October

1998, Japan presented the Miyazawa Plan, launched by Finance Minister Kiichi Miyazawa. The plan offered $30 billion in aid to the crisis-struck Asian economies but was careful to do so as part of a larger aid effort involving the G-7 countries, the IMF, and the World Bank. At that time, the IMF was running out of funds and the U.S. Congress was waffling on approval of further U.S. funding. The Miyazawa Plan gained the support of even the IMF. The U.S. administration was less enthusiastic, but it did not oppose the plan.

There are some tentative indications that a coalition supporting the idea of an Asian financial institution is forming within Asia.[48] This consensus appears to be taking shape within the context of "ASEAN Plus Three." ASEAN Plus Three meetings are discussions between the ASEAN-Ten and Japan, South Korea, and China about the financial architecture of the Asia Pacific. These have become a regular and increasingly important part of Asia-Pacific institutional activity. These meetings were initiated in 1996 to help the Asian participants prepare for the Asia-Europe Meeting (ASEM). However, due to the urgency of the economic crisis, ASEAN Plus Three immediately began to address issues of regional finance. The 2000 ASEAN Plus Three meeting promoted economic and technological exchange within the region, the idea of Asian unity in any future regional crises, and the long-term goal of creating a common market and monetary union.

The suggestion that ASEAN Plus Three can serve as the basis for a regional financial mechanism has led, naturally, to renewed discussion of the AMF concept. Ali Alatas, former Indonesian foreign minister, has argued that an ASEAN Plus Three should "vigorously pursue . . . the establishment of an Asian Monetary Fund."[49] The following discussion will focus primarily upon the political problems facing the creation of an AMF, but the same arguments would hold for any attempt to create an effective regional financial institution.

In the aftermath of the crisis, Japan continues quietly to promote its idea of an AMF. The ASEAN countries are reluctant to antagonize the United States, so they have offered only guarded support to the AMF idea, at least at the official level. However, China, which was opposed to the idea when Japan first proposed it, is now endorsing the AMF concept. It is also putting considerable emphasis upon ASEAN Plus Three or, as the Chinese refer to it, "Ten Plus Three."

This show of Asian unity has many obstacles to overcome before it can be a reality. Despite its soundings on the AMF idea, Japan may not be ready to face down the United States in a contest over the established international political economy. The AMF may simply become a regional extension of the IMF. For Asia to unify to support its own vision of the international economy, Asian states will first have to overcome the considerable tensions that exist between them. While the need for economic unity could well promote conciliation in the security realm, the obstacles are significant.[50] Moreover, there is no clear Asian economic model that an AMF could defend or promote, though all Asian states strongly support a Westphalian understanding of the international system, and most agree that the state potentially has an extensive role to play in the organization of the domestic economy. Even if these obstacles could be overcome, the long-term implications for ASEAN remain uncertain. While ASEAN may have an initially important role to play in creating an Asian financial mechanism, the effectiveness of such an instrument is contingent on relations between the major Asian powers. If these countries did resolve their differences enough to make an Asian financial institution a real possibility, ASEAN's political role as a regional intermediary would decline.

The Idea of an Asian Monetary Fund

Most observers argue that an AMF should be, essentially, an Asian arm of the IMF—better able to act quickly and effectively, not dependent on the U.S. Congress for its funds, but still guided by, and subordinate to, the principles and policies articulated by the IMF. The alternative view is more militant: the AMF should replace the IMF in Asia. It should promote and defend a model of "Asian developmental capitalism" that is more appropriate for Asia than the Anglo-American model promoted by the IMF. Considerable political obstacles stand in the way of either AMF model becoming a reality.

AMF and IMF

The recent string of international financial and economic crises have demonstrated the volatility and interdependence of the world economy. An economic catastrophe in one part of the world is almost certain to have powerful repercussions around the globe.[51] An AMF could serve various stabilizing functions. The Asian crisis showed the weakness of the IMF's surveillance capacities. An AMF could serve as an early warning mechanism and watchdog over Asian economies. Most importantly, the IMF had limited resources with which to face the Asian crisis. It had to mobilize financial support from bilateral sources and other international organizations and contend with the U.S. Congress over the need for more funds. An AMF would provide financial support to Asian states without going outside the region. Asians have very little influence in the creation and definition of the rules and institutions shaping the world system, despite the enormous global importance of the region. To many Asians, the "international community" and its various instruments are impositions of the Western world. The Asian crisis brutally reinforced this perception.

The argument that an AMF should complement and be subordinate to the IMF appears to contradict the feeling of growing East Asian regionalism identified by Bergsten. Nonetheless, a subordinate role for the AMF is widely promoted by analysts inside and outside of the region.[52] Ramkishen Rajan notes at least six good reasons to create an AMF (though there is some overlap between the six).[53] First, past economic crises have been regional in nature, and the bailout packages organized by the IMF have been heavily financed by regional powers. Rajan cites the Latin American and East Asian crises as examples. Having a regional body to coordinate such rescues is not a great departure from established practice and increases efficiency. Second, there is an undeniable East Asian demand for a regional economic facility, and the resources to fulfill this demand are clearly present. Third, an AMF can complement other East Asian efforts to facilitate regional economic development and interaction. Fourth, a regional economic facility can improve the East Asian voice in the international financial architecture. Fifth, there is no strong regional hegemon in Asia or regional monetary institution, in contrast to the dominant role of the United States in the Americas, or the EU in Europe. Sixth, whatever the avenues of transmission, it is clear that economic crises in one part of the region easily spread to other parts and beyond. Dealing with these contagion effects is another strong reason for enhancing regional economic cooperation.

Rajan argues that an AMF should focus on crisis prevention, leaving the tasks of crisis management and resolution to the IMF. An AMF could protect regional currencies under attack from speculators. To be an effective deterrent, the AMF must provide its members access to a large pool of funds, built through appropriate donations from the regional states. The ability to access these funds "ought to be conditional on/tied to member economies maintaining some pre-determined standards of macroeconomic and financial stability. . . . If and when necessary, the members must be willing to subject themselves to regional peer pressure to undertake necessary policy adjustments. . . . Promotion of policy dialogue will be a key function of such a facility."[54]

Rajan sees the AMF as the coordinating regional body that would work with the IMF and other international institutions to coordinate bilateral aid, ensure speedy disbursements of aid, and suggest "the appropriateness of various policies/conditionalities, given its knowledge of regional circumstances."[55] This latter function addresses the charges that the IMF is often unaware of the local economic conditions before it begins imposing solutions and that "outsiders" impose its conditionality. Conditionality would clearly be set with the IMF, though the AMF could lend funds separately, in order to bypass the IMF's system of quotas for individual economies. Rajan sees the IMF as lending its experience and expertise to the AMF in helping it to fulfill its crisis prevention function. However, he also notes that any regional facility must have the ability to force members to "take appropriate actions if domestic weaknesses and imbalances are apparent."[56]

Rajan presents these ideas as fairly unproblematic. However, questions of conditionality and its enforcement would create ideological and political tensions around the AMF idea. Moreover, the primary role assigned to the IMF assumes that the goals of the IMF and AMF would be the same. Those who argue that the AMF should complement the IMF privilege a view of the world economy as a unified whole, with the IMF as the necessary and appropriate shepherd of monetary and economic cohesion. This vision is being challenged by some Asian states.

The political and ideological issues aside, it is not clear that the vision of the AMF, articulated by Rajan and others, could ever work. Even if the institution started out as an adjunct of the IMF, its financial independence would probably ensure that it would soon strike off on its own. An Asian-funded AMF would not likely stay under the IMF thumb for long, especially if the IMF advocated policies that most AMF members opposed. From this perspective, any effective version of an AMF would evolve to challenge U.S. and IMF domination of the structures of the world economy.

The AMF and "Asian Capitalism"

When Eisuke Sakakibara first proposed an AMF in 1997, he explicitly argued that the AMF would defend the "Asian model" of economic development by providing emergency funds to Asian states without IMF-like conditionality. Earlier, Sakakibara had argued that the "Asian model" was more favorable to development than the liberal Anglo-American model supported by international financial institutions. In this incarnation, the AMF can serve as a vehicle that can support and further an "Asian" conception of the regional economy. As such, it would compete directly with the IMF and the U.S. vision of the world economy.

As discussed in Chapter 6, there is no clear "Asian model" of economic development that all Asian states follow. Only a few Asian countries have possessed the proper mixture of state capacity and social cohesion to duplicate the Japanese version of "alliance capitalism." Throughout the 1990s, Asian states have moved toward an Anglo-American liberal model of business. However, governments continue to accept the principle that the state has a legitimate role to play in managing economic and social relations.[57] If there is an enduring Asian model of development, it is represented by this commitment, which an AMF may act to preserve.

The United States and the IMF have promoted an approach to international economics that accepts as an article of faith that the international flow of capital should be left to relatively unregulated market forces.[58] There are few compelling reasons to accept this approach and far more to believe that the free flow of international capital (as opposed to the open trade of goods) is inherently destabilizing and particularly dangerous to the comparatively fragile states of the developing world. This neoliberal position also rejects the notion that the state has anything but the most basic legitimate interventionary role to play in the economy. Many Asians perceive that the United States is using the IMF to take advantage of the crisis and open up Asian economies to unrestricted U.S. and foreign ownership and domination.[59]

Asians argue that an AMF should act as a buffer against future currency crises. It should shield Asian economies from the vagaries of the international market by providing emergency funds to threatened economies. In doing this it would implicitly protect these economies from being forced into structural adjustments that would run contrary to the political and social goals of the state government. The activities of the IMF and the U.S. Treasury during the crisis were based, in part, on the belief that Western financial markets needed to be involved in regional resource allocation. However, the failures of Western financial institutions in allocating resources in Asia helped fuel the speculative bubble; their panicked rush to the exits, even when Asian economic fundamentals remained strong, undermines their claim to any special economic insights or privilege. According to Wade, "the economic performance of the emerging Asian economies prior to the crisis suggests that Asian governments and their financial institutions can allocate resources more efficiently" than Western actors.[60]

An AMF that acted to protect Asian economies might well preserve economic inefficiencies and the political and social dominance of existing, and often corrupt, domestic elites. The call for an AMF may be an attempt by these elites to preserve themselves against the forces of change. However, an AMF independent of the IMF might also prevent the catastrophic effects of a future investor panic or the other kinds of economic instability produced by the volatile world financial system. It could serve the positive social purpose of protecting the weakest members of Asian society from social and economic disaster. For states that are dependent upon "performance legitimacy," that is, economic success , in order to preserve political stability, this is a fundamental concern.[61]

In the aftermath of the crisis, Asians remain committed to a globalized world economy. At the same time, however, many Asian states are pursuing economic solutions to the effects of the crisis that lead to greater government involvement in their economies. Bank restructuring in Japan, South Korea, and the affected Southeast Asian states, is extending government control and ownership of the financial sector. Malaysia's capital controls have elicited considerable regional support and have not prevented the country from undergoing a dramatic economic recovery, illustrating that adherence to the received Western economic wisdom may not be necessary after all.

Throughout all of Asia, government resources are fueling recovery and restructuring. Asian governments have agreed that they need to restructure their countries' financial systems radically and to promote economic transparency, but restructuring has been proceeding very slowly in most of the crisis-affected states. As regional economies recover and political and social opposition to economic restructuring solidifies, Asian governments are finding it more difficult to implement extensive economic reform.

Obstacles to the AMF

The first major problem confronting the idea of an AMF is its leadership. The obvious leader of an Asian Monetary Fund is Japan. Despite being locked in a ten-year recession, Japan is still the richest state in Asia. It possesses enormous reserves of wealth and foreign exchange. Japan would be the primary source of funds for an AMF. In 1997, Japan was willing to put $50 billion into the project, half the proposed AMF's budget. Japan has also quietly and persistently pursued the idea since its initial rejection by the West. Nonetheless, it is unlikely that Japan is prepared to exercise regional leadership or that other Asian states would accept its leadership.

Leading an AMF would probably lead Japan into conflict with the United States. Is Japan prepared for such a showdown? Little in the post–World War II record suggests that Japan is willing to antagonize the United States. So long as the Asia Pacific remains dependent upon the U.S. market to absorb its exports and the U.S. military to maintain regional stability, the relationship with the United States remains key to the economic and political health of the region—though it is important to note that the economic relationship between the United States and Asia is one of mutual vulnerability. The AMF may be the first step toward creating a more dynamic and internally focused Asian economic region that is less dependent on the U.S. market. If there is an East Asian region emerging, however, it is still in a nascent stage and is complicated by historical distrust and uneven economic interdependence among the Asian countries.

The leadership of an AMF requires some resolution of the rivalry between Japan and China. China rejected the original AMF proposal because it was unprepared to accept a Japanese-dominated economic institution that might be the first step toward creating a "yen bloc." China is now an active supporter of the AMF idea. It feels that curbing U.S. economic influence is more important than containing Japan. While the reasons for this shift are unclear, Paul Bowles suggests that NATO's war against Yugoslavia in 1999, and the bombing of the Chinese embassy in Belgrade during that conflict, caused China to redefine its perception of the U.S. role in the Asia Pacific.[62] Nonetheless, China's wariness of Japan continues. China's concerns about Japanese power have the potential to sabotage any efforts at creating effective regional institutions. Japan's uncertainty about China's regional intentions and influence are also relevant factors and will become more pronounced if and when China becomes more assertive in the Asia Pacific.

The tensions between the two most powerful Asia-Pacific states provide ASEAN with an opportunity to play an important role in the creation of new regional institutions. The ASEAN Plus Three meetings have resulted in the signing of currency-swap agreements that may be enough to combat future currency crises. The May 2000 meeting of ASEAN Plus Three was initially billed as an effort to discuss an AMF. In the end, a lack of support from the major economic powers forced the AMF onto the regional back burner. Yet, the swap agreement may be the first step toward an AMF.

ASEAN's Role in an Asian Monetary Fund

While neither China nor Japan would be willing to accept the dominance of the other, both can compromise and accept ASEAN as the fulcrum on which regional cooperation turns. As in the ARF, ASEAN's relative weakness makes it a suitable platform on which to build a new institution. Its intermediary position provides it with potentially considerable political influence within whatever institution may emerge. The Asian economic crisis placed ASEAN's institutional viability in serious jeopardy; it is unlikely that the organization can be reformed sufficiently to play a major role in future economic crises. However, the great-power realities of the Asia Pacific may create a new and important role for ASEAN in the larger region.

Nonetheless, the boost that ASEAN can gain from its intermediary position in the AMF should not be exaggerated. First, if there were an actual crisis that demanded action from the AMF, the new institution would create deep strains within ASEAN itself. There were significant differences between the ASEAN states on how to handle the Asian crisis. Singapore's leaders, in particular, were unsympathetic to the travails of their ASEAN neighbors. Their general attitude was that the crisis revealed important structural deficiencies and inefficiencies (such as rampant corruption) in the neighboring states, and they were reluctant to offer assistance outside of the confines of an IMF-approved bailout. In contrast, Malaysia has pushed for the establishment of an AMF that would provide unconditional loans to Asian countries. As Singapore is in a position to make a significant contribution to an AMF, it is unlikely that it would agree to what it might see as a waste of its resources. (A similar issue may arise with the existing currency-swap agreement). ASEAN is likely to break down along the lines of borrowers and lenders within an AMF.

The possibility of such divisions within a prospective AMF underlines another crucial consideration: how would the AMF operate? Some Asian states envision a mechanism that lends without conditionality. However, it has been clear from the outset that an AMF would attach some conditions to its loans—the conditions would just be less onerous than the IMF, more sensitive to Asian realities and stages of development, and more likely to allow greater periods of adjustment. The issues of how these terms are defined and who defines them, however, remain open and are potential time bombs within the AMF structure. Singaporean senior minister Lee Kuan Yew has argued that any Asian fund would need the backing of the IMF simply because the IMF is able and willing to deliver the hard medicine to its "patients":

> When you go into a country and impose discipline, it is going to be painful, whether it is in Thailand, in Indonesia or in Korea. Interest groups will rebel. Governments will be accused of having caved in. I do not see any Asian group in the ASEAN Regional Forum (ARF) strong enough to tell President Suharto, "You will do this or we will not support you." If you don't say that and do support him, that's money down the drain. So, we have to face the awful fact that in order to fix something wrong, bitter medicine has to be administered. If you ask me, I think you'd better get a doctor that is accustomed to administering bitter medicine. So, I'm not against the idea of an Asian Monetary Fund. But if you're gonna have one, we have to be very careful deciding on what terms it will be extended and who is administering the conditionalities.[63]

Once Asian members accept that some kind of conditionality must be attached to the AMF, the question of leadership comes, again, to the fore. ASEAN cannot define the terms of conditionality. ASEAN itself is too divided in the nature, economic outlooks, and political conditions of its members. As a group, the ASEAN states lack the economic clout to legitimately dominate the decisions of an AMF. But if ASEAN cannot lead the AMF, the question remains, who will? Even if China and Japan could somehow agree on a sharing of leadership, would the smaller, weaker regional states accept the dictates of the powerful regional players? Would Asians prefer the dictates of local powers over the IMF? Or would historical tensions make such a situation even more unpalatable than taking the IMF's medicine?

The second way in which ASEAN's limitations are made bare by the issue of leadership is in the inapplicability of ASEAN's methods of interaction to the proposed AMF. It is clear that the Asian model of institution building, as exemplified in ASEAN, has considerable limitations. Jeffrey Lewis argues that Asian proposals for the AMF imply an institution based around ASEAN-like methods of interaction. In his view, "An Asian Monetary Fund would eschew conflict with Asian governments, while its offers of aid would undercut the IMF's ability to pressure intransigent economies into mounting difficult but essential economic reforms . . . the appeal of an AMF largely appears to be a desire to avoid difficult reforms required by the IMF."[64]

Such a view of the competence of the IMF and Western liberal economics in the aftermath of the crisis is simplistic. Nonetheless, an AMF is not likely to adopt the "ASEAN way" of interaction. A critical difference between the AMF idea and ASEAN or APEC is that the AMF will be dependent upon wealthier members to provide emergency funds to members in more dire straits. This imbalance automatically creates an imbalance in power and resources that greatly complicates the dynamic of an AMF. The willingness of stronger and richer states to support an AMF would undoubtedly be contingent on their ability to set terms for the use of their resources in times of crisis. Consensus-oriented decisionmaking cannot work under such conditions.

ASEAN's political acceptability to others provides it with an advantageous position in any regional dialogue. However, in this position, ASEAN could not occupy a leadership role. The Asia Pacific would remain dominated by non-ASEAN powers. So long as China and Japan remain wary of each other, ASEAN can be an important intermediary. However, meaningful institutional development in the Asia-Pacific region will only be possible once the dominant regional powers learn to collaborate. If that happens, then ASEAN would find its intermediary position compromised.

This argument suggests that ASEAN's most meaningful role in the region for the foreseeable future is as a bridge between China and the rest of the Asia Pacific. This is an important role, but one contingent upon China's own political uncertainties and perceptions. Moreover, many ASEAN countries are still trying to determine what their relationship with China should be, especially in light of Chinese provocations in the South China Sea and their existing relationships with the United States. How individual ASEAN states resolve these questions has implications for intra-ASEAN unity, which is necessary to any influence ASEAN may have on regional developments. Nonetheless, acting as a bridge to China may present ASEAN with the focus that it needs to redefine itself after the economic crisis.

The prospects that an AMF, or some kind of regionally based financial institution, will take form are quite good. How effective it will be, however, is a different matter. Its chances of becoming a meaningful regional institution hinge on how Asia-Pacific states see the future. Are external financial shocks sufficiently threatening to their stability and independence that they would unite within an organization that would require them to sacrifice some sovereignty to larger regional actors? This is unclear. The Asian states are very jealous of their sovereignty. Most of them are still deeply engaged in the process of state building and feel too unstable to sacrifice sovereign capacity.[65] Yet, these same concerns with sovereignty, state building, and security could be what draw East Asia together and teach it to cooperate; these fundamental qualities are at risk if these states remain vulnerable to the international financial system. It may well take another destructive economic shock, or series of shocks, before the regional states decide that the sacrifices necessary to create an effective regional financial mechanism are worth making for longer-term economic and political independence. Ultimately, regional cooperation may be the best way to enhance the long-term sovereignty of the Asia-Pacific states.

The creation of an AMF does not mean that Asia will come into conflict with the economic vision of the United States and the West. The levels of interdependence and cooperation between the regions are very great. However, interregional tensions and a greater push toward various kinds of regionalism would probably increase. To offset the drive for an AMF, the West must be more accommodating and willing to compromise on the diversities of capitalism and culture that it considers acceptable. It will need to accept East Asia and its perspectives within the structures of the international system. (Many European states share many characteristics with "Asian capitalism" and would probably be happy to compromise.) Peter Preston argues that Asia is one of three economic blocs in the world (along with North America and Europe) that the international economy must accommodate. He argues that the economic crisis did not create enough of an upheaval to force cultural change within Asia, which is what is necessary for Asians to renounce their own economic and social arrangements and adopt a Western approach. Institutions such as the IMF, which reflect only one ideological and cultural disposition, require reform.[66] If existing structures, such as the IMF, prove willing to incorporate East Asian ideas and concerns, then the drive for Asian institutions may be deflated. However, such accommodation seems unlikely. The IMF represents an ideological position that has been at the root of U.S. perceptions about its own interests. In many ways, it is not an exaggeration to say that the United States fought the Cold War for the sake of its economic model. It may be unwilling to compromise on what it considers as core principles, especially at a time when it sees itself as the sole and ascendant world power.

During its formative period, the AMF needs an acceptable compromise candidate to serve as its foundation. ASEAN is ideal for this purpose, and this is a role that would greatly enhance its faltering prestige and utility. Over time, however, ASEAN would have to be supplanted by other actors. Ultimately, an AMF will only work if the largest and wealthiest powers in the region can reach an acceptable understanding regarding their own roles in the AMF. If they cannot, the AMF will not amount to an effective organization. If they can, they will no longer need ASEAN's good offices to alleviate tensions. In addition, the different levels of development, economic philosophy, and political dispositions within ASEAN are likely to cause further friction within the institution between the have and have-not Southeast Asian states. These divergent views would undermine ASEAN's ability to function as a united bloc. Ultimately, the AMF would end up supplanting many of ASEAN's functions as an economic organization, particularly if it ends up becoming the basis for a larger East Asian economic region and the foundation for a common Asian currency. ASEAN, the organization, would become lost within such a structure.

Even if ASEAN has difficulties in playing a leading role in the Asia Pacific, this does not preclude its individual members from implementing financial policies designed to protect them from international financial instability. In the aftermath of the crisis, the most affected regional economies are experiencing fairly rapid recoveries, though rates of unemployment and other social indicators have not yet recovered to precrisis levels in many states. All of the major crisis-affected states have liberalized their policies designed to encourage FDI. In most cases, this liberalization was part of IMF-sponsored restructuring, but the governments of the affected states have willingly adopted the policies. These strategies have been relatively successful in attracting FDI. However, most of this FDI has taken the form of mergers and acquisitions, particularly in the financial sector. Western investors are buying up Asian assets at fire-sale prices, precisely the kind of activity feared by political and figures and economic nationalists in Asian countries. Moreover, political and social opposition to these activities is beginning to develop in all the affected states, particularly South Korea and Thailand.[67]

ASEAN countries are suspicious of outside actors. The economic crisis has simply reinforced this tendency, albeit in a nontraditional and much more complex security area. The crisis has also underscored the vulnerability of ASEAN states to international economic forces. Countries such as Indonesia and Malaysia are not ideologically committed to economic liberalism and capitalist development. Anne Marie Murphy notes that most

Table 7.1   Mergers and Acquisitions by Foreign Firms in Affected Countries, 1998–2000, Announced Value (U.S.$ millions)

	1998	1999	2000
Indonesia	35.98	545.69	1,441.51
Republic of Korea	1,864.65	3,914.24	3,723.58
Malaysia	1,334.46	867.38	250.23
Philippines	1,478.64	293.03	1,126.69
Thailand	829.24	1,014.58	314.27

Source: Asian Development Bank, *Asia Recovery Report 2001* (Manila, Phillipines: Asian Development Bank, 2001), 83.

Indonesians find the idea of free markets and their associated effects to be questionable. This is especially the case in a country where a massive proportion of the national wealth lies in the hands of an ethnic minority, the Chinese community. Indonesians see the operation of free markets under such conditions to favor the advantages that already lie with wealthy ethnic Chinese and neo-imperialistic foreigners. Similarly, the Malaysian government has explicitly pursued policies meant to take advantage of "globalization" to serve specific political and economic goals. If the market does not operate to fulfill those goals, there is no reason to think that the government will simply facilitate the market.

If another economic crisis hits Southeast Asia in the future, it is far more likely that the ASEAN states, including Thailand, will implement policies of capital control and economic insulation, following the example of Malaysia in the 1997–1999 crisis. Attracting foreign investment to fuel regional development is not necessarily a goal worth pursuing at any price.[68] Moreover, implementing such policies may not be as detrimental to business investment as many neoliberal economists argue. The markets have not punished Malaysia for putting social and political stability before economic orthodoxy.

Even if East Asia does not succeed in creating a regional financial mechanism, local states will consider many other options before going to the IMF in the future. These alternative measures could include bilateral and multilateral currency swap agreements, as well as state-to-state loans between smaller states and the larger regional powers. China and Japan may well find their competition for regional influence determined by which country is more willing to offer financial support in time of crisis.

Conclusion

A mixed picture of ASEAN emerges from the East Asian economic crisis. The crisis revealed serious limitations in the organization. Those limitations were always present, but they were well concealed behind a facade of ASEAN unity. In the economic crisis, the ASEAN states were faced with direct threats to their domestic and regional economic and political stability. Under these conditions, their first instincts were to turn inward and away from regional responses. ASEAN's inability to deal with the environmental and security issues that arose during the course of the crisis accentuated the tension between its established practices and the new demands being placed upon it in a more complex regional environment. ASEAN was unable to adapt to these new realities.

The crisis did create a demand for regional financial architecture, however, which may give ASEAN a new lease on life. However, political and economic divisions within the Asia-Pacific region must be overcome before a regional financial mechanism can be truly effective. ASEAN can contribute to this process, but it is still limited by the weaknesses of its individual members.

Notes

1. The discussion in this section draws mostly upon the following sources: Ruland, 2000; Soesastro, 1999; Harris, 2000; Chang and Rajan, 1999; Denoon and Colbert, 1998–1999; Wesley, 1999; and Ahmad and Ghoshal, 1999.

2. "Hanoi Plan of Action," ; "Statement on Bold Measures, 6th ASEAN Summit, Hanoi, 16 December 1998," http: //www.asean.or.id/economic/invest/sum_bold.htm.

3. ASEAN Secretariat, 2000.

4. "Beggars and Choosers," 1997: 43–44.

5. Quoted in Soesastro, 1999: 164.

6. Chang and Rajan, 1999: 265.

7. Furtado and Storey, 2001: 2–3.

8. "At Arm's Length," 1998: 25. Singapore was also concerned that relinquishing firm control of its currency could make it much more vulnerable to regional economic forces.

9. Wesley, 1999: 59.

10. Thai Ministry of Foreign Affairs, 2000: pp. xx.

11. Ibid.

12. In September 2000, there were news reports that Thailand had suggested convening the Troika to try to bridge gaps between the SPDC government in Myanmar and the National League for Democracy (NLD), represented by Aung San Suu Kyi. Myanmar's government immediately rejected this proposal, and the Thai foreign ministry quickly pointed out that UN secretary-general Kofi Annan, not Thailand, had made the suggestion for Troika intervention. See Baruah, 2000; Thai Ministry of Foreign Affairs, 2000.

13. Nesadurai, 2000.

14. Ruland, 2000: 436.

15. "Limits of Politeness," 1998: 43–44.

16. Miller, 1997: 79–80; "Meanwhile," 1997: 41–42; Jayasankaran, 1998: 99; Ravenhill, 2000.

17. Ching, 1998: 32.

18. "Out of Its Depth," 1998: 25–26.

19. Ramcharan, 2000: 74–76.

20. Haake, 1999: 583.

21. Ibid.: 586–587. Haake makes it clear that other domestic and international political considerations also pushed Thailand's support of flexible engagement.

22. Tay, 1998; Cotton, 1999.

23. Cotton, 1999: 332.

24. Ibid., 333. The figure tallies $3.1 billion for fire damage and $1.4 billion for haze costs. This estimate is based on very conservative assumptions. It does not include the final toll by the end of 1998, or such things as ultimate health costs or consideration of costs to biodiversity. The burned area considered was also limited to 5 million hectares. The actual costs, therefore, are likely far higher.

25. Tay, 1998: 110.

26. Cotton, 1999: 348.

27. This comes to approximately 200,000 people. See East Timor Action Network, 2000.

28. Note that Singapore, initially, was uneasy about Indonesia's invasion of East Timor in 1975. It did not support Indonesia in the first UN vote on the invasion, in order to register its discomfort. The idea of a large state invading a smaller neighbor was too close to Singapore's own situation. Subsequently, however, it fell in line with the other ASEAN states.

29. In the referendum, 98.5 percent of eligible voters cast ballots; 78 percent voted for independence. Taylor, 1999: xiv.

30. Dupont, 2000.

31. Ibid.: 165.

32. Japan provided US$100 million of a $107 million INTERFET fund established to help developing countries cover expenses. Ibid.: 166.

33. Ibid.: 167. For further commentary, see Lee Kim Chew, 1999.

34. Suh, 1999.

35. East Timor Action Network, 2000: 2.

36. Vatikiotis and Dolven, 1999: 14, 16.

37. For a further discussion of how the Asian economic crisis has affected the regional security dialogue, see Cheeseman, 1999.

38. This discussion of the aftermath of the crisis draws primarily upon the following: Narine, 1999; Nischalke, 2000; Kurus, 1995; and Kurus, 1993.

39. Smith, 1999.

40. In this respect, ASEAN is in keeping with its traditional orientation. In the past, the organization focused on external security issues, such as the Vietnamese invasion of Cambodia, because it could not directly address intra-ASEAN conflicts. Keeping an external focus allowed the ASEAN states to develop better cooperative ties, while avoiding issues of contentions. See Narine, 1998.

41. Bergsten, 2000.

42. Higgott and Phillips, 2000.

43. See Higgott, 2000; Beeson, 2000; Rhodes and Higgott, 2000; Weiss, 2000; Pempel, 1999; Reich, 2000; Wade, 1998b; Kapstein, 1998; Radelet and Sachs, 1997; Haas and Litan, 1998; Bhagwati, 1998; Granville, 1999; Bird and Joyce, 2001; Sachs, 1997; Stiglitz, 2000; and Krugman, 1998.

44. The following discussion of the AMF is based upon, but not limited to, the following sources: Narine, 2001; Cumings, 1999: 25–30; Wessel and Davis, 1999; Bello, 1998b; Kristof and WuDunn, 1999; Hamada, 1998.

45. Wade and Veneroso, 1998b: 19–21.

46. Nordhaug, 2000.

47. Larry Summers, quoted in Wessel and Davis.

48. Examples of this are cited in Feinberg, 2000; Swain, 2000; "Common Interests," 1999; "Japan Investigates," 1999; "Thailand Pushes," 2000.

48. Bergsten, 2000: 23.

49. Alatas, 2001: 3.

50. Acharya, 1999; Christensen, 1999.

51. Montes and Popov, 1999.

52. Bergsten, 1998; Rose, 1999.

53. Rajan, 2000: 2–4.

54. Ibid.: 12.

55. Ibid.: 13.

56. Ibid.: 14.

57. Stubbs, 1995; Crawford, 2000; Beeson, 2000.

58. Helleiner, 1994; Bhagwati, 1998.

59. Dittmer, 2000.

60. Wade and Veneroso, 1998b: 21.

61. See chapters in Alagappa, 1995, and Alagappa, 1998.

62. Bowles, 2000: 21–27. Bowles also argues that China's irritation over not being given full credit by the United States for the Chinese role in promoting regional stability during the crisis as another contributing factor to China's change of attitude.

63. Lee Kuan Yew, quoted in Doronila, 2000.

64. Lewis, 1999.

65. Ayoob, 1995; Dauvergne, 1998.

66. Preston, 1998: 256–257; Higgott, 1998: 1–30.

67. Asian Development Bank, 2001: 76–86; For an excellent rundown on the economics of the crisis, see the *Asian Recovery Reports.*

68. Murphy, 2000; Welsh, 2000; Ho, 1998.

8

ASEAN in
the Twenty-First Century

A SEAN is at a threshold in its history. It may reform itself to become a much more formal and binding institutional structure. It may fade into irrelevance. It may continue to be a loosely structured organization, representing Southeast Asia in international forums on uncontentious issues on which its members have reached consensus. However, in the context of the changing international system, the status quo is probably unsustainable. ASEAN is too important as a symbol of political stability and regional cooperation in Southeast Asia to be easily discarded. Maintaining that symbolic value is contingent upon ASEAN functioning at a much higher level of efficacy than it has in the past. In order to be a unified, powerful voice for Southeast Asia on the international stage, ASEAN needs to demonstrate that it can manage regional economic and security issues. If it cannot do this, its credibility and legitimacy in the eyes of the international community will erode until the organization means little to either the international community or ASEAN's members.

ASEAN is dedicated to protecting and enhancing the sovereignty of its member states. This is its fundamental purpose and cannot be altered without destroying the organization. The reason that ASEAN is so preoccupied with sovereignty is because most of its member states are—or perceive themselves to be—institutionally weak. Their political legitimacy is usually under threat from within their own borders. The reform of ASEAN is limited by the capacity, legitimacy, and stability of its constituent parts. Only when the ASEAN states are confident of their own survival will they tolerate the risks involved in allowing ASEAN to function as a strong institution. It may be generations before most of the states possess the durability needed to make meaningful sacrifices of sovereignty. ASEAN, the organization, can assist in the state-building process—indeed, this is one of its primary functions. In the past, ASEAN has fulfilled this function by protecting its members from external intervention. ASEAN's ability to protect its members is linked to the respect that it enjoys on the international stage. That respect is dependent on ASEAN's effectiveness as a regime, which is tied to its members' willingness to concede to the organization significant powers and authority. Again, the reality of the ASEAN states' weakness becomes an obstacle to such reform.

The major impediment to ASEAN's institutional reform is the lack of common economic and political interests between its member states. The states have agreed on basic principles of international interaction in the past. These principles form the basis of ASEAN's normative structures. However, this agreement does not extend to more detailed issues of economic and political policies or perceptions of security needs. If the ASEAN countries could identify binding common interests in the economic and political spheres, then the organization stands a far greater chance of maturing into a potent regime. However, common interests cannot be easily invented or imagined. The basic interests of states emanate from domestic political and social considerations. If domestic factors push the ASEAN states toward greater international cooperation, then ASEAN may be the object of meaningful reform. On the other hand, if ASEAN members find their domestic concerns pushing them in incompatible directions, the organization will remain moribund.

Sovereignty and Identity

Over its history, ASEAN has evolved to serve two distinct (but related) and important purposes for its member states. The first is to provide a forum in which its members can meet on a regular basis. The organization does not directly address issues of contention between its members, but it has facilitated regular contacts that have alleviated the tensions between members. Still, observers may have exaggerated this alleviation effect. The ASEAN-Five countries had relatively little to fight about after the creation of ASEAN in 1967 and the various political and economic developments that have reinforced intra-ASEAN peace since that time occurred without the direct involvement of the organization. Nonetheless, the states accept that ASEAN, by its very existence, promotes regional peace.[1] Ironically, ASEAN's inability to address internal conflicts between its members means that the organization functions best when it has an external focus to its activities. An external focus allows ASEAN's members to meet on a regular basis and undergo the socialization process without having to contend with the tensions that might arise if the organization tried to address internal conflicts. ASEAN's handling of the Cambodian conflict is the best example of this dynamic at work.

ASEAN's second essential purpose has been to provide its members with a much louder and more influential voice on the international stage than any single ASEAN state could enjoy on its own. ASEAN's members were impressed by their ability to wield influence within international forums when dealing with Vietnam's invasion of Cambodia. This experience later helped motivate ASEAN's expansion to include Cambodia, Laos, Myanmar, and Vietnam and prompted those states to join ASEAN on the assumption that a unified ASEAN-Ten could wield even more influence than the ASEAN-Six.

In recent years, a third factor has reinforced ASEAN's appeal to its members. The international trend toward regional economic arrangements has caused ASEAN's members to see it as a potentially important economic organization. With the creation of AFTA, ASEAN may be on the verge of becoming a functional economic regime, albeit one that is meant to attract foreign investment rather than to facilitate regional economic integration. ASEAN's economic functions are also creating the need for a more deeply institutionalized and bureaucratized organization. ASEAN's importance to its members as an economic regime has increased accordingly.

ASEAN was designed to enhance and protect the sovereign rights of its member states. Its first two functions tie directly into this purpose. Alleviating tensions between members involves encouraging them to adhere to the institutions' basic rules, primary among these the principle of nonintervention. ASEAN's norms expand upon nonintervention and explicitly forbid certain kinds of behavior that would violate the sovereignty of member states. For example, ASEAN prohibits its members from using force to settle disputes. This norm contributes to regional peace and security, but it is also a direct extension of the focus on state sovereignty. States at peace are not violating each other's sovereign rights.

Today, the international community is debating the meaning and implications of sovereignty.[2] The idea that sovereignty is limited by considerations of human rights, and subject to the interpretation of outside organizations and states, has been widely disseminated by Western states in the post–Cold War world. This is a concept most ASEAN states vehemently reject. Nonetheless, coming to terms with the changing attitudes and norms of the Western world is a political necessity for ASEAN. Its global influence is connected to its members' legitimacy in the eyes of the international community, and the West constitutes a fundamentally important part of that community. The pressure upon ASEAN's understanding of sovereignty does not only come from without, however. Thailand and the Philippines have been at the forefront of efforts to introduce changes to the principle of nonintervention. The impact that domestic events can have upon regional neighbors was dramatically demonstrated during the 1990s.

ASEAN's continuing relevance—both to the outside world as well as some of its own members—is linked to how effectively it can manage these regional issues.

Can ASEAN undertake meaningful reform? The answer depends upon whether or not ASEAN is more than an instrumental institution to its members; does it, in fact, constitute a regional identity? If so, does this identity affect ASEAN's behavior? The answer to the first question is "yes." The answer to the second is a qualified "no." ASEAN does embody a regional identity, but that identity is too weak to alter its members' actions.

Amitav Acharya argues that regional community is formed around the basis of shared norms and the ASEAN states have shown a high degree of compliance with ASEAN's regulatory norms. However, the collective action that these norms encourage promotes the ability of states to act as separate, sovereign entities. In the case of ASEAN, the norms that are shared by the member states actually have the effect of limiting the sense of regional community. Jusuf Wanandi has argued that the ASEAN concept of "regional resilience" actually provides a bridge between ASEAN's focus on sovereignty and the ASEAN leaders' explicit desire to create a sense of Southeast Asian regionalism: "If each member nation can accomplish an overall national development and overcome internal threats, regional resilience will automatically result much in the same way as a chain derives its overall strength from the strength of its constituent parts."[3]

This argument does not hold up under scrutiny. The push for "national resilience," the concept described by Wanandi, does not automatically translate into a strong sense of regionalism. National resilience may eventually lead to a collection of strong states but not necessarily a strong region. Admittedly, as the concept of "regional resilience" implies, building individually strong states is probably a prerequisite to building a strong sense of regionalism. It is not apparent, however, that these two processes can occur concurrently or that they are complementary. In practice, ASEAN's norms conflict with the development of a strong Southeast Asian regionalism. ASEAN's leaders have always expressed the desire to create a regional identity, but at the time of the organization's creation, its members were too suspicious of each other to make the sacrifices necessary to make regionalism possible. More than three decades later, most member states appear no more ready to sacrifice sovereign power to a larger regional organization.

The argument of whether or not ASEAN embodies a regional identity is often addressed in terms of its cultural practices. Evidence that ASEAN's regional interactions are governed by cultural norms would be powerful evidence of a strong sense of regional identity. However, the evidence supporting this contention is unconvincing. Nikolas Busse recognizes the importance of ASEAN's commitment to sovereignty in determining its organizational imperatives. In discussing the development of ASEAN's norms, he notes, "the normative ideal of sovereignty became the standard prescription for almost every political disease in the region and the cornerstone of ASEAN's attempts at creating a regional order."[4] He goes on to argue that the cultural norms embodied in ASEAN, particularly the supposed Asian aversion to confrontational behavior, has significantly affected how the ASEAN states have dealt with regional issues. ASEAN's decision to oppose Vietnam's invasion of Cambodia through diplomatic means was in keeping with its "deepseated cultural dislike for confrontational social behaviour."[5] ASEAN's attempt to "socialize" China to regional norms through positive engagement reflects the same cultural predisposition against confrontation. Busse's points should not be dismissed out of hand. ASEAN's processes do reflect cultural considerations. However, neither ASEAN's diplomatic response to the invasion of Cambodia nor its attempt to engage China can be understood simply—or even primarily—as cultural responses to regional relations.

In the case of the Cambodian conflict, ASEAN's reaction was complex. First, it is actually not true that ASEAN avoided military force in its response to the invasion. Its organization of the Coalition Government of Democratic Kampuchea (CGDK) meant that it indirectly sponsored military action against the Kampuchean government. Numerous other factors accounted for ASEAN's approach, among these the inability of the ASEAN states to agree on security perceptions and the fact that most of the ASEAN countries did not feel militarily threatened by Vietnam. If Vietnam had actually posed a true military challenge to the ASEAN states, it may have provided ASEAN's members with the incentive to form a military alliance. It is much more likely, however, that ASEAN's members would have forged individual pacts with external security providers, much as Thailand did with China. The case of the Cambodian conflict does not demonstrate a cultural predisposition toward nonconfrontational behavior as much as it does a complex interweaving of divergent security and political interests and perceptions and the limited nature of the Vietnamese threat.

The China situation is equally complex. As discussed in Chapter 4, ASEAN does not know how to interpret China's future intentions. Treating China like an enemy is the surest way to make it one, which runs the additional risk of putting ASEAN on the wrong side of a major economic power. Moreover, individual ASEAN states have different interests in their dealings with China. There is no consensus on how to approach China, nor is there likely to be one. Finally, ASEAN states cannot be certain of the U.S. commitment to their security. There is no ally that ASEAN can depend upon to balance China in the region. Under these circumstances, attempting to engage and socialize China is the most appealing and viable option.

ASEAN's preference for nonlegalistic methods of interaction is also described as a manifestation of cultural differences between Asian and

Western approaches to multilateralism. Cultural considerations affect its informal and nonconfrontational approaches. However, such approaches are also well suited to an organization that places state sovereignty at the top of its hierarchy of values and interests. Consensus decisionmaking and a refusal to push reluctant partners toward common positions protect national prerogatives. Miles Kahler argues that Asian states, particularly those in ASEAN, reject legalization of regional institutions when it is to their disadvantage, not because of culturally distinct approaches to legalism. In organizations such as the ARF and APEC, Asians have resisted binding legal instruments because these would place too much influence in the hands of the most powerful nations, particularly the United States. Kahler argues that ASEAN is becoming more legalized as it is pushed by the requirements of AFTA. According to Kahler,

> the choice of legalization [for Asian states] is both *instrumental* and *strategic*. The choice of legalized institutions is instrumental in that it does not express deeper cultural preferences (or aversions). Instead, legalized institutions are primarily a means to other ends . . . The national choice of legalization in a particular context . . . results from a calculus that legalized institutions serve those goals, even when costs (particularly sovereignty costs) are taken into account.[6]

The analysis of this book supports this contention. Claims about the cultural distinctiveness of ASEAN's methods are overstated.

Throughout ASEAN's history, the ASEAN states have consistently placed national interests ahead of regional interests. Tobias Nischalke, in an attempt to "contribute to the debate about the essential nature of state interaction in Southeast Asia," reviews twenty of ASEAN's major foreign policy initiatives from across its first thirty years and comes to some unsurprising conclusions.[7] Of the twenty cases, seven clearly violated ASEAN's established methods. Policies that had significant regional consequences were advanced or implemented without consultation with other ASEAN states. Among these were the Thailand-China alliance of 1979, the Kuantan Declaration, and Thailand's policy reversal in 1988 in respect to Vietnam. Thirteen cases were resolved using the "ASEAN way" of consultation and consensus. However, there are considerable reasons to doubt that these cases reflect a sense of ASEAN identity, that states did not cooperate out of a sense of belonging to ASEAN, but for other reasons. In six of the thirteen cases, consensus emerged without the need for extensive negotiations. In these cases, the issues at stake were either widely accepted ASEAN principles or involved very little cost to individual ASEAN members. In the remaining seven cases substantial negotiations were necessary to achieve consensus. In these cases, Nischalke notes that ASEAN consensus was the product of external influences, usually external threat. The ASEAN states have usually only consulted each other in cases where ASEAN agreement was necessary to achieve state goals. When it was possible to achieve state objectives through unilateral initiatives, the ASEAN states did so.[8] ASEAN has, for the most part, not been motivated by sentiments of community or "we feeling." These qualities may exist, but they play relatively little role in explaining the actions of ASEAN's members.

ASEAN does form the basis for a regional identity. Its actual influence is difficult to demonstrate, but the fact that state actors believe the organization has positive effects on regional interaction is an important consideration. But how *important* is the ASEAN identity to its member states? Every state is constituted by many different and overlapping identities. These identities are frequently complementary, but they are also often competitive. Demonstrating the existence of an ASEAN identity says nothing about where this identity falls in the structure of identities that define the ASEAN countries.

The question of identity is central to the domestic and international politics of most ASEAN states. The ASEAN countries support Mohammed Ayoob's argument that the developing world is characterized by weak states that are attempting to create themselves as strong states.[9] Most of the ASEAN countries are contending with divisive forces within their borders. These divisions center around different ethnic, religious, and linguistic identities. The process of state building requires that states forge common national identities out of these divergent parts. The ASEAN states are, to varying degrees, caught up in this state-building process. Their focus on *constructing* national identities helps to explain the primacy of sovereignty within ASEAN. It also underscores the point that it is difficult to create an influential regional identity when national identities are still in the process of formation.

Most of the ASEAN states have only a tentative grip upon their sovereignty. Those that have a firm grip on sovereignty are relatively few, and are unconvinced of their own stability.[10] Indonesia is a newly emerging democratic state, besieged by political instability, ethnic tensions, and numerous separatist movements, which are looking for weakness in Jakarta in order to press their own advantages and agendas.[11] Malaysia is stable in comparison to Indonesia, but it is experiencing renewed ethnic tensions in the wake of the economic crisis. Demands from minorities for greater rights and less favoritism toward the Malay majority have been met by counter-demonstrations from Malays. Attempts by Malaysian political parties to court the Chinese minority's vote create a risk of unleashing an ethnic Malay backlash. Malaysia's history of ethnic conflict always bubbles just below the surface.

Singapore is well aware of the ethnic instability in its neighboring states. The ruling People's Action Party (PAP) insists on maintaining a firm grip on power, even though many observers feel that the PAP can afford to loosen that grip. The government itself remains unconvinced, however, and is still mired in a perception—not entirely unjustified—that Singapore is caught within a hostile external environment.[12] The Philippines is also afflicted with political instability and separatist violence. Its status as a democratic state relieves some of the pressure on the government but cannot still the forces of religious and ethnic separatism. Moreover, the durability of the Philippines democratic institutions is uncertain; in 2001, Philippine president Estrada was removed from power by unconstitutional means, even if the action was popular with much of the public. Brunei remains a monarchy that is uncertain of its status among regional states.

Among the newest ASEAN members, the situations are much the same. Vietnam and Laos are nominally communist states, with regimes that hold firmly to power but cannot be certain of their legitimacy among their own people. Cambodia is a multiparty state, but its political instability is obvious and manifest in political violence and continuing tensions between contending factions. Myanmar is led by a government that much of the international community condemns as illegitimate. The SPDC government has crushed the democratic movement in Myanmar and continues to be wary of the many separatist movements that have fought perpetual wars against the center for most of Myanmar's modern history.

Of all the ASEAN states, only Thailand is relatively secure as a state that is widely accepted as legitimate by its population. Thailand has relatively little to contend with in the way of serious separatist movements; it has managed to deal effectively with other ethnic tensions; and it is a vibrant and growing democracy. Thailand is also the state that has pushed most vigorously for ASEAN's institutional reform, particularly as it has been most directly affected by the policies of Myanmar. Of all the member states, Thailand can most afford to endure institutional reform and has the least to fear from organizational intervention in its domestic affairs.

ASEAN states resist ASEAN reform because almost every governing regime is seriously concerned about its hold on power. Most of them feel that they simply cannot afford to risk losing their hold on the reins of power. Many of these weak states may also lack the capacity to implement agreements that they might make within a more institutionally interventionist ASEAN. This argument is not concerned with the actual legitimacy of the governments in power within ASEAN states. What is important is that most of these governments resist ASEAN reform out of their sense of weakness.

As ASEAN countries become more democratic, their concern with their legitimacy should become less of an issue. However, the spread of democracy within ASEAN is a long-term process. Moreover, it hardly guarantees the institutional development of ASEAN. Whether they are democratic or not, ASEAN's members must recognize strong common interests before they will agree to grant ASEAN binding powers. Given the external economic orientation of ASEAN and the different economic and social policies followed by many of its members, it is unlikely that these countries will coordinate their policies in the near future. This kind of cooperation might evolve over time, but it would probably take many years to truly take root and would be contingent on external factors pushing a confluence of policies.

The reality that ASEAN is directed toward enhancing its members' sovereignty has not prevented the organization's ideals from occasionally coming into conflict with its members' perceptions of the actual requirements of sovereignty. ASEAN's members have usually not allowed ASEAN ideals to stop them from doing what they felt necessary. ASEAN, itself, is an ideal. Its principles and stated objectives reflect values and aspirations that may be shared, to differing degrees, by member states. However, attaining that ideal is not always possible. Circumstances and political realities force the states to compromise on the principles of ASEAN. Even in these cases, they are usually motivated by a general desire to enhance their sovereignty, though doing so might put them at odds with some of ASEAN's stated objectives.

This dynamic is illustrated by the disagreements within ASEAN over the issue of foreign bases. The ASEAN states that wished to maintain foreign bases insisted on this point because they recognized that their own security was best ensured through arrangements with foreign powers. In taking this position, they compromised the norm of regional autonomy. However, they enhanced their own security and thus their status as sovereign states. ASEAN represents only one part of the foreign policies of its member states. Usually, it is an important part but other interests often take precedence over ASEAN interests.

Acharya argues that socialization processes around the "ASEAN way" have contributed to a degree of "we feeling" within ASEAN. The ASEAN states share "a common feeling of regional belonging [that has] led to claims about institutional exceptionalism underpinning constructs such as the ASEAN way."[13] The ASEAN states do share an institutional culture that has helped relieve various tensions. ASEAN has tried, over the years, to consciously differentiate its politics and processes of interaction from other regional actors and organizations. This sense of ASEAN exceptionalism "has become a key aspect of ASEAN security discourse, and has facilitated community building."[14] However, Acharya concludes that ASEAN has contributed to a sense of collective identity in Southeast Asia but that the ASEAN members have not moved "decisively away from their identity as sovereignty-bound actors."[15] Ultimately, Acharya argues that events in the post–Cold War era are presenting ASEAN with challenges to its basic norms and practices that it may not be able to manage. ASEAN may be an institution that reached a peak as a nascent security community and is now in a state of decline. The argument presented here is not that ASEAN is in decline but, rather, that it has been fairly consistent in its application of its principles and its approach to issues of sovereignty. In the post–Cold War era, the changing nature of the international environment has exposed ASEAN to challenges that its basic approach cannot meet. Its limitations are not new, however, nor are they a product of interaction with the changing environment. They have been apparent and have affected the organization's development from its inception.

The Question of Socialization

The idea that ASEAN has "socialized" its member states into becoming part of a regional identity is generally accepted within the organization. However, who or what is truly socialized by the ASEAN process? It appears that it is the foreign policy elites within the foreign affairs ministries and academic institutions of the ASEAN countries who end up sharing a common identity with their counterparts across the region. This ASEAN identity is not necessarily shared by officials in other ministries, such as the defense and economic establishments. Indeed, Nischalke notes in his survey that most of the ASEAN state initiatives that disregarded the procedures of the ASEAN way were situations where states' foreign ministries *were not* involved.[16] ASEAN members' foreign ministries are the repositories of the ASEAN way.

Over time, this may change. Greater effort on the part of ASEAN to create regular meetings between economic and defense officials may create similar bonds. However, this development cannot be taken for granted. The attitudes of different officials to intraregional cooperation are influenced by their predispositions. While regular contacts between officials of different states can mitigate tensions, defense officials are conditioned to think in terms of protecting the territorial interests of their states. For many ASEAN countries, ongoing territorial disputes and other tensions may make extending the ASEAN identity into the defense establishment far more difficult. It should be less difficult to do so in the area of economics, but this will also be affected by the extent to which intra-ASEAN trade becomes a relevant factor.

The process of ASEAN socialization has also been at work, in a somewhat different way, between the leaders of the ASEAN states. The personal relationships of ASEAN leaders have been very important in helping to create a common ASEAN identity. The idea that ASEAN is most effective as an informal instrument, and that much of its business is carried out on the golf courses and in the corridors between meetings, is directly related to the personal relationships between regional leaders. If so much of ASEAN's stock is related to these personal connections, what happens when leadership changes?

As some ASEAN countries become more democratic, their leadership changes more rapidly, and the value of personal relationships between leaders is reduced. To date, ASEAN has been an elite-driven institution. Governments that are accountable to their electorates are more susceptible to public pressure and have less room in which to maneuver. The introduction of democracy in key ASEAN countries invites other complications. One of the reasons that Thailand's relations with Myanmar deteriorated throughout the 1990s and part of Thailand's motivation in calling for ASEAN institutional reform is because its democratically elected government is attempting to establish its democratic credentials with Western countries.[17] Within ASEAN, the situation is further complicated by the fact that none of the leaders and few of the bureaucrats who were present when ASEAN was first created are still in positions of power. The younger generation replacing them has a limited institutional memory and no recollection of the nature of regional relations before ASEAN. Their commitment to ASEAN is wanting.

The ASEAN identity is not part of the general public consciousness within the ASEAN states. Most citizens in member states have little idea of what the organization is or does; these people are still divided from their regional neighbors by languages, ethnicities, and other historical factors. The ASEAN identity is, therefore, quite shallow.

If democratically elected governments continue to spread in ASEAN states, the tensions between the democracies and the dictatorships within ASEAN will continue to grow. Moreover, the democratic states will find their own relationships deeply complicated by the realities of electoral politics. Pressure from human rights and political organizations within ASEAN democracies will influence intra-ASEAN relations. Pressure from vested interests which are competing with opposing interests in other ASEAN states will create other divisions. These developments support the contention that ASEAN needs to create solid institutional structures in order to manage the increasingly complex relations between its members that can be expected in the future. The informal mechanisms that have worked until now are too dependent upon too few people to guarantee the organization's future viability.

The importance of socialization to the ASEAN process raises questions about the role and influence of the newest members on the organization's social dynamic. Cambodia, Laos, Myanmar, and Vietnam are all too new to ASEAN to feel part of its corporate identity, however weak that identity might be. Such an identification can only develop over a long period of time and requires much more favorable interactive circumstances. In the meantime, these states have the potential to seriously disrupt ASEAN's functions, or at least delay the development of a more coherent and effective regional institution.

ASEAN in the Twenty-First Century

As ASEAN moves into the twenty-first century, it is faced with numerous difficulties. ASEAN's inability to address the Asian economic crisis effectively, however unfair that expectation may have been, has provided further impetus to demands that the organization reform its established methods of interaction to allow for greater intervention. The economic crisis, and other events from around the same time, such as the problem of regional haze and the East Timor situation, drove home the reality that the domestic circumstances in one ASEAN state can have repercussions across the rest of the region. To foreign investors in particular, Southeast Asia is a regional bloc. Under such conditions, the only way for the ASEAN countries to exercise some level of control or influence over regional events is for them to reform the organization and provide it with the capabilities to deal with regional problems. This implies creating an organization that is far more institutionalized and "legalized" than ASEAN's traditional structures allow. It also implies a "pooling of sovereignty" within ASEAN, rather than the "enhancing of sovereignty" that has characterized the organization until now.

Despite the apparent need to reform ASEAN to make it more relevant and effective in the modern world, it is highly unlikely that such reform is possible. A strongly institutionalized and binding ASEAN with the ability to intervene in, or even comment upon, the domestic politics and policies of its member states is diametrically opposed to everything that ASEAN has represented. ASEAN's principle of nonintervention has been the single greatest factor accounting for the association's durability. It is not simply that reforming ASEAN to be more institutionalized would be difficult for its member states; rather, any serious attempts to implement such reforms are virtually guaranteed to destroy ASEAN. ASEAN has survived because it has never pushed its members beyond what they are willing to accommodate. Its fundamental rules and practices have encouraged its members to put their own interests before any regional concerns. This focus on national interests is what made it appealing and nonthreatening to the newest ASEAN states. Reforming ASEAN to make it more intrusive will undermine the foundations of the organization's durability and abrogate the principles on which it was built.

If ASEAN cannot be reformed into a more intrusive and demanding—but more effective—organization, what are its prospects for the twenty-first century? ASEAN can continue to serve as a representative for Southeast Asia within international bodies, so long as its members can reach consensus on the relevant issues. Beyond this, however, its prospects for institutional growth do not look good. Its inability to reform is not just the result of a lack of political will on the part of ASEAN's leaders, or an example of entrenched elites holding onto power, though elements of both of these factors may be at work. Rather, ASEAN's limited capacity for reform reflects the domestic political realities of the ASEAN countries.

Given the importance of sovereignty, reform would be possible if ASEAN states could be convinced that being part of a more institutionalized ASEAN enhances their individual sovereignty. If faced with an environment where some significant erosion of sovereign power is inevitable, the ASEAN states might recognize that banding together and pooling their sovereignty into a more legalized, restrictive, and intrusive regime might actually be the lesser of two undesirable alternatives. Maintaining some element of independent action and interacting within an institution with compatible states that are sensitive to mutual problems would be far more desirable than being left as individual states to deal with political and economic pressures from the outside world.

There are a number of problems with this position. First, the ASEAN states would require conclusive demonstrations of their own inability to influence regional events, along with convincing evidence that a more united ASEAN can improve their ability to influence regional affairs. The latter point may be difficult to demonstrate, particularly as the nature of the forces affecting regional affairs changes. For example, no reform of ASEAN would have been enough to offset the devastating effects of the Asian economic crisis. ASEAN simply lacked the financial resources to deal directly with that problem, and its internal disunity would have prevented any concerted action even if the resources had been available. Yet, a credible argument can be made that ASEAN may have been able to have an indirect influence on the crisis. A strongly united ASEAN could possibly have bargained more effectively with the IMF. Perhaps a Thailand supported by the foreign reserves of all the ASEAN states might have been enough to dissuade currency speculators and reassure foreign investors, thereby nipping the economic crisis in the bud. Given the psychological factors that contributed to the crisis, and bearing in mind that currency-swap arrangements between the ASEAN states did exist before the crisis, an effective intra-ASEAN financial arrangement may have had the desired effect. However, there are no guarantees that a more united ASEAN could have had this kind of influence. Given the history of the institution, it is clear that ASEAN members would not accept a significant reform of the organization without a very convincing case that the associated sacrifices would be clearly beneficial.

Beyond this practical problem, however, there are more fundamental difficulties with reform. These center on the different economic and political outlooks of ASEAN's members. Divergent economic, security, and political interests have limited intra-ASEAN cooperation from the inception of the organization. In the future, attaining sophisticated regional economic cooperation will require a level of policy coordination and compatibility between the ASEAN states that does not exist. For example, the ASEAN states do not share a consensus over the causes of the economic crisis, let alone how to address it. These kind of disagreements need to be overcome before any fully integrated ASEAN regime can become a reality. This development is very far down the road.

This argument suggests that ASEAN is, for all practical purposes, largely incapable of substantive reform. For most ASEAN states, the gains to be had by making significant sacrifices of sovereignty to a restructured ASEAN are simply too uncertain to justify those sacrifices. This individualistic approach may leave the ASEAN states at the mercy of international forces. However, for the individual ASEAN states, other relationships might afford them better protection than their membership in ASEAN.

The operation of international economic forces poses a serious threat to the stability and integrity of many ASEAN countries. These economic forces also have the potential to undermine the development of democracy within ASEAN. However, access to international capital also has the potential to further state and economic development in Southeast Asia. As the Asian economic crisis demonstrated, the proper management of international economic forces requires a strong and, preferably, legitimate state to mediate the effects of these forces on society. For the most part, ASEAN states recognize these factors, but they are unsure of how to deal with them. ASEAN countries need to find a position that allows them to benefit from the inflow of international capital and investment while still maintaining the ability to direct those benefits toward social and economic development. The ASEAN states are faced with the necessity of creating themselves as strong states while contending with many factors, such as domestic ethnic, religious, and linguistic divisions, that mitigate against the creation of strong states.

If the ASEAN states were able to coordinate economic, social, and political goals among themselves, the organization could form the basis of a significant "point of resistance" to the current operation of global capitalism. Their lack of consensus on these issues, however, means that resistance to Western-style capitalism, which is developing in some parts of Southeast Asia, will have to focus around powerful outside actors. China stands as the state most able to fulfill this role. It is a real and potential economic powerhouse, which has its own distinct understanding of regional economics, supports the right of sovereign states to manage their domestic affairs without external intervention, and already understands its traditional regional role as being protector of the smaller Asian countries. China's ambivalent relationship with many ASEAN states is an impediment to its assuming a leadership role in the region. However, if it employs a careful diplomacy that is sensitive to the fears of Southeast Asian states, it may be able to overcome local suspicions of its intentions. The emergence of Chinese leadership in Southeast Asia may undermine ASEAN, but it may provide the basis for a stronger East Asian community.

In the aftermath of the economic crisis, many non-ASEAN states have realized that ASEAN is a far less coherent body than they had thought, and these states may be willing to exploit that evident weakness. If this happens, then ASEAN's value to its members, which lies largely in its ability to project international influence, will erode further. ASEAN enjoys the loyalty and support of most of its members largely because it promises them international influence. If ASEAN cannot fulfill this promise, then many of its members, particularly the newest ones, will cease to support the organization. Yet, ASEAN's influence is contingent on the support and unity of its members. The organization is caught in a catch-22 situation: without demonstrable international influence, it will lose the commitment of its members; yet, without that commitment it cannot be a major international actor.

If ASEAN has run into its limits as a political organization, it may be breaking new ground as an economic entity. AFTA seems to be slowly but inexorably evolving into a more stable and institutionalized mechanism. If this trend continues, AFTA may begin to define ASEAN, and through it ASEAN may become a functional regime, an organization focused around a well-defined purpose and embodying clear rules and procedures. Over time, this economic cooperation could form the basis for more institutionalized and sustainable political cooperation. However, it is important not to exaggerate AFTA's importance or its potential as the basis for more extensive cooperation within ASEAN. The relatively low level of intra-ASEAN trade remains a constant reminder that the ASEAN countries' economies are oriented outward. Singapore, has diligently pursued trading agreements with its major trading partners, such as Japan and the United States. Other ASEAN states can be expected to follow suit. Unless intra-ASEAN trade becomes ever more important, ASEAN will remain of secondary economic importance to its members. This will limit what the organization can achieve in terms of political and economic integration.

Conclusion

ASEAN's prospects for institutional reform in the twenty-first century are not encouraging. The emerging international environment requires that states band together and work cooperatively if they hope to control or mitigate the effects of global economic and political forces. Yet the ASEAN states are too divided in their economic and political outlooks and levels of development to agree on common positions. Moreover, even if the ASEAN states could agree on shared economic and political interests, the kind of coordination required of states cooperating within a strong international institution may be beyond the capacity of many ASEAN members.

ASEAN forms the foundation of a regional identity in Southeast Asia. However, that identity is very weak, especially when compared to the various ethnic, religious, and linguistic identities that crisscross the region. ASEAN's established members favor and encourage the growth of regionalism, but their more pressing priority is in creating national identities among their own domestic constituencies. A sense of regionalism does exist in Southeast Asia, but it is too weak to be reliably invoked, and it rarely motivates the actions of ASEAN's members.

ASEAN has always walked a narrow line between encouraging a sense of regionalism while implementing practices and promoting norms that emphasize the value and primacy of state sovereignty. These two approaches are incompatible but managed to coexist so long as expectations of ASEAN were low and its activities could be focused outside of its own membership. In an era when the Asia Pacific, despite its strategic uncertainty, is more peaceful than it has been in decades, ASEAN no longer has an external focus. The issues that now demand regional management are emanating from within the ASEAN region itself or are directly and significantly affecting the domestic politics of its member states. ASEAN was never designed to deal with these kinds of concerns.

ASEAN remains an important symbol of political and economic stability in Southeast Asia. The institution will continue to exist for the foreseeable future. However, as an active and meaningful international institution, it is at risk of fading into irrelevance. ASEAN's greatest potential for real development is in the realm of regional economics. If AFTA prospers, ASEAN's institutional raison d'être may be satisfied. Over time, as other factors promote intra-ASEAN economic development, the organization may find itself capable of building on a strong foundation of common interest between its members. However, it is more likely that the economic development of the ASEAN states will be toward the rest of East Asia and the Western world.

ASEAN is an organization that has run up against its own inherent limitations. These limitations have always been present and consistent in their effects. In the contemporary period, they are simply more obvious. ASEAN has never been able to shape the interests of its members. The objectives that they pursue have always reflected their own particular agendas and concerns and have been determined mostly by domestic political and economic considerations. Today, ASEAN needs a level of commitment from its members that they are unwilling to give.

Notes

1. For discussion of these issues, see Kurus, 1993: 819–829, and Kurus, 1995.
2. See, for example, Philpott, 2001, and Krasner, 2000.
3. Wanandi, quoted in Acharya, 2001: 58.
4. Busse, 1999: 47.
5. Ibid., 50.
6. Kahler, 2000: 562.
7. Nischalke, 2000: 90.
8. Ibid.: 103–106. Most of the cases that Nischalke discusses and categorizes have been mentioned in this book.
9. Ayoob, 1995. Also, see Dauvergne, 1998.
10. See chapters in Alagappa, 1998, and Alagappa, 1995.
11. MacDonald and Lemco, 2001.
12. Leifer, 2000.
13. Acharya, 2001: 202.
14. Ibid.: 203.
15. Ibid.
16. Nischalke, 2000: 104.
17. Haake, 1999: 587–592; Snitwongse, 1997: 96–99.

Abbreviations

ABM	Anti-Ballistic Missile
ABRI	Armed Forces of Indonesia
ACU	ASEAN Cooperation Unit
ADB	Asian Development Bank
AFTA	ASEAN Free Trade Area
AIA	ASEAN Investment Area
AIC	ASEAN Industrial Complementation Scheme
AIPs	ASEAN Industrial Projects
AMM	Annual Ministerial Meeting
ANS	Armée Nationale Sihanoukiste
APEC	Asia-Pacific Economic Cooperation Forum
ARF	ASEAN Regional Forum
ARF-SOM	ARF Senior Officials Meeting
ASA	Association of Southeast Asia
ASCU	ASEAN Surveillance Coordinating Unit
ASEAN	Association of Southeast Asian Nations
ASEAN-ISIS	ASEAN-Institutes of Strategic Studies
ASEAN-PMC	ASEAN-Post-Ministerial Conferences
ASEM	Asia-Europe Summit Meeting
ASC	ASEAN Standing Committee
ASP	ASEAN Surveillance Process
ASPAC	Asian Pacific Council
ASTSU	ASEAN Technical Support Unit
CBC	Central Bank of China
CGDK	Coalition Government of Democratic Kampuchea
CLOB	Central Limit Order Book
CPP	Cambodian People's Party
CSCA	Council for Security and Cooperation in Asia
CSCE	Council for Security and Cooperation in Europe

DFAT	Australian Department of Foreign Affairs and Trade
DRV	Democratic Republic of Vietnam
DSG	deputy secretary-general
DSM	disputes settlement mechanism
ECAFE	Economic Commission for Asia and the Far East
EEC	European Economic Community
EEZs	Exclusive Economic Zones.
EU	European Union
EVSL	Early Voluntary Sectoral Liberalization
FDI	foreign direct investment
FPDA	Five Power Defence Arrangement
FUNCINPEC	Front Uni pour un Cambodge Independent, Neutre et Pacifique
GDP	gross domestic product
ICJ	International Court of Justice
ICK	International Conference on Kampuchea
IISS	International Institute for Stategic Studies
IMF	International Monetary Fund
INTERFET	International Force for East Timor
ISG	Inter-Sessional Support Group
ISM	Inter-Sessional Meetings
JIM	Jakarta Informal Meetings
KPNLF	Khmer People's National Liberation Front
KR	Khmer Rouge
MAPHILINDO	Malaya-Phillipines-Indonesia
MCP	Malayan Communist Party
MDT	Mutual Defence Treaty
MFN	most-favored nation
MST	Mutual Security Treaty
NAFTA	North American Free Trade Agreement
NICs	Newly Industrialized Countries
NLD	National League for Democracy
ODA	offical development assistance
OECD	Organization for Economic Cooperation and Development
PAP	People's Action Party
Perm-Five	Permanent Members of the UN Security Council
PICC	Paris International Conference on Cambodia
PKI	Communist Party of Indonesia
PLA	People's Liberation Army
PPP	purchasing power parity
PRC	People's Republic of China
PRK	People's Republic of Kampuchea

PTA	preferential trading arrangements
SEAARC	Southeast Asian Association for Regional Cooperation
SEAC	South-East Asia Command
SEATO	Southeast Asian Treaty Organization
SEOM	Senior Economic Officials Meeting
SLORC	State Law and Order Restoration Council
SNC	Supreme National Council
SOC	Senior Officials Committee
SOC	State of Cambodia
SOM	Senior Officials Meeting
SPDC	State Peace and Development Council
SRV	Socialist Republic of Vietnam
TAC	Treaty of Amity and Co-operation in Southeast Asia
UNCLOS	United Nations Convention on the Law of the Sea
UNTAC	United Nations Transitional Authority in Cambodia
ZOPFAN	Zone of Peace, Freedom and Neutrality
ZOPIGN	Zone of Peace, Independence and Genuine Neutrality

References

Abdulgaffar, Peang-Meth. (1992) "The United Nations Peace Plan, the Cambodian Conflict, and the Future of Cambodia." *Contemporary Southeast Asia,* vol. 14, no. 1 (June): 33–46.

Acharya, Amitav. (1990) *A Survey of Military Cooperation Among the ASEAN States: Bilateralism or Alliance?* Occasional Paper no. 14. Toronto: Centre for International and Strategic Studies.

———. (1993) *A New Regional Order in South-East Asia: ASEAN in the Post–Cold War Era.* Adelphi Paper no. 279. London: International Institute for Strategic Studies.

———. (1994) *An Arms Race in Post–Cold War Southeast Asia? Prospects for Control.* Pacific Strategic Paper no. 8. Singapore: Institute of Southeast Asian Studies.

———. (1995a) "A Regional Security Community in Southeast Asia?" *Journal of Strategic Studies,* vol. 18, no. 3 (September): 175–200.

———. (1995b) "Transnational Production and Security: Southeast Asia's 'Growth Triangles.'" *Contemporary Southeast Asia,* vol. 17, no. 2, September: 173–185.

———. (1996) "Defence Cooperation and Transparency in Southeast Asia." In Bates Gill and J. N. Mak, eds., *Arms, Transparency, and Security in Southeast Asia,* SIPRI Research Report no. 13, Oxford University Press, 1997: 49–62.

———. (1999) "A Concert of Asia?" *Survival,* vol. 41, no. 3 (Autumn): 84–101.

———. (2000) *The Quest For Identity: International Relations of Southeast Asia.* Singapore: Oxford University Press.

———. (2001) *Constructing a Security Community in Southeast Asia.* London: Routledge.

Acharya, Amitav, and Paul Evans. (1994) *China's Defence Expenditures: Trends and Implications.* Toronto: Joint Centre for Asia-Pacific Studies.

Aggarwal, Vinod K. (1993) "Building International Institutions in Asia-Pacific." *Asian Survey,* vol. 33, no. 11 (November): 1029–1042.

Ahmad, Zakaria Haji, and Baladas Ghoshal. (1999) "The Political Future of ASEAN After the Asian Crisis." *International Affairs,* vol. 75, no. 4: 759–778.

Alagappa, Muthiah. (1988) "Japan's Political and Security Role in the Asia-Pacific Region." *Contemporary Southeast Asia* vol. 10, no. 1 (June): 17–54.

———. (1989) "U.S.-ASEAN Security Relations: Challenges and Prospects." *Contemporary Southeast Asia,* vol. 11, no. 1 (June): 1–39.

———. (1990) "The Cambodian Conflict: Changing Interests." *The Pacific Review,* vol. 3, no. 3: 266–271.

———. (1991a) "The Dynamics of International Security in Southeast Asia: Change and Continuity." *Australian Journal of International Affairs,* vol. 45 (May): 1–37.

———. (1991b) "Regional Arrangements and International Security in Southeast Asia: Going Beyond ZOPFAN." *Contemporary Southeast Asia,* vol. 12, no. 4: 269–305.

———. (1993) "Regionalism and the Quest for Security: ASEAN and the Cambodian Conflict." *Journal of International Affairs,* vol. 46, no. 2 (Winter): 439–467.

———, ed. (1995) *Political Legitimacy in Southeast Asia.* Stanford, Calif.: Stanford University Press.

———, ed. (1998) *Asian Security Practice.* Stanford, Calif.: Stanford University Press.

Alatas, Ali. (2001) *"ASEAN Plus Three" Equals Peace Plus Prosperity.* Singapore: Institute of Southeast Asian Studies.

Almonte, Jose. (1997–1998) "Ensuring Security the 'ASEAN Way.'" *Survival,* vol. 39, no. 4 (Winter): 80–92.

Amer, Ramses. (1993) "Sino-Vietnamese Relations and Southeast Asian Security." *Contemporary Southeast Asia,* vol. 14, no. 4 (March): 314–331.

———. (1999) "Conflict Management and Constructive Engagement in ASEAN's Expansion." *Third World Quarterly,* vol. 20, no. 5: 1031–1048.

"America and Japan: Friends in Need." (1996) *The Economist,* April 13: 17–19.

"America's Chinese Puzzle." (1996) *The Economist,* May 25: 35–36.

"Anger of a Nation." (1995) *Far Eastern Economic Review,* March 30: 24.

Antolik, Michael. (1990) *ASEAN and the Diplomacy of Accommodation.* Armonk, N.Y.: M. E. Sharpe.

———. (1994) "The ASEAN Regional Forum: The Spirit of Constructive Engagement." *Contemporary Southeast Asia,* vol. 16, no. 2 (September):117–136.

Anwar, Dewi Fortuna. (1993a) "The Rise in Arms Purchases: Its Significance and Impacts on South East Asian Political Stability." Unpublished paper, University of Toronto, April.

———. (1993b) "Sijori: ASEAN's Southern Growth Triangle: Problems and Prospects." Unpublished paper, University of Toronto, April.

Arif, Mohamed. (1996) "Outlooks for ASEAN and NAFTA Externalities." In Shoji Nishjima and Peter H. Smith, eds., *Cooperation or Rivalry? Regional Integration in the Americas and the Pacific Rim.* Boulder, Colo.: Westview Press, 209–224.

Arif, Mohamed, and Hal Hill (1985) *Export-Oriented Industrialisation: the ASEAN Experience.* Sydney: Allen and Unwin.

ASEAN Secretariat. (1997) "Chapter Five: Co-operation within a Narrower Framework: Growth Triangles in ASEAN," in *ASEAN Economic Co-operation.* Singapore: Institute of Southeast Asian Studies, 137–156.

———. (2000) "The ASEAN Secretariat: Basic Mandate, Functions and Composition," (http://www.aseansec.org).

Asian Development Bank. (2000) *Asian Development Outlook 2000.*

———. (2001) "Tracking Asia's Recovery—A Regional Overview." *Asia Recovery Report 2001.* Manila, Phillipines: Asian Development Bank.

"Asia's Economic Crisis: How Far is Down?" (1997) *The Economist,* November 15: 19–21.

"Asia's Economies: On Their Feet Again?" (1999) *The Economist,* August 21: 16–18.

"Asia's Flagging Alliance." (1996) *The Economist,* April 13:13–14.

"At Arm's Length." (1998) *Far Eastern Economic Review,* February 19: 25.

"Austerity Overdose." (1998) *Far Eastern Economic Review,* January 22: 21.

Australian Department of Foreign Affairs and Trade. (1997) *The New ASEANs: Vietnam, Myanmar, Cambodia and Laos.* Canberra: Department of Foreign Affairs and Trade (www.dfat.gov.au./eaau/new_asia.pdf).

Ayoob, Mohammed. (1995) *The Third World Security Predicament.* Boulder, Colo.: Lynne Rienner Publishers.

Ba, Alice. (1997) "The ASEAN Regional Forum: Maintaining the Regional Idea in Southeast Asia." *International Journal,* vol. 52, no. 4 (Autumn): 635–656.

"Bah, Humbug." (1998) *Far Eastern Economic Review,* December 25, 1997–January 1: 5.

Baker, Richard. (1998) "The United States and APEC Regime Building." In Vinod Aggarwal and Charles Morrison, eds., *Asia Pacific Crossroads: Regime Creation and the Future of APEC.* New York: St. Martin's Press.

Baker, Richard, and Charles E. Morrison, eds. (2000) *Asia Pacific Security Outlook 2000.* Tokyo: Japan Center for International Exchange.

Bandow, Doug. (2001) *Needless Entanglements: Washington's Expanding Security Ties in Southeast Asia.* Policy Analysis no. 401 (May 24). Washington, D.C.: Cato Institute.

Bank for International Settlements. (1998) *68th Annual Report, Chapter VII: Financial Intermediation and the Asian Crisis.* Manila: Bank for International Settlements (http://www.bis.org./publ/).

Baruah, Amit. (2000) "Thai Move for 'Truce' in Myanmar." *The Hindu,* September 27.

Beeson, Mark. (1999) "Reshaping Regional Institutions: APEC and the IMF in East Asia." *The Pacific Review,* vol. 12, no. 1: 1–24.

———. (2000) "The Political Economy of East Asia at a Time of Crisis." In Richard Stubbs and Geoffrey Underhill, eds., *Political Economy and the Changing Global Order,* 2d ed. Toronto: Oxford University Press, 352–361.

"Beggars and Choosers." (1997) *The Economist,* December 6: 43–44.

Bello, Walden. (1998a) "The End of a Miracle." *Multinational Monitor,* January/February: 10–16.

———. (1998b) Testimony of Walden Bello before Banking Oversight Subcommittee, Banking and Financial Services Committee, U.S. House of Representatives, April 21.

Berger, Mark T. (1999) "APEC and Its Enemies: The Failure of the New Regionalism in the Asia-Pacific." *Third World Quarterly,* vol. 20, no. 5: 1013–1030.

Bergsten, Fred. (1998) "Reviving the 'Asian Monetary Fund.'" *International Economics Policy Brief,* December.

———. (2000) "East Asian Regionalism: Towards a Tripartite World." *The Economist,* July 15–21: 23–26.

Bernstein, Richard, and Ross H. Munro. (1997) "China I: The Coming Conflict with China." *Foreign Affairs,* vol. 76, no. 2 (March/April): 18–32.

Bert, Wayne. (1993) "Chinese Policies and U.S. Interests in Southeast Asia." *Asian Survey,* vol. 33, no. 3 (March): 320–321.

Bhagwati, Jagdish. (1998) "The Capital Myth." *Foreign Affairs,* vol. 77, no. 3, (May/June): 7–12.

Bird, Graham, and Joseph P. Joyce. (2001) "Remodeling the Multilateral Financial Institutions." *Global Governance,* vol. 7, no. 1 (January–March): 75–93.

Bowles, Paul. (1997) "ASEAN, AFTA and the 'New Regionalism.'" *Pacific Affairs,* vol. 70, no. 2 (Summer): 219–233.

————. (2000) *Asia's Post-Crisis Regionalism: Bringing the State Back In, Keeping the (United) States Out.* Mimeograph (October). Prince George, B.C.: University of Northern British Columbia.

Bowles, Paul, and Brian Maclean. (1996) "Understanding Trade Bloc Formation: The Case of the ASEAN Free Trade Area." *Review of International Political Economy,* vol. 3, no. 2 (Summer): 319–348.

Breckon, Lyall. (2001) "Solid in Support of the U.S. . . . So Far." *Comparative Connections,* vol. 3, no. 3, (October):10 (http://www.csis.org/pacfor/cc/0103Qus_asean.html).

Busse, Nikolas. (1999) "Constructivism and Southeast Asian Security." *The Pacific Review,* vol. 12, no. 1: 39–60.

Buszynski, Leszek. (1990) "Declining Superpowers: The Impact on ASEAN." *The Pacific Review,* vol. 3, no. 3: 259–260.

————. (1992) "Southeast Asia in the Post–Cold War Era." *Asian Survey,* vol. 32, no. 9 (September): 830–847.

Caballero-Anthony, Mely. (1998) "Mechanisms of Dispute Settlement: The ASEAN Experience." *Contemporary Southeast Asia,* vol. 20, no1 (April): 38–66.

Castro, Amado. (1982) "ASEAN Economic Co-operation." In Alison Broinowski, ed., *Understanding ASEAN.* New York: St. Martin's Press, 70–91.

Chaiwhat Khamchoo. (1991) "Japan's Role in Southeast Asian Security: 'Plus ca change . . . '" *Pacific Affairs,* vol. 64, no. 1 (Spring): 7–22.

Chalmers, Malcolm. (1997) "ASEAN and Confidence Building: Continuity and Change after the Cold War." *Contemporary Security Policy,* vol. 18, no. 1 (April): 36–56.

Chanda, Nayan. (1986) *Brother Enemy: The War After the War.* New York: Harcourt Brace Jovanovich.

————. (1990) "Vietnam's Withdrawal from Cambodia: The ASEAN Perspectives." In Gary Klintworth, ed., *Vietnam's Withdrawal from Cambodia: Regional Issues and Realignments.* Canberra Papers on Strategy and Defense no. 64. Canberra: Australian National University, 75–91.

————. (1995) "Fear of the Dragon." *Far Eastern Economic Review,* April 13: 24–28.

Chanda, Nayan, Rigoberto Tiglao, and John McBeth. (1995) "Territorial Imperative." *Far Eastern Economic Review* February 23: 14–16.

Chang Ha-Joon. (1998) "South Korea: The Misunderstood Crisis." In K. S. Jomo, ed., *Tigers in Trouble.* London: Zed Books: 222–231.

Chang Li Kin and Ramkishen S. Rajan. (1999) "Regional Responses to the Southeast Asian Financial Crisis: A Case of Self-Help or No Help?" *Australian Journal of International Affairs,* vol. 53, no. 3: 261–281.

Chang Pao-Min. (1987) "China and Southeast Asia: The Problem of a Perceptional Gap." *Contemporary Southeast Asia* vol. 9 , no. 3 (December): 181–193.

————. (1990) "A New Scramble for the South China Sea Islands." *Contemporary Southeast Asia,* vol. 12, no. 1 (June): 20–39.

Chatterjee, Srikanta. (1990) "ASEAN Economic Co-operation in the 1980s and 1990s." In Alison Broinowski, ed., *ASEAN into the 1990s.* London: Macmillan, 58–82.

Cheeseman, Graeme. (1999) "Asian-Pacific Security Discourse in the Wake of the Asian Economic Crisis." *The Pacific Review,* vol. 12, no. 3: 333–356.

Chen Jie. (1994) "China's Spratly Policy: With Special Reference to the Philippines and Malaysia." *Asian Survey,* vol. 34, no. 10 (October): 893–903.

Chen Qimao. (1993) "New Approaches in China's Foreign Policy." *Asian Survey,* vol. 33, no. 3, (March): 237–251.

Cheng, Joseph Y. S. (1999) "China's ASEAN Policy in the 1990s: Pushing for Regional Multipolarity." *Contemporary Southeast Asia,* vol. 21, no. 2 (August): 176–204.

Cheung, Tai Ming. (1990) *Growth of Chinese Naval Power: Priorities, Goals, Missions, and Regional Implications.* Pacific Strategic Paper no. 1. Singapore: Institute of Southeast Asian Studies.

Chia Siow Yue. (1998) "The ASEAN Free Trade Area." *The Pacific Review,* vol. 11, no. 2: 213–232.

Chin Kin Wah. (1993) "Regional Perceptions of China and Japan." In Chandran Jeshurun, ed., *China, India, Japan and the Security of Southeast Asia.* Singapore: Institute for Southeast Asian Studies, 3–25.

———. (1995) "ASEAN: Consolidation and Institutional Change." *The Pacific Review,* vol. 8, no. 3: 424–439.

———. (1997) "ASEAN: The Long Road to 'One Southeast Asia.'" *Asian Journal of Political Science,* vol. 5, no. 1 (June): 1–19.

Ching, Frank. (1998) "Are Asian Values Finished?" *Far Eastern Economic Review,* January 22: 32.

Christensen, Thomas J. (1999) "China, the U.S.-Japan Alliance, and the Security Dilemma in East Asia." *International Security,* vol. 23, no. 4 (Spring): 49–80.

Chu, Yun-han. (1999) "Surviving the East Asian Financial Storm: The Political Foundations of Taiwan's Economic Resilience." In T. J. Pempel, ed., *The Politics of the Asian Economic Crisis,* Ithaca, N.Y.: Cornell University Press, 184–202.

"Common Interests." (1999) *Asiaweek,* vol. 25, no. 49 (December 10).

Cossa, Ralph. (2000) "Multilateralism Sputters Along, as North Korea Continues to Grab the Spotlight." *Comparative Connections,* vol. 2, no. 2 (October): (http://www.csis.org/pacfor/).

———. (2001) "Ushering in the Post Post Cold War Era." *Comparative Connections,* vol. 3, no. 3, (July–September): (http://www.csis.org/pacfor/cc/0103Qoverview.html).

Cotton, James. (1999) "The 'Haze' over Southeast Asia: Challenging the ASEAN Mode of Regional Engagement." *Pacific Affairs,* vol. 72, no. 3 (Fall): 331–351.

Crawford, Darryl. (2000) "Chinese Capitalism: Cultures, the Southeast Asian Region and Economic Globalisation." *Third World Quarterly,* vol. 21, no. 1: 69–86.

Cribb, Robert. (1998) "Myanmar's Entry into ASEAN: Background and Implications." *Asian Perspective,* vol. 22, no. 3: 49–62.

Crone, Donald. (1992) "The Politics of Emerging Pacific Cooperation." *Pacific Affairs,* vol. 65, no. 1 (Spring): 68–83.

Cumings, Bruce. (1999) "The Asian Crisis, Democracy, and the End of 'Late' Development." In T. J. Pempel, ed. *The Politics of the Asian Economic Crisis.* London: Cornell University Press, 17–44.

Dauvergne, Peter, ed. (1998) *Weak and Strong States in Asia-Pacific Societies.* Canberra: Allen and Unwin.

Demetriades, Panicos O., and Bassam A. Fattouh. (1999) "The South Korean Financial Crisis: Competing Explanations and Policy Lessons for Financial Liberalization." *International Affairs,* vol. 75, no. 4: 779–792.

Deng, Yong. (1999) "Conception of National Interests: Realpolitik, Liberal Dilemma and the Possibility of Change." In Yong Deng and Fei-Ling Wang, eds., *In the Eyes of the Dragon.* Lanham, Md.: Rowman and Littlefield, 47–72.

Deng, Yong, and Fei-Ling Wang. (1999) "Introduction: Toward an Understanding of China's Worldview." In Yong Deng and Fei-Ling Wang, eds., *In the Eyes of the Dragon.* Lanham, Md.: Rowman and Littlefield, 1–19.

Denoon, David B. H., and Evelyn Colbert. (1998–1999) "Challenges for the Association of Southeast Asian Nations (ASEAN)." *Pacific Affairs,* vol. 71, no. 4 (Winter): 505–523.

Denoon, David B. H., and Wendy Frieman. (1996) "China's Security Strategy: The View from Beijing, ASEAN and Washington." *Asian Survey,* vol. 36, no. 4: 422–439.

Dibb, Paul. (1995) *Towards a New Balance of Power in Asia.* Adelphi Paper no. 295 (May). London: International Institute for Strategic Studies.

Dibb, Paul, David D. Hale, and Peter Prince. (1998) "The Strategic Implications of Asia's Economic Crisis." *Survival,* vol. 40, no. 2 (Summer): 5–26.

Dills, Barry K., and Dong-Sook S. Gills. (2000) "South Korea and Globalization: The Rise to Globalism?" In Samuel S. Kim, ed., *East Asia and Globalization.* Lanham, Md.: Rowman and Littlefield: 81–104.

Dittmer, Lowell. (2000) "Globalization and the Asian Financial crisis." in Samuel S. Kim, ed., *East Asia and Globalization,* New York, Rowman and Littlefield: 31–53.

Djalal, Hasjim, and Ian Townsend-Gault. (1999) "Managing Potential Conflicts in the South China Sea: Informal Diplomacy for Conflict Prevention." In Chester A. Crocker, Fen Osler Hampson, and Pamela Aall, eds., *Herding Cats.* Washington, D.C.: United States Institute of Peace, 109–133.

Doronila, Amando. (2000) "An Asian Fund Needs IMF Backing." *Philippine Daily Inquirer Interactive,* June 14.

Dosch, Jorn. (1997) *PMC, ARF and CSCAP: Foundations for a Security Architecture in the Asia Pacific?* Strategic and Defence Studies Centre Working Paper no. 307 (June). Canberra: Strategic and Defence Studies Centre.

Drysdale, Peter, and Andrew Elek. (1997) "APEC: Community-Building in East Asia and the Pacific." In Donald C. Hellman and Kenneth B. Pyle, eds., *From APEC to Xanadu.* Armonk, N.Y.: M. E. Sharpe, 37–69.

Dupont, Alan. (2000) "ASEAN's Response to the East Timor Crisis." *Australian Journal of International Affairs,* vol. 54, no. 2: 163–170.

East Timor Action Network. (2000) "ASEAN's Commitment to New Nation Tested." East Timor Action Network.

Economy, Elizabeth C. (1999) "Reforming China." *Survival,* vol. 41, no. 3 (Autumn): 21–42.

Eichengreen, Barry. (1999) "Appendix C: Understanding Asia's Crisis," in *Toward A New International Financial Architecture.* Washington, D.C.: Institute for International Economics, 143–169.

Emmerson, Donald K. (1984) "'Southeast Asia': What's in a Name?" *Journal of Southeast Asian Studies,* vol. 15, no. 1 (March): 1–21.

Evans, Grant, and Kelvin Rowley. (1990) *Red Brotherhood at War: Vietnam, Cambodia and Laos Since 1975.* London: Verso.

Feinberg, Richard. (2000) "Distrustful Asia Looks Inward for Financial Solutions." *Straits Times Interactive,* July 1.

Ferguson, Joseph. (2001) "Will Terrorism Be a Salve for Bilateral Relations?" *Comparative Connections,* vol. 3, no. 3 (July–September): (http://www.csis.org/pacfor/cc/0103Qus_rus.html).

Findlay, Trevor. (1994) "South-East Asia and the New Asia-Pacific Security Dialogue," in *SIPRI Yearbook 1994.* Oxford: Oxford University Press, 125–147.

Foot, Rosemary. (1998) "China in the ASEAN Regional Forum." *Asian Survey,* vol. 38, no. 5 (May): 425–440.

Frost, Frank. (1990) "Introduction: ASEAN Since 1967—Origins, Evolution and Recent Developments." In Alison Broinowski, ed., *ASEAN into the 1990s*. London: Macmillan, 1–31.

Furtado, Xavier. (1999) "International Law and the Dispute over the Spratly Islands: Whither UNCLOS?" *Contemporary Southeast Asia*, vol. 21, no. 3 (December): 386–404.

Furtado, Xavier, and Jim Storey. (2001) "Peering into Darkness: Evaluating the Prospects for an Economic and Financial Monitoring and Surveillance Mechanism in the Asia Pacific Region." Unpublished paper.

Gallagher, Michael G. (1994) "China's Illusory Threat to the South China Sea." *International Security*, vol. 19, no. 1 (Summer): 169–194.

Gallant, Nicole, and Richard Stubbs. (1997) "APEC's Dilemmas: Institution-Building Around the Pacific Rim." *Pacific Affairs*, vol. 70, no. 2 (Summer): 203–218.

Ganesan, N. (1995) "Testing Neoliberal Institutionalism in Southeast Asia." *International Journal*, vol. 50, no. 4 (Autumn): 779–804.

———. (1999) *Bilateral Tensions in Post–Cold War ASEAN*. Pacific Strategic Papers no. 9. Singapore: Institute of Southeast Asian Studies.

Garner Noble, Lela. (1977) *Philippine Policy Toward Sabah: A Claim to Independence*. Tucson: University of Arizona Press.

Garofano, John. (1999) "Flexibility or Irrelevance: Ways Forward for the ARF." *Contemporary Southeast Asia*, vol. 21, no. 1 (April): 74–94.

Garrett, Banning, and Bonnie Glaser. (1994) "Multilateral Security in the Asia-Pacific Region and its Impact on Chinese Interests: Views from Beijing." *Contemporary Southeast Asia*, vol. 16, no. 1 (June): 13–34.

Glaser, Bonnie S. (1993) "China's Security Perceptions: Interests and Ambitions." *Asian Survey*, vol. 33, no. 3 (March): 252–271.

———. (2001) "Terrorist Strikes Give U.S.-China Ties a Boost." *Comparative Connections*, vol. 3, no. 3 (July–September): (http://www.csis.org/pacfor/cc/0103Qus_china.html).

Goad, G. Pierre. (1999a) "An Upgrade for Asia." *Far Eastern Economic Review*, September 30: 67.

———. (1999b) "Wiser in Washington." *Far Eastern Economic Review*, October 7: 86.

Granville, Brigitte. (1999) "Bingo or Fiasco? The Global Financial Situation Is Not Guaranteed." *International Affairs*, vol. 75, no. 4: 713–728.

Green, Michael J., and Benjamin L. Self, (1996) "Japan's Changing China Policy: From Commercial Liberalism to Reluctant Realism." *Survival*, vol. 38, no. 2 (Summer): 35–58.

Guan, Ang Cheng. (2000) "The South China Sea Dispute Revisited." *Australian Journal of International Affairs*, vol. 54, no. 2: 201–215.

Haake, Jurgen. (1999) "The Concept of Flexible Engagement and the Practice of Enhanced Interaction: Intramural Challenges to the 'ASEAN Way.'" *The Pacific Review*, vol. 12, no. 4: 581–611.

Haas, Michael. (1991) *Genocide by Proxy: Cambodian Pawn on a Superpower Chessboard*. New York: Praeger.

Haas, Richard N., and Robert E. Litan. (1998) "Globalization and Its Discontents." *Foreign Affairs*, vol. 77, no. 3 (May/June): 2–6.

Hamada, Koichi. (1998) "IMF Special: Keeping Alive the Asian Monetary Fund." *Capital Trends*, vol. 3, no. 10 (September 25).

Hanggi, Heiner. (1991) *ASEAN and the ZOPFAN Concept*. Singapore: Institute of Southeast Asian Studies.

Harding, Harry. (1997) "Agenda for the ASEAN Regional Forum." *ISEAS Trends,* October 25–26: 1.

Harris, Stuart. (2000) "Asian Multilateral Institutions and Their Response to the Asian Economic Crisis: The Regional and Global Implications." *The Pacific Review,* vol. 13, no. 3: 495–516.

Helleiner, Eric. (1994) "From Bretton Woods to Global Finance: A World Turned Upside Down." In Richard Stubbs and Geoffrey Underhill, eds., *Political Economy and the Changing Global Order.* Toronto: McClelland and Stewart, 163–175.

Hellman, Donald C., and Kenneth B. Pyle, eds. (1997) "Appendix I: Chronology of Significant Events in APEC's History," in *From APEC to Xanadu.* Armonk, N.Y.: M. E. Sharpe, 203–208.

Henderson, Jeannie. (1999) *Reassessing ASEAN.* Adelphi Paper no. 328 (May). London: International Institute for Strategic Studies.

Hiebert, Murray. (1995) "Comforting Noises." *Far Eastern Economic Review,* August 10: 14–16.

———. (1997) "All for One." *Far Eastern Economic Review,* August 7: 26.

Hiebert, Murray, and Adam Schwartz. (1995) "But Can They Sing Karaoke?" *Far Eastern Economic Review,* August 3: 23–24.

Higgott, Richard. (1998) *The Asian Economic Crisis: A Study in the Politics of Resentment.* CSGR Working Paper no. 02/98 (March). Warwick, UK: Centre for the Study of Globalisation and Regionalisation.

———. (2000) "Regionalism in the Asia-Pacific: Two Steps Forward, One Step Back?" In Richard Stubbs and Geoffrey Underhill, eds., *Political Economy and the Changing Global Order,* 2d ed. Toronto: Oxford University Press: 254–263.

Higgott, Richard, Andrew Fenton Cooper, and Jenelle Bonnor. (1990) "Asia-Pacific Economic Cooperation: An Evolving Case-Study in Leadership and Co-operation Building." *International Journal,* vol. 45 (Autumn): 823–866.

Higgott, Richard, and Nicola Phillips. (2000) "Challenging Triumphalism and Convergence: The Limits of Global Liberalization in Asia and Latin America." *Review of International Studies,* vol. 26 (July): 359–379.

Hill, Hal. (1999) "An Overview of the Issues." In H.W. Arndt and Hal Hill, eds., *Southeast Asia's Economic Crisis: Origins, Lessons and the Way Forward.* Singapore: Institute of Southeast Asian Studies, 1–15.

Hinds, Antonia, and Oliver Sprague. (1996) "Arms Transfers in East Asia." *Pacific Research,* 22 (August): 22–24.

Ho Khai Leong. (1998) "Malaysia's Conceptions of Security: Self-Resilience, Sovereignty and Regional Dynamics." *Asian Perspective,* vol. 22, no. 3: 63–101.

Hoang Anh Tuan. (1994) "Vietnam's Membership in ASEAN: Economic, Political and Security Implications." *Contemporary Southeast Asia,* vol. 16 (December): 259–273.

Holloway, Nigel. (1995) "Missed Opportunity: U.S. and Japan Postpone Their Defence Declaration." *Far Eastern Economic Review,* November 30: 16.

Hornik, Richard. (1994) "Bursting China's Bubble." *Foreign Affairs,* vol. 73, no. 3 (May/June): 28–49.

Hu Weixing. (1995) "China's Security Agenda After the Cold War." *The Pacific Review,* vol. 8, no. 1: 117–135.

Hutchcroft, Paul. (1999) "Neither Dynamo nor Domino: Reforms and Crises in the Philippine Political Economy." In T.J. Pempel, ed., *The Politics of the Asian Economic Crisis.* Ithaca, N.Y.: Cornell University Press, 163–183.

Huxley, Tim. (1990) "ASEAN Security Co-operation—Past, Present and Future." In Alison Broinowski, ed., *ASEAN into the 1990s.* London: Macmillan, 83–111.

————. (1993) *Insecurity in the ASEAN Region.* London: Royal United Services Institute for Defence Studies.

"If Nanny Retires." (1990) *The Economist,* May 12: 38.

"Innocents Abroad: Bill Clinton's Commitment to Asia." (1996) *Far Eastern Economic Review,* May 2: 2.

International Institute for Strategic Studies. (1997) *The Military Balance 1997/98.* Oxford: Oxford University Press.

————. (1998) *The Military Balance 1998/1999.* Oxford: Oxford University Press.

————. (1999) *The Military Balance 1999/2000.* Oxford: Oxford University Press.

————. (2000) *The Military Balance 2000/2001.* Oxford: Oxford University Press.

Irvine, Roger. (1982) "The Formative Years of ASEAN: 1967–1975." In Alison Broinowski, ed., *Understanding ASEAN.* New York: St. Martin's Press, 8–36.

"Japan Investigates the Creation of an Asian Monetary Fund." (1999) Stratfor.com, February 11.

"Japan Makes a Stand, Sort Of." (1997) *The Economist,* December 20: 47.

"Japan's Stumble Felt Around the Globe." (1998) *The Globe and Mail,* June 13: A1, A16.

Jayasankaran, S. (1998) "Blah, Blah." *Far Eastern Economic Review,* November 26: 99.

Johnson, Chalmers. (1997) "The Chinese Way." *The Bulletin of Atomic Scientists,* January–February: 23.

Johnston, Alistair Iain. (1999) "The Myth of the ASEAN Way? Explaining the Evolution of the ASEAN Regional Forum." In Helga Haftendorn, Robert O. Keohane, Celeste A. Wallander, eds., *Imperfect Unions.* New York: Oxford University Press, 287–324.

Jomo, K. S. (1997) *Southeast Asia's Misunderstood Miracle,* Boulder, Colo.: Westview Press.

————. ed. (1998) *Tigers in Trouble.* London: Zed Books.

Jorgenson-Dahl, Arnfinn. (1982) *Regional Organisation and Order in Southeast Asia.* London: Macmillan.

Kahler, Miles. (2000) "Legalization as Strategy: The Asia-Pacific Case." *International Organization,* vol. 54, no. 3 (Summer): 549–571.

Kapstein, Ethan B. (1998) "Global Rules for Global Finance." *Current History,* vol. 97, no. 622 (November): 355–360.

Karp, Aaron. (1990) "Military Procurement and Regional Security in Southeast Asia." *Contemporary Southeast Asia,* vol. 11, no. 4 (March): 334–362.

Kattoulas, Velisarios. (2001) "Sorry is the Hardest Word." *Far Eastern Economic Review,* March 8: 56–59.

Khoo How San. (1993) "ASEAN and the South China Sea Problem." In Chandran Jeshurun, ed., *China, India, Japan and the Security of Southeast Asia.* Singapore: Institute of Southeast Asian Studies, 181–207.

Klare, Michael. (1993) "The Next Great Arms Race." *Foreign Affairs,* vol. 72, no. 3 (Summer): 136–152.

————. (1997) "East Asia's Militaries Muscle Up," *The Bulletin of Atomic Scientists,* January–February: 56–61.

Kraft, Herman Joseph S. (2000) "ASEAN and Intra-ASEAN Relations: Weathering the Storm?" *The Pacific Review,* vol. 13, no. 3: 453–472.

Krasner, Stephen D. (2000) *Problematic Sovereignty.* New York: Columbia University Press.

Krauss, Ellis S. (2000) "Japan, the US, and the Emergence of Multilateralism in Asia." *The Pacific Review,* vol. 13, no. 3: 473–494.

Kristof, Nicholas. "Beware the Dragon Armed to the Teeth." (1993) *The Globe and Mail,* January 12, p. A7.

―――. (1998) "The Problem of Memory." *Foreign Affairs,* vol. 77, no. 6 (November/December): 37–49.

Kristof, Nicholas D., and Sheryl WuDunn. (1999) "Of World Markets, None an Island." *New York Times,* February 17: A1.

Krugman, Paul. (1998) "The Confidence Game." *The New Republic,* November 5.

Kumar, Rajiv, and Bibek Debroy. (1999) *The Asian Crisis: An Alternate View.* Economic Staff Paper no. 59. Manila, Phillipines: Asian Development Bank.

Kumar, Sree. (1994) "Johor-Singapore-Riau Growth Triangle: A Model of Subregional Cooperation." In Myo Thant, Min Tang, and Hiroshi Kakazu, eds., *Growth Triangles in Asia.* Hong Kong: Oxford University Press: 175–217.

Kurus, Bilson. (1993) "Understanding ASEAN: Benefits and Raison d'Etre." *Asian Survey,* vol. 33, no. 8 (August): 819–831.

―――. (1995) "The ASEAN Triad: National Interest, Consensus-Seeking, and Economic Co-operation." *Contemporary Southeast Asia,* vol. 16, no. 4 (March): 404–419.

Lampton, David. (1998) "China: Think Again." *Foreign Policy,* no. 110 (Spring): 13–27.

Lasater, Martin L. (1996) *The New Pacific Community.* Boulder, Colo.: Westview Press.

Lauridsen, Laurids S. (1998) "Thailand: Causes, Conduct, Consequences." in K. S. Jomo, ed., *Tigers in Trouble.* London: Zed Books, 137–161.

"Law of the Gun." (1997) *Far Eastern Economic Review,* July 17: 14–15.

Lawrence, Susan V., and Bruce Gilley. (1999) "Bitter Harvest." *Far Eastern Economic Review,* April 29: 22 (www.feer.com/1999/9904_29/p22china.html).

Lee Kim Chew. (1999) "Politics Behind ASEAN's Inaction." *Straits Times,* October 17.

Lee Lai To. (1995) "ASEAN and the South China Sea Conflicts." *The Pacific Review,* vol. 8, no. 3: 531–543.

Lee, Yeon-ho. (2000) "The Failure of the Weak State in Economic Liberalization: Liberalization, Democratisation and the Financial Crisis in South Korea." *The Pacific Review,* vol. 13, no. 1: 115–131.

Leifer, Michael. (1968) *The Philippine Claim to Sabah.* Zug, Switzerland: Inter-Documentation/University of Hull.

―――. (1989) *ASEAN and the Security of Southeast Asia.* London: Routledge, 1989.

―――. (1993) "Indochina and ASEAN: Seeking a New Balance." *Contemporary Southeast Asia,* vol. 15 (December): 269–279.

―――. (1996) *The ASEAN Regional Forum.* Adelphi Paper no. 302 (July). London: International Institute for Strategic Studies.

―――. (1999) "The ASEAN Peace Process: A Category Mistake." *The Pacific Review,* vol. 12, no. 1: 25–38.

―――. (2000) *Singapore's Foreign Policy: Coping with Vulnerability.* New York: Routledge.

Lewis, Jeffrey. (1999) "Asian vs. International: Structuring an Asian Monetary Fund." *Harvard Asia Quarterly,* Autumn.

Lim, Linda Y. C. (1999) "Free Market Fancies: Hong Kong, Singapore, and the Asian Financial Crisis." in T. J. Pempel, ed., *The Politics of the Asian Economic Crisis.* Ithaca, N.Y.: Cornell University Press: 101–115.

Lim, Robyn. (1998) "The ASEAN Regional Forum: Building on Sand." *Contemporary Southeast Asia,* vol. 20, no. 2 (August): 115–136.

"The Limits of Politeness." (1998) *The Economist,* February 28: 43–44.

Luhulima, C. P. F. (1994) "The Performance of ASEAN Economic Cooperation." *The Indonesian Quarterly*, vol. 22, no. 1: 15–21.

MacDonald, Scott, and Jonathan Lemco. (2001) "Indonesia: Living Dangerously." *Current History*, vol. 100, no. 645 (April): 176–182.

MacIntyre, Andrew. (1997) "South-East Asia and the Political Economy of APEC." In Garry Rodan, Kevin Hewison, and Richard Robison, eds., *The Political Economy of South-East Asia*. Melbourne: Oxford University Press: 225–246.

———. (1999a) "Political Institutions and the Economic Crisis in Thailand and Indonesia." In H. W. Arndt and Hal Hill, eds., *Southeast Asia's Economic Crisis: Origins, Lessons and the Way Forward*. Singapore: Institute of Southeast Asian Studies, 142–157.

———. (1999b) "Political Institutions and the Economic Crisis in Thailand and Indonesia." In T. J. Pempel, ed., *The Politics of the Asian Economic Crisis*. Ithaca, N.Y.: Cornell University Press: 143–162.

———. (2001) "Institutions and Investors: The Politics of the Economic Crisis in Southeast Asia." *International Organization*, vol. 55, no. 1 (Winter): 81–122.

Mack, Andrew, and Desmond Ball. (1992) "The Military Build-up in Asia-Pacific." *The Pacific Review*, vol. 5, no. 3: 197–208.

Mackie, J. A. C. (1974) *Konfrontasi: The Indonesia-Malaysia Dispute, 1963–1966*. London: Oxford University Press.

Mak, J. N. (1991) "The Chinese Navy and the South China Sea: A Malaysian Assessment." *The Pacific Review*, vol. 4, no. 2: 150–161.

———. (1994) "Armed but Ready? ASEAN Conventional Warfare Capabilities." *Harvard International Review*, vol. 16, no. 2: 20–24.

———. (1995) "The ASEAN Naval Build-up: Implications for the Regional Order." *The Pacific Review*, vol. 8, no. 2: 303–325.

Martin, Linda G., ed. (1987) *The ASEAN Success Story*. Honolulu: University of Hawaii Press.

Martin, Marie Alexandrine. (1994) *Cambodia: A Shattered Society*. Berkeley and Los Angeles: University of California Press.

McCarthy, Stephen. (2000) "Ten Years of Chaos in Burma: Foreign Investment and Economic Liberalization Under the SLORC-SPDC 1988–1998." *Pacific Affairs*, vol. 73, no. 2 (Summer): 233–262.

McNally, Christopher A., and Charles E. Morrison, eds. (2001) *Asia Pacific Security Outlook 2001*. Tokyo: Japan Center for International Exchange.

"Meanwhile, Back Where the Wagons are Circling. . . ." (1997) *The Economist*, November 29: 41–42.

Menon, Jayant. (1996) *Adjusting Towards AFTA*. Singapore: Institute of Southeast Asian Studies.

Miller, Matt. (1997) "APEC: Which Way Ahead?" *Far Eastern Economic Review*, November 27: 79–80.

Moffett, Sebastian. (1995) "Presidential Priorities." *Far Eastern Economic Review*, November 30: 15.

Moller, Kay. (1998) "Cambodia and Myanmar: The ASEAN Way Ends Here." *Asian Survey*, vol. 38, no. 12 (December): 1087–1104.

Montes, Manuel F. (1998) *The Currency Crisis in Southeast Asia*. Singapore: Institute of Southeast Asian Studies.

Montes, Manuel F., and Muhammad Ali Abdusalamov. (1998) "Indonesia: Reaping the Market." In K. S. Jomo, *Tigers in Trouble*. London: Zed Books, 162–180.

Montes, Manuel F., and Vladmir V. Popov. (1999) "Chapter Five: The Currency Crises in East Asia," in *The Asian Crisis Turns Global.* Singapore: Institute of Southeast Asian Studies, 67–90.

Morrison, Charles E., ed. (1999) *Asia Pacific Security Outlook 1999.* Tokyo: Japan Center for International Exchange.

Murphy, Ann Marie. (2000) "Indonesia and Globalization." In Samuel S. Kim, ed., *East Asia and Globalization.* Lanham, Md.: Rowman and Littlefield, 209–232.

Nagara, Bunn. (1995) "The Notion of an Arms Race in the Asia-Pacific." *Contemporary Southeast Asia,* vol. 17, no. 2 (September): 186–206.

Naidu, G. (1994) "Johor-Singapore-Riau Growth Triangle: Progress and Prospects." In Myo Thant, Min Tang, and Hiroshi Kakazu, eds., *Growth Triangles in Asia.* Hong Kong: Oxford University Press: 218–242.

Naidu, G. V. C. (2000) *Indian Navy and Southeast Asia.* New Delhi: Institute for Defence Studies and Analyses.

Narine, Shaun. (1997) "ASEAN and the ARF: The Limits of the 'ASEAN Way.'" *Asian Survey,* vol. 37, no. 10 (October): 961–978.

———. (1998) "ASEAN and the Management of Regional Security." *Pacific Affairs,* vol. 71, no. 2: 195–214.

———. (1999) "ASEAN into the Twenty-First Century: Problems and Prospects." *The Pacific Review,* vol. 12, no. 3: 357–380.

———. (2001) "ASEAN and the Idea of an 'Asian Monetary Fund': Institutional Uncertainty in the Asia Pacific." In Andrew T. H. Tan and J. D. Kenneth Boutin, eds., *Non-Traditional Security Issues in Southeast Asia.* Singapore: Select Publishing-IDSS, 227–256.

Nesadurai, Helen E. S. (2000) "In Defence of National Economic Autonomy? Malaysia's Response to the Financial Crisis." *The Pacific Review,* vol. 13, no. 1: 73–113.

———. (2001) "Cooperation and Institutional Transformation in ASEAN: Insights for Regional Governance from the AFTA Project." In Andrew Tan and Kenneth Boutin, eds., *Non-Traditional Security Issues in Southeast Asia.* Singapore: Select Publishing-IDSS, 197–226.

"New Illness, Same Old Medicine." (1997) *The Economist,* December 13: 65–66.

Nguyen, Thach Hong. (1996) "How Will ASEAN and China Solve the Spratly Conflict?" *Pacific Research* August: 15–16.

Nischalke, Tobias Ingo. (2000) "Insights from ASEAN's Foreign Policy Co-operation: The 'ASEAN Way,' a Real Spirit or a Phantom?" *Contemporary Southeast Asia,* vol. 22, no. 1 (April): 89–112.

"No Help Here." (1997) *Far Eastern Economic Review,* November 20: 60–61.

Nordhaug, Kristen. (2000) "Asian Monetary Fund Revival?" *Focus on Trade,* no. 51 (June).

Nye, Joseph S. (1997–1998) "China's Re-emergence and the Future of the Asia-Pacific." *Survival,* vol. 39, no. 4 (Winter): 65–79.

———. (2001) "The 'Nye Report': Six Years Later." *International Relations of the Asia-Pacific,* vol. 1, no. 1: 95–103.

Ohiorhenuan, John F. E., ed. (1999) *Cooperation South,* Special Issue: Rethinking the International Financial System, no. 1 (June).

Oldham, Peter, and Robin Wettlaufer. (2000) "The Long Haul: Institution Building and the ASEAN Regional Forum." *Cancaps Bulletin,* no. 27 (November): 9–10.

"On the Rocks." (1998) *The Economist,* March 7: 5–7.

Ortuoste, Maria Consuelo. (1999) "Security Cooperation in the Asia Pacific: The ASEAN Regional Forum Experiment." *FSI Quarterly,* vol. 1, no. 1 (January–March): 43–73.

————. (2000) "The Establishment of the ASEAN Regional Forum." Paper prepared for the *Multilateral Institutions in Asia* conference, Asia-Pacific Center for Security Studies, Honolulu, Hawaii, July 14, 2000.

"Out of Its Depth." (1998) *Far Eastern Economic Review,* February 19: 25–26.

Paal, Douglas H. (2000) "The United States in Asia in 1999." *Asian Survey,* vol. 40, no. 1: 1–15.

Palmer, Norman. (1991) "Regionalism in Southeast Asia: Focus on ASEAN." In Norman D. Palmer, ed., *The New Regionalism in Asia and the Pacific.* Toronto: Lexington Books, 59–74.

Park, Innwon. (1995) *Regional Integration Among the ASEAN Nations.* London: Praeger.

Parrenas, Julius Caesar. (1998) "ASEAN and Asia Pacific Economic Cooperation." *The Pacific Review,* vol. 11, no. 2: 233–249.

Pempel, T. J., ed. (1999), *The Politics of the Asian Economic Crisis.* Ithaca, N.Y.: Cornell University Press.

Philpott, Daniel. (2001) *Revolutions in Sovereignty: How Ideas Shaped Modern International Relations.* Princeton, N. J.: Princeton University Press, 2001.

Pollack, Jonathan D. (1996) "The United States and Asia in 1995: The Case of the Missing President." *Asian Survey,* vol. 36, no. 1 (January): 1–12.

Preston, Peter W. (1998) "Reading the Asian Crisis: History, Culture and Institutional Truths." *Contemporary Southeast Asia,* vol. 20, no. 3 (December): 241–260.

Pryzstup, James. (2000) "Waiting for Zhu. . . ." *Comparative Connections,* vol. 2, no. 3 (October).

Radelet, Steven and Jeffrey Sachs. (1997) "Asia's Reemergence." *Foreign Affairs,* vol. 76, no. 6 (November/December): 44–59.

Ramcharan, Robin. (2000) "ASEAN and Non-interference: A Principle Maintained." *Contemporary Southeast Asia,* vol. 22, no. 1 (April): 74–76.

Rajan, Ramkishen S. (2000) *Examining the Case for an Asian Monetary Fund.* ISEAS Working Papers no. 3. Singapore: Institute of Southeast Asian Studies.

Ravenhill, John. (1995) "Economic Cooperation in Southeast Asia." *Asian Survey,* vol. 35, no. 9 (September): 850–866.

————. (1999) "APEC and the WTO: Which Way Forward for Trade Liberalization?" *Contemporary Southeast Asia,* vol. 21, no. 2 (August): 220–237.

————. (2000) "APEC Adrift: Implications for Economic Regionalism in Asia and the Pacific." *The Pacific Review,* vol. 13, no. 2: 319–333.

"Rebuilding Asia." (1998) *Far Eastern Economic Review,* February 12: 46–47.

Reich, Simon. (2000) "Miraculous or Mired? Contrasting Japanese and American Perspectives on Japan's Economic Problems." *The Pacific Review,* vol. 13, no. 1: 163–193.

"Rescuing Asia." (1997) *Business Week,* November 17: 118.

Rhodes, Martin, and Richard Higgott. (2000) "Introduction: Asian crises and the Myth of Capitalist 'Convergence.'" *The Pacific Review,* vol. 13, no. 1: 1–19.

Rodan, Garry, Kevin Hewison, and Richard Robison, eds. (1997) *The Political Economy of Southeast Asia.* Melbourne: Oxford University Press.

Rolls, Mark G. (1991) "ASEAN: Where from or Where to." *Contemporary Southeast Asia,* vol. 13, no. 3 (December): 313–332.

Rose, Andrew K. (1999) "Is There a Case for an Asian Monetary Fund?" *FRBSF Economic Letter,* no. 99-37 (December 17): (http://www.sf.frb.org/econrsrch/wklyltr/wklyltr99/el99–37.html).

Ross, Robert. (1997) "China II: Beijing as a Conservative Power." *Foreign Affairs,* vol. 76, no. 2 (March/April): 33–44.

————. (2000) "The 1995–96 Taiwan Strait Confrontation." *International Security,* vol. 25, no. 2 (Fall): 87–123.

Roy, Denny. (1993) "Consequences of China's Economic Growth for Asia-Pacific Security." *Security Dialogue,* vol. 24, no. 2: 181–191.

———. (1994) "Hegemon on the Horizon? China's Threat to East Asian Security." *International Security,* vol. 19, no. 1 (Summer): 149–168.

———. (1996) "The 'China Threat' Issue." *Asian Survey,* vol. 36, no. 8 (August): 758–771.

Rudner, Martin. (1995) "APEC: The Challenges of Asia Pacific Economic Cooperation." *Modern Asian Studies* vol. 29, no. 2 (May): 403–437.

Ruland, Jurgen. (2000) "ASEAN and the Asian Crisis: Theoretical Implications and Practical Consequences for Southeast Asian Regionalism." *The Pacific Review,* vol. 13, no. 3: 421–451.

Sachs, Jeffrey. (1997) "The Wrong Medicine for Asia." (http://www.stern.nyu.edu/~nroubini/asia/AsiaSachsOp–EdNYT1197.html), November 3: A2.

Samuels, Marwyn S. (1982) *Contest for the South China Sea.* New York: Methuen.

Saravanamuttu, Johan, and Shaun Narine, eds. (1998) *The Engagement of Civil Society in the APEC Process.* Penang, Malaysia: Canadian International Development Agency.

SarDesai, D. R. (1994) *Southeast Asia: Past and Present,* 3d ed. Boulder, Colo.: Westview Press.

Schwartz, Adam. (1994) "Bigger is Better." *Far Eastern Economic Review,* July 28: 24.

Segal, Gerald. (1994) *China Changes Shape: Regionalism and Foreign Policy,* Adelphi Paper no. 287. London: International Institute for Strategic Studies.

———. (1995) "Tying China into the International System." *Survival,* vol. 37, no. 2 (Summer): 60–73.

Selin, Shannon. (1994a) *Asia Pacific Arms Buildups, Part One: Scope, Causes and Problems.* Working Paper no. 6 (November). Vancouver: Institute of International Relations.

———. (1994b) *Asia Pacific Arms Buildups, Part Two: Prospects for Control.* Working Paper no. 7 (November). Vancouver: Institute of International Relations.

Shambaugh, David. (1992) "China's Security Policy in the Post–Cold War Era." *Survival,* vol. 34, no. 2 (Summer): 88–106.

———. (1999–2000) "China's Military Views the World." *International Security,* vol. 24, no. 3 (Winter): 52–79.

Sharma, Shalendra D. (1998) "Asia's Economic Crisis and the IMF." *Survival,* vol. 40, no. 2, (Summer): 27–52.

Sheng Lijun. (1995) "China's Foreign Policy Under Status Discrepancy, Status Enhancement." *Contemporary Southeast Asia,* vol. 17, no. 2 (September): 101–125.

Sikorski, Douglas. (1999) "The Financial Crisis in Southeast Asia and South Korea: Explanations and Controversies." *Global Economic Review,* vol. 28, no. 1 (Spring): 117–124.

Simon, Sheldon W. (1992) "The Regionalization of Defence in Southeast Asia." *The Pacific Review* vol. 5, no. 2: 112–124.

———. (1993) "U.S. Strategy and Southeast Asian Security: Issues of Compatibility." *Contemporary Southeast Asia,* vol. 14, no. 4 (March): 301–313.

———. (1998) "Security Prospects in Southeast Asia: Collaborative Efforts and the ASEAN Regional Forum." *The Pacific Review,* vol. 11, no. 2: 195–212.

———. (1999) "Is There a U.S. Strategy for East Asia?" *Contemporary Southeast Asia,* vol. 21, no. 3 (December): 325–343.

Simone, Vera. (2001) *The Asian Pacific,* 2d ed. New York: Longman.

"Singapore's Trade Initiatives Undermine ASEAN Economic Policy." (2000) *Global Intelligence Update,* Stratfor.com, November 28: (http://www.stratfor.com).

Singh, Bilveer. (1993) "ASEAN's Arms Procurements: Challenge of the Security Dilemma in the Post–Cold War Era." *Comparative Strategy*, vol. 12: 199–223.

Smith, Anthony. (1999) "Indonesia's Role in ASEAN: The End of Leadership?" *Contemporary Southeast Asia*, vol. 21, no. 2 (August): 238–260.

Snitwongse, Kusuma. (1995) "ASEAN's Security Cooperation: Searching for Regional Order." *The Pacific Review*, vol. 8 no. 3: 523–524.

———. (1997) "Thailand and ASEAN: Thirty Years On." *Asian Journal of Political Science*, vol. 5, no. 1 (June): 87–101.

Snyder, Craig. (1995) *Making Mischief in the South China Sea*. CANCAPS Papier no. 7 (August). Toronto: Canadian Consortium on Asia Pacific Security.

Soesastro, Hadi. (1995a) "ASEAN and APEC: Do Concentric Circles Work?" *The Pacific Review*, vol. 8, no. 3: 475–493.

———. (1995b) "ASEAN Economic Cooperation: The Long Journey to AFTA." *The Indonesian Quarterly*, vol. 23, no. 1 (First Quarter): 25–37.

———. (1999) "ASEAN During the Crisis." in H. W. Arndt and Hal Hill, eds., *Southeast Asia's Economic Crisis: Origins, Lessons and the Way Forward*. Singapore: Institute of Southeast Asian Studies, 158–169.

"Soft Border, Soft Wars." (1995) *Far Eastern Economic Review*, April 13: 28.

"Soft Targets." (1998) *Far Eastern Economic Review*, February 12: 20.

Solomon, Richard H., and William M. Drennan. (2001) "The United States and Asia in 2000." *Asian Survey*, vol. 41, no. 1: 1–11.

Speed, Elizabeth. (1995) *Chinese Naval Power and East Asian Security*, Working Paper No. 11. Vancouver: Institute of International Relations, August.

Stiglitz, Joseph. (2000) "The Insider." *The New Republic*, April 17.

Stuart, Douglas T., and William T. Tow. (1995) *A US Strategy for the Asia-Pacific*. Adelphi Paper no. 299 (December). London: International Institute for Strategic Studies.

Stubbs, Richard. (1989) "Geopolitics and the Political Economy of Southeast Asia." *International Journal*, vol. 44 (Summer): 517–540.

———. (1991) "Reluctant Leader, Expectant Followers: Japan and Southeast Asia." *International Journal*, vol. 46 (Autumn): 647–667.

———. (1995) "Asia Pacific Regionalization and the Global Economy." *Asian Survey*, vol. 35, no. 9 (September): 785–797.

———. (1998) "Asia-Pacific Regionalism Versus Globalization: Competing Forms of Capitalism." In William D. Coleman and Geoffrey R. D. Underhill, eds., *Regionalism and Global Economic Integration*. London: Routledge, 68–80.

———. (2000) "Signing on to Liberalization: AFTA and the Politics of Regional Economic Cooperation." *The Pacific Review*, vol. 13, no. 2: 297–318.

Sudo, Sueo. (1991) *Southeast Asia in Japaneses Security Policy*, Pacific Strategic Paper no. 3, Singapore: Institute of Southeast Asian Studies.

Suh, Sangwoh. (1999) "Unease over East Timor." *Asiaweek*, vol. 25, no. 41: (http://www.asiaweek.com/asiaweek/magazine/99/1015/easttimor.html).

Sundararaman, Shankari. (1998) "The ASEAN Regional Forum: Reassessing Multilateral Security in the Asia Pacific." *Strategic Analysis*, vol. 22, no. 4: 655–665 (http://www.idsa.india.org/an-jul8-11.html).

Suriyamongkol, Marjorie L. (1988) *Politics of ASEAN Economic Co-operation*. Singapore: Oxford University Press.

Swain, Sitanshu. (2000) "Mr. Yen Calls for an Asian Monetary Fund." *The Financial Express*, March 30.

Swaine, Michael D. (1993) "The PLA and China's Future." *Far Eastern Economic Review*, March 4: 25.

Tan, Joseph L. H. (1996) "Introductory Overview: AFTA in the Changing International Economy." In Joseph L. H. Tan, ed., *AFTA in the Changing International Economy*. Singapore: Institute of Southeast Asian Studies, 1–18.

Tang, Min, and Myo Thant. (1994) "Growth Triangles: Conceptual and Operational Considerations." In Myo Thant, Min Tang, and Hiroshi Kakazu, eds., *Growth Triangles in Asia*. Hong Kong: Oxford University Press, 1–28.

Tay, Simon S. C. (1998) "What Should Be Done About the Haze." *The Indonesian Quarterly,* vol. 26, no. 2: 99–117.

Taylor, John. (1999) *East Timor: The Price of Freedom.* New York: Zed Books.

Thai Ministry of Foreign Affairs. (1999) "The ASEAN Troika," press release.

———. (2000) "Clarification on News Reports Concerning ASEAN Troika," press release.

"Thailand Pushes Asian Monetary Fund to Head Off New Crises." (2000) *Detroit News,* May 6.

Thambipillai, Pushpa. (1998) "The ASEAN Growth Areas: Sustaining the Dynamism." *The Pacific Review,* vol. 11, no. 2: 249–266.

Thayer, Carlyle. (1990) "ASEAN and Indochina: the Dialogue." In Alison Broinowski, ed., *ASEAN into the 1990s.* London: Macmillan, 138–161.

———. (1995) *Beyond Indochina.* Adelphi Paper no. 297. London: International Institute for Strategic Studies.

———. (1999) "Some Progress, along with Disagreements and Disarray." *Comparative Connections,* vol. 1, no. 1 (July).

———. (2000) *Multilateral Institutions in Asia: The ASEAN Regional Forum.* Honolulu: Asia-Pacific Center for Security Studies.

———. (2001) "Developing Multilateral Cooperation." *Comparative Connections,* vol. 3, no. 3 (October). (http://www.csis.org/pacfor/cc/0103Qchina_asean.html).

Tilman, Robert O. (1987) *Southeast Asia and the Enemy Beyond.* Boulder, Colo.: Westview Press.

Townsend-Gault, Ian. (1994) "Testing the Waters: Making Progress in the South China Sea." *Harvard International Review,* vol. 16, no. 2 (Spring): 16–19.

"Treacherous Shoals." (1992) *Far Eastern Economic Review,* August 13: 15.

Tripathi, Salil. (1998) "In the Hot Seat." *Far Eastern Economic Review,* May 14: 65.

Turley, William S. (1993) "'More Friends, Fewer Enemies': Vietnam's Policy Toward Indochina-ASEAN Reconciliation." In Sheldon W. Simon, ed., *East Asian Security in the Post–Cold War Era.* Armonk, N.Y.: M. E. Sharpe, 167–193.

Tyabji, Amina. (1990) "The Six ASEAN Economies: 1980–88." In Alison Broinowski, ed., *ASEAN into the 1990s.* London: Macmillan, 32–57.

Um, Khatharya. (1991) "Thailand and the Dynamics of Economic and Security Complex in Mainland Southeast Asia." *Contemporary Southeast Asia,* vol. 13, no. 3 (December): 245–270.

Valencia, Mark J. (1995) *China and the South China Sea Disputes.* Adelphi Paper no. 298. London: International Institute for Strategic Studies.

Van der Kroef, Justus M. (1971) *Indonesia After Sukarno.* Vancouver: University of British Columbia Press.

———. (1988) "Cambodia: The Vagaries of 'Cocktail' Diplomacy." *Contemporary Southeast Asia,* vol. 9, no. 4 (March): 300–320.

———. (1990) "Thailand and Cambodia: Between 'Trading Market' and Civil War." *Asian Profile,* vol. 18, no. 3 (June): 227–238.

Vatikiotis, Michael. (1995) "Care to Join Us?" *Far Eastern Economic Review,* December 7: 23.

————. (1997) "Friends and Fears." *Far Eastern Economic Review*, May 8: 4.

————. (1998) "Fund Under Fire." *Far Eastern Economic Review*, May 14: 60–63.

Vatikiotis, Michael, and Ben Dolven. (1999) "Missing in Action." *Far Eastern Economic Review*, September 30: 14, 16.

Vogel, Ezra. (1991) *The Four Little Dragons*. Cambridge, Mass.: Harvard University Press.

Wade, Robert. (1998a) "From Miracle to Meltdown: Vulnerabilities, Moral Hazard, Panic and Debt Deflation in the Asian Crisis." Russell Sage Foundation Working papers (June).

————. (1998b) "The Asian Crisis and the Global Economy: Causes, Consequences and Cure." *Current History*, vol. 97, no. 622 (November): 361–373.

————. (1998c) "The Asian Debt-and-Development Crisis of 1997–?: Causes and Consequences." *World Development*, vol. 26, no. 8: 1535–1553.

Wade, Robert, and Frank Veneroso. (1998a) "The Asian Crisis: The High Debt Model vs. the Wall Street-Treasury-IMF Complex." *New Left Review*, March–April: 3–23.

————. (1998b) "The Resources Lie Within." *The Economist*, November 7–13: 19–21.

Wanandi, Jusuf. (1997) "A Lesson for ASEAN." *Far Eastern Economic Review*, July 24: 34.

Wang, Fei-Ling. (1999) "Self-Image and Strategic Intentions: National Confidence and Political Insecurity." In Yong Deng and Fei-Ling Wang, eds., *In the Eyes of the Dragon*. Lanham, Md.: Rowman and Littlefield, 21–46.

Wang, Jianwei. (1999) "Managing Conflict: Chinese Perspectives on Multilateral Diplomacy and Collective Security." In Yong Deng and Fei-Ling Wang, eds., *In the Eyes of the Dragon*. Lanham, Md.: Rowman and Littlefield, 73–96.

Wattanayagorn, Panitan. (1995) "ASEAN's Arms Modernization and Arms Transfers Dependence." *The Pacific Review*, vol. 8, no. 3: 494–507.

Wattanayagorn, Panitan, and Desmond Ball. (1995) "A Regional Arms Race?" *Journal of Strategic Studies*, vol. 18, no. 3 (September): 147–174.

Weiss, Linda. (2000) "Developmental States in Transition: Adapting, Dismantling, Innovating, Not 'Normalizing.'" *The Pacific Review*, vol. 13, no. 1: 21–55.

Welsh, Bridget. (2000) "Malaysia and Globalization: Contradictory Currents." In Samuel S. Kim, ed., *East Asia and Globalization*. Lanham, Md.: Rowman and Littlefield: 233–254.

Wesley, Michael. (1999) "The Asian Crisis and the Adequacy of Regional Institutions." *Contemporary Southeast Asia*, vol. 21, no. 1 (April): 54–73.

————. (2001) "APEC's Mid-Life Crisis? The Rise and Fall of Early Voluntary Sectoral Liberalization." *Pacific Affairs*, vol. 74, no. 2 (Summer): 185–204.

Wessel, David, and Bob Davis. (1998) "Limits of Power." *The Wall Street Journal*, September 24: A1, A10.

Winters, Jeffrey A. (1999) "The Determinants of Financial Crisis in Asia." In T. J. Pempel, ed., *The Politics of the Asian Economic Crisis*. Ithaca, N.Y.: Cornell University Press: 79–97.

Woo-Cumings, Meredith. (1999) "The State, Democracy, and the Reform of the Corporate Sector in Korea." In T. J. Pempel, ed., *The Politics of the Asian Economic Crisis*. Ithaca, N.Y.: Cornell University Press: 116–142.

Wortzel, Larry M. (1994) "China Pursues Traditional Great-Power Status." *Orbis*, Spring: 157–175.

You Ji and You Xu. (1991) "In Search of Blue Water Power: The PLA Navy's Maritime Strategy in the 1990s." *Pacific Review*, vol. 4, no. 2: 137–149.

Yu, Peter Kien-hong. (1990) "Protecting the Spratlys." *The Pacific Review,* vol. 3, no. 1: 78–83.

Yuan, Jing-Dong. (1995) "China's Defence Modernization: Implications for Asia-Pacific Security." *Contemporary Southeast Asia,* vol. 17, no. 1 (June): 67–84.

Zhang Ming. (1999) "Public Images of the United States." In Yong Deng and Fei-Ling Wang, eds., *In the Eyes of the Dragon.* Lanham, Md.: Rowman and Littlefield, 141–158.

Index

About the Book

Is ASEAN the foundation of a strong regional community in Southeast Asia? Or is it no more than an instrument used by its members to advance their individual interests? Addressing these questions, Shaun Narine offers a comprehensive political analysis of ASEAN from its creation in 1967 through the events of 2001.

Reflecting both the accomplishments and the limitations of the organization, Explaining ASEAN explores issues of regional security, economic stability—and the growing expectations of the international community. Narine's trenchant analysis makes it clear that, unless ASEAN can resolve the problems of inadequate resources and disagreements among the member states, its future as an effective, active international regime is doubtful.

Shaun Narine is Killam Postdoctoral Fellow at the University of British Columbia.